India Mutiny to Mahatma and Swaraj
(A History of Hundred Years)

India Mutiny to Mahatma and Swaraj

(A History of Hundred Years)

Kamini Krishna
The University of Zambia, Lusaka
School of Humanities and Social Sciences

GYAN

ISBN : 978-81-212-1322-6

Price : ₹ 950

First Published: 2016

Published by

Gyan Publishing House
5, Ansari Road
Daryaganj, New Delhi-110002
Phone: 9811692060
E-mail: books@gyanbooks.com

Printed at: G. Print Process, Delhi.

Cataloging in Publication Data—DK
Courtesy: D.K. Agencies (P) Ltd. <docinfo@dkagencies.com>

Krishna, Kamini, author.
India mutiny to Mahatma and swaraj : a history of hundred years / Kamini Krishna.
pages cm
Includes bibliographical references.
ISBN 9788121213226

1. India—History—British occupation, 1765-1947. 2. India—Politics and government—1765-1947. 3. India—Politics and government—20th century. I. Title.

DS463.K75 2015 DDC 954.03 23

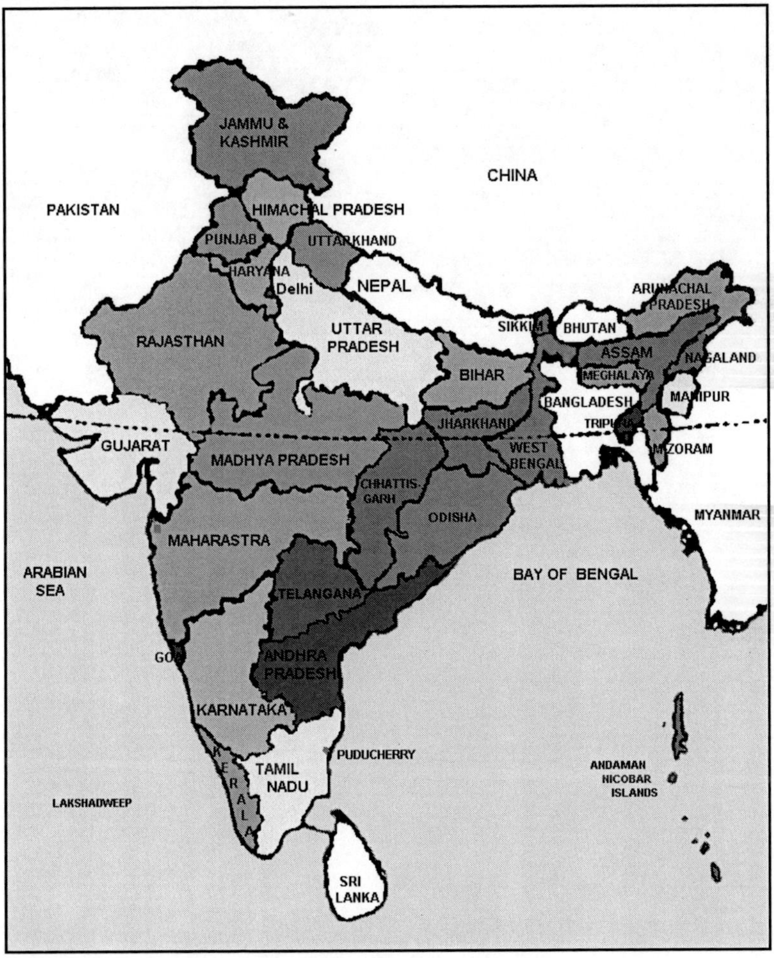

Map 1: India 2015 (29 states and 7 Union Territories)

Dedication

In the loving memory of my parents who taught me compassion and gave me wisdom

Late Rajendra Prasad
Late Draupadi Prasad

Contents

List of Maps

List of Plates

Preface

India is often referred to as a sub-continent because of her great size and its separation from the continent of Asia by a large body of water. To discuss the history of India, it is important to remember that the original name of India is 'Bharat'. However, Indians called their country 'Bharat' after a legendary monarch, named *Bharat*. When Bharat was invaded by the Muslims (1000 AD onwards), from the North-West, they changed its name and started calling it Hindustan (country of Hindus). The Europeans colonised India (1600 onwards) and this country was renamed as 'India'. It is argued by the historians that the Europeans mispronounced the word Sindhu as Indus and they called the people living on the banks of the Sindhu River as Indus. Now, the country is popularly known as India rather than her original name 'Bharat'.

It is equally important to note that India or Bharat was predominantly a Hindu country which was captured and controlled by the Mughals and then by the Europeans. These two encroachers ruled over a vast diverse land of desert, large navigable rivers and thick forests, mountains, with the physical barriers that separated various linguists, religion, and ethnic groups for about 500 and 190 years by the Mughals and then by the British, respectively. No doubt that the history of India is quite complex and intertwine with a number of events.

Different chapters in this book deal with various themes which in turn comprises several sub-themes. It begins with the European's arrival in India and finally the colonisation of India by the British East India Company. Book highlights the outstanding features of

Indian culture and society before the British colonisation of India. This is followed by the Reform Movements and Westernisation between 1820 and 1857 which explains how the Indian societies overcame to various evils and mythical prejudices, due to the introduction of European education. This period witnessed a remarkable outburst of intellectuals and radical transformations in her social and religious sectors in the Indian folk. The European education and westernisation had both positive and negative impacts on the Indian society.

The British East India Company ruled India both directly and indirectly. Princely or Native states were given a sovereign entity of India numbering about 600 (about 40 per cent) of India's total land. The remaining of them (about 60 per cent) was ruled directly by the British East India Company.

The Indian neighbouring countries from three sides like, Afghanistan, Nepal and Tibet were also captured by the British to thwart the Russian intrusion. To secure trading monopoly in Burma and in China the British rulers, whether under Company or Crown, invaded above neighbouring countries ruthlessly.

The East India Company ruled India for about 100 years and then was forced to hand over its power to the British Crown after the 1857 mutiny. The book also examines the Indian mutiny of 1857 that marked the end of East India Company rule and its aftermath Impacts. The period from 1857 to 1950 has a great significance in the history of India. During this period, Indians struggled to throw off the yoke of the British colony. A number of important events took place ranging from revolt of 1857, the renaissance movements, formation of the Indian National Congress and Muslim League, Revolution movements and appearance of Mahatma Gandhi.

The historians argue that the British ruled India through the 'divide and rule' policy. Following such policy Hindu and Muslim communities were divided, to make it easier for them to manipulate and rule the country effectively.

The book contains a chapter on India's participation and its effects on India during the two World Wars. It even discusses the National

Movements and the role of Mahatma Gandhi (arrived India in 1915 from South Africa) and the emergence of mass politics from 1919 to 1939 that laid the foundation of independent India. Mahatma convinced Indian freedom fighters to change their strategies to adopt non-violence and passive resistance (*Satyagraha*). During this period, he protested British rule (government) with his unique tactics like non-cooperation, boycott of foreign goods, civil disobedience etc.

Due to the hard work of nationalists, finally, came independence and division of India on 15th August 1947. Two dominions were created out of what had been the one country known as India. One dominion kept the name India and the other took the name Pakistan (with two wings: East Pakistan and West Pakistan). Their boundaries were fixed according to two different religions, Hinduism and Islam.

This period (1947–1957) equally has great significance in the history of modern India. When India attained independence she had a lot of challenges to face in each sector of her country for the reconstruction of India and bring her as one of the largest democracy in the world. India's "tryst with destiny" began on August 15, 1947 amidst many challenges. The most formidable task was to overcome the colonial legacy, which had left the sub-continent socially fragmented and economically crippled.

Book focuses on 'Pandit Jawaharlal Nehru', the first Prime Minister of India. Nehru dominated the Indian political scene for about half a century and was the most popular leader India has produced during modern time. His personality had glamour, a charm which at times kept even his opponents spell-bound. He remained the Prime Minister of India for seventeen years till his death. He played an important role during the writing of Indian Constitution and spoke for a democratic country with a free press and for opposition party. He always looked forward to make India scientifically advanced and an industrialised country. Finally book evaluates the impact of British colonial rule that did not settle in India but utilised India's economic resources for the benefit of their motherland, Great Britain. The last topic assesses the impact of British rule in India and the legacy which India had to overcome.

1

Europeans as Explorers

Introduction

Portuguese discoverer and navigator, Vasco da Gama, made an eleven months journey around Africa and dropped anchor at Calicut in 1498, on the south western coast of India. He was restoring a link between Europe and the east that had existed many centuries previously. Portuguese were the first agents of this renewal contact, because they were among the few Europeans nations to possess both the navigational know-how and the necessary motivation for the long sea voyage. They opened route for other Europeans in search of spices, silk and other commodities. By the seventeenth century, traders from various European nationalities started struggling one against the other to gain the monopoly of Indian trade.

British East India Company

The English venture to India was entrusted to the East India Company (included a group of London merchants), which received monopoly right of trade in 1660, landed in the eastern part of India whose sole object was prompt cash when the Mughal Empire broke up in the eighteenth century. The power of the company grew and by 1757, India went under the British company, this time neither under Hindu nor Islamic but under the British rule.

In the early days of being in India, the British made little progress. The situation of East India Company in India remained insecure during the entire first half of the seventeenth century. Far from finding an outlet in Indian markets for fabrics, linen goods, and other English products, it was forced on the company to buy textiles from Indians so as to exchange them for spices. Spices had preservative and medicinal value much needed in Europe at that time.

The voyages undertaken by Fitch and Lancaster precipitated the interest to colonise India by the British. These voyages led to the foundation of the trading company known as East India Company. On 31st December 1600, the Charter was issued granting trade rights, to the Governor and Company of merchants of London, to the East Indies. Trade between India and Britain started slowly and by 1613 the British were allowed to found or establish an agency or a 'factory' for trade at Surat. In the beginning trade by the company was lucrative in India. According to Carrington, the trade of the company was at first very profitable. One cargo of cloves bought in Amboyana for 2,948 pounds was sold in London for 36,827 pounds, profits averaged 150 per cent on each successful voyage.

The first East Indian Company voyage left London in1601. The four ships on the trip returned home by 1603, with lots of pepper. Other successful voyages followed. One voyage in 1612 was so profitable that the investors in the venture got back the money they had invested in the voyage plus 220 per cent profit. The East India Company was a commercial enterprise and traded from 1600 until 1833. The company slowly took over India and governed it on behalf of the British Government until 1857.

It is argued that the British Colonial Policy's turning point was in 1651. This was when the British Parliament resorted to attempts to win over the colonies through trading privileges and favourable tarriffs. An attempt was also made to build up a closely-knit imperial unit. Parliamentary legislation, enforced by the navy, aimed at increasing colonial production to supply England with all her needs.

By the year 1640, colonial products re-exported from England equalled in value all British exports other than textiles. In the end, England became interested in the colonial expansion to reorient the colonial trade and make London an entrepot for re-exports of colonial products. This was so in order to shift the world commercial capital from Amsterdam to London. The addition of more than 200 ships to the British navy was a deliberate move to increase British Commercial advantages between 1651 and 1660. India, therefore became a candidate for commerce and her rapid growing population in Britain.

The need for free market for European manufactured goods especially those from Britain, was another major reason that made Britain to capture India, a far flung country. Due to her early industrialisation, Britain was able to produce cheap goods in huge quantities and she had the largest merchant navy for easy transportation to the Asian markets such as India, China and Indonesia. These territories were ready markets for the British manufactured products. For this reason the British manufacturers were attracted to colonise India in 1757. Thus profits, adventure and prestige encouraged many English people to go to India. Furnivall states that, "many men from Britain went to India for a variety of reasons, to make money, for adventure and prestige." In other words India became a powerful and good destination for marketing European goods.

In addition, the need for cheap raw materials for the British manufacturing industries was yet another factor that made the British capture or colonise India. There were a number of items available in India at the time most of which were not found in Europe. This promted the British merchants to go to far away places in search of raw materials to use. In words of Guicharnaud, "India at that time provided spices and pepper, silk, cotton goods, sugar, copper, coffee and tea." Malacca was a well known centre of trade during this time. It was a land of Alexandria on the Indian Ocean. As a consequence, the British held it in high esteem. India also had gold.

Besides India was endowed with huge quantities of untapped wealth and other natural resources. On their own, it was not easy for mechants to control the untapped wealth, labour and other raw materials. For this reason, the traders asked their home governments to take over the control of India. This would drive away traders from other countries and British merchants would monopolise trade in India and became wealthier. This would make traders trade in a safe environment since the government would help to maintain law and order. Brown contends that, "The British manufacturing class and the traders demanded much greater parliamentary control over Indian affairs." This increased pressure from Briitsh industrialists and traders made the British government to take a meticulous step to colonise India for her market and raw materials as well as her available cheap labour.

Furthermore, imperial British wanted the Indian economy to be developed on the classical colonial representation. Therefore the economic policies of India in agriculture, heavy industry, finance, foreign investment, trade, banking, tarriffs, and so on were all tailored to suit the colonial economy. The English began depriving the India cotton. There was an introduction of a twist into Hindustan and eventually the country was flooded with cotton. The cottage industry was destroyed because India was force to accept goods from Britain without recourse.

It is also vital to state that the British interest to spread Christianity in Asia was another important factor that made this small country to colonise this huge or vast country. The British colonised Indian in order to drive away muslims. Mukherjee posit that "India provided a great field of activity for Christian missionaries. From the very early period of contact, priests travelled to Asia. They looked for convers…" Among the religious groups that went to India, earlier were the Jesuits, who proved to have a profound zeal of missionary work. These combined their religious duties with commerce. The works of the Jesuits were felt especially after the arrival of St. Francis Xavier in 1542.

With passage of time Christianity spread in India through the Roman Catholic missionaries. The works of St. Francis Xavier, Father Matteo Ricci and Father Ignatius Loyola encouraged and worked as agents for the British government to capture India.

Finally, between 1772 and 1857, India became the subject of discussion in the British parliament, both in the legislative and judicial councils. This was so due to her raw materials, market, religious aspect, and so on. The state (England) was to take over the control of administration of India, but the trade monopoly was to be left in the hands of the East India Company. Suffice it to say that after 1858, India became officially a British Colony as the British Crown took over control of the company. The British Crown put a Secretary of State for India in charge of India. Later India was divided into three adminstrative zones namely Bengal, Madras and Bombay. Then the British introduced a number of legal and adminstrative changes.

As such, Britain captured India as a colony not only for availability of spices, silver, silk, copper and other natural resources but it also provided cheap labour for the British Crown. The spread of Christianity by missionaries was yet another reason the British colonised a far flung country in the East. Although Spain, Holland and Portugal were the first countries to develop trade links with India, the British trade relations with India surpassed them leading to its eventual colonisation.

The British Conquest of India

The edifice of the Mughal central structure began to crumble in the eighteenth century under the weight of its own inner contradictions. Whatever the level of its military and cultural achievements, the Mughal rulers failed to create any national feeling or corporate spirit among its heterogeneous population. Revolts and desertions assumed alarming proportions in the eighteenth century when weak Mughal emperors succeeded one another in quick succession. In fact, the pricinciple of 'survival of the weakest' became operative among the Mughal princes. The emperors became playthings in the hands of powerful and intriguing nobles. The power-hungry subhadars of Bengal, Oudh and the Deccan behaved as semi-independent rulers, sought political partners without any scruples, solicited the help of traditional enemies of the Mughal empire and engaged. European companies in the game of territorial aggrandisement.

Nadir Shar's invasion of India in 1739 left the Mughal empire prostrate and bleeding apart from demonstrating to the world that a political vacuum was fast developing in Northern India.

Competition in North and South India

In Northern India, a triangular struggle for an empire ensued between three contenders – the Mughals, the Afghans and the Marathas. The Afghans under Ahmad Shah Abdali, the Maeathas under the Peshwas humbled the Mughal emperors and decimated the size of the Mughal empire; later Abdali defeated the Marathas at Panipat (1761) but withdrew from India because of internal commotion in Afgahanistan. In the tragic drama, the Rohilla chiefs, the nawabs of Oudh, the Jats and the Rajputs played a subsidiary role but added to the political confusion. The East India Company did not take any part in the struggle for an Empire in the eighteenth century. However, the Indian powers weakened one anoher in this internecine struggle, facilitating the political ambitions of the East India Company. Hindustan was left without a strong ruler. In a typically imperialist style P. Spear sums up, "It was in this way that the British proved to be the residuary legatees of the unclaimed estate of Hindustan."

In the South too a triangular struggle for political supremacy ensured between three Indian powers – the Marathas, the Nizams and the Mysoreans. Another triangular contest between three Europeans Companies – the Dutch, the English and the French – complicated the political scenario. This six powers entered into intrigues and cospiracies, organised plots and counterplots and formed combinations and alliances which baffle all political analysts.

The European companies added largely to the political confusions because they changed their political alliances and alignments in India at the dictates of their Home Governments in Europe. The Dutch had eliminated the Portuguese from India, Ceylon and the Spice Islands, but faced contenders in the English and the French. Finding it impossible to protect their interests in India and the Spice Islands (Modern Indonesian Islands). The Dutch withdrew from India and concentrated their attention upon the Spice Islands. The residual two European powers – the English and the French – fought three Carnatic wars in which the English emerged victorious. The successful English got the better of the Indian powers in the South and humbled or subordinated the Nizams, the Mysoreans and the Marathas. By the second decade of the nineteenth century the whole of India barring the states of Assam (in north eastern India), Punjab and Sind (in north western India) passed under direct British rule or English protectorate.

In another wave of aggressive wars the East India Company conquered Assam, Arakan and Tenasserim in 1824, Sind in 1843, Punjab in 1849 and Lower Burma in 1852. Lord Dalhousie's annexations gave the map of modern India. All the same, British imperialism continued to extend its stranglehold on neighbouring countries of India in the nineteenth century and capture whole India. It is intresting to know that how the tiny island-nation of Great Britain, situated thousands of miles away, was able to conquer and rule the vast Asian continent of India. The answer lies in the fact that the British conquered India in stages (figure shown below).

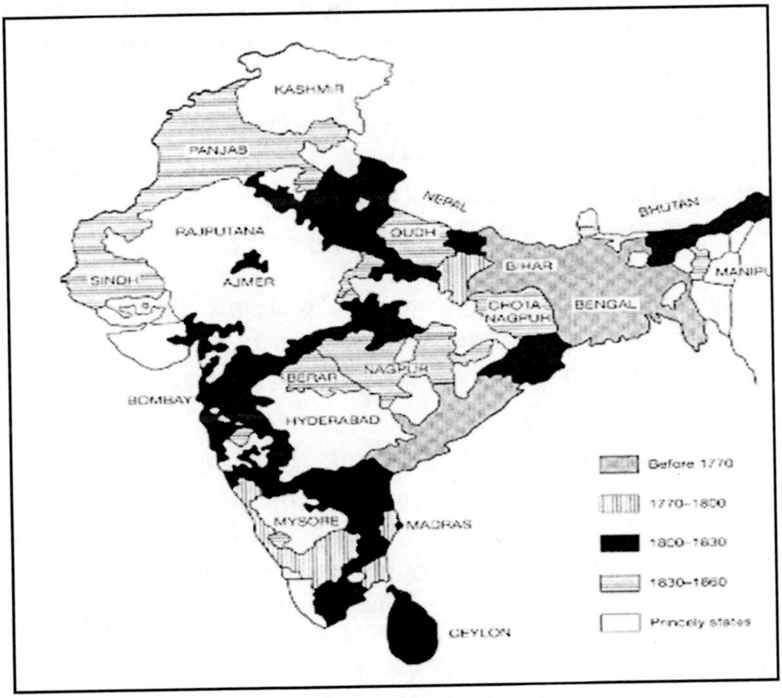

Map 2: The British Penetration of India (1750–1860)

Forces and Factors for British Success in India

The process of British conquest of various parts of India extended over a period of nearly a century. The English suffered many diplomatic failures and some military reverses but ultimately emerged victorious. A number of causes explain the victory of the British against their Indian adversaries.

First and foremost, the British were superior in arms, military tactics and strategy. The firearms used by Indian powers in the eighteenth century were slow firing and cumbrous and were outclassed by cannons used by the English. Again, European infantry could fire three times more quickly than the heavy Indian cavalry could close and ire. True, many Indian rulers, including the Nizam, the Mysoreans and the Marathas imported European arms, employed European officers to train their troops in the use of European arms. Unfortunately, Indian military officers and the rank and file never rose above the level of amateurs and as such could be no match for English officers and English trained armies.

On top of that, the English had the advantage of military discipline. The Company ensured loyalty of sepoys by strict discipline and regular payment of salaries. On the other hand, most of the Indian rulers suffered the chronic problem of lack of means to pay regular salaries; some of the Maratha chiefs had to divert their campaigns for collecting revenue to pay their troops. More often the Indian rulers depended on personal retinues of mercenary soldiers who were deficient in military discipline and could mutiny or desert to the enemy when victory seemed doubtful.

The English had the advantage of civil discipline of the Company's servants. The Company's army was directed by men themselves under discipline without any hereditary connections or ties. Further, European military officers were given command of armies only after rigorous discipline, they were reliable as well as skilful and given overall direction of affairs. In contrast Indian military command was usually given on caste basis to relatives whose military competence was doubtful and who could prove refractory or disloyal to subserve their personal ambitions.

No doubt that brilliant leadership gave the English another advantage. R. Clive, Warren Hastings, Elphinstone Munro, Wellesley, Lord Hastings, Dalbousie displayed rare qualities of leadership. They had the advantage of a long list of secondary leaders like Sir Eyre Coote, Lord Lake, Arthur Wellesley who fought not for the leader but for "cause and glory of their country." The Indian side too had brilliant leaders like Haider Ali, Tipu Sultan, Chin Kulich Khan, Madhao Rao Sindhia, Jaswant Rao Holkar, Nana Fadnavis, Ranjit Singh, but they more often lacked a team of second line trained personnel. Worst of all, the Indian leaders were as much fighting against one another as against the British. Their lieutenants too were notorious for desertions and for changing sides when the destiny of the leaders seemed in doubt. The Indian leaders were fighting for personal or dynastic advancement and the spirit of fighting for higher cause or for their country was altogether absent. Percival Spear, an English writer comments, : "A victory of an Indian leader was a victory for himself; victory of an English General was a victory for England."

Additionally, the British were superior in economic resources. The East India Company never ignored their trade and commerce. Towards the end of the eighteenth century the Company's foreign trade crossed 10 crore dollars with an annal favourable balance of trade figure of 7.5 crore dollars. The East India Company earned enough profits in India to pay dividends to their shareholders and finance their military campaingns in India. In due course the British used their political clout to earn fabulous profits from their trade with India. England was also earning fabulous profits from her trade with the rest of the world. These national resources in money, stores and troops were available to the British India in times of thanks to the advantage of superior sea power that Britain possessed.

Above all, a dynamic English people (in the vanguard of material civilisation) and motivated by a common ideal of fighting for national glorification faced a static Indian society still steeped in medieval ideals of religious complexes and altogether bereft of political nationalism of modern type. In fact, India was left far behind Europe in the race for material civilisation and thus lost her political independence.

Robert Clive,was the military and administrative genius largely responsible for giving Great Britain its Empire in India. He established the military and political supremacy of East India Company in Bengal. Together with W. Hasting.They were the key figures in the creation of British India.

Plate 1

Robert Clive (By courtesy of National Gallery, London)

British Conquest of India : An Analysis

Broadly, there are two theories regarding the British conquest of India. The first theory was popularised by John Seeley (British historian and essayist) who maintained that the British conquest of India was made "blindly, unintentionally and accidently" and "in a fit of absent-mindedness." According to this view, the British came to India for trade and commerce and had no political ambitions; they desired no territories nor wanted to squander their profits on wars, but were driven into the political troubles of India and annex territories. The protagonists of the second theory believe that the British came to India with plans to occupy territory after territory and determined to lay the foundation of a strong and stable empire. They carried out their grand design bit by bit. The supporters of this view decry the British proclamations of peace and political neutrality as a cheap propaganda device to befool their citics.

There is an element of exaggeration in both the opposing theories. Perhaps, it will be more correct to suggest that the process of conquest of India, to begin with, was accidental but in the later stages the design of an Indian Empire gripped the imagination of both British politiicans and Indian administrators. In the seventeenth century, the traders of the English East India Company were lured by the fabulous profits from trade in the spices of the East. A similar motivation attracted the traders of Holland, France and other European companies. The British Flag followed the British trader. As the British conquest of India extended over a long period of a century, different circumstances and a large number of factors – quick profits, personal ambitions of individual military leaders, Governors-General, contemporary European political developments, national chauvinism etc., etc.,— contributed to extension of British political sphere in India. Sometimes the British waged wars as a 'defensive device', at other times to save some Indian prince from some other aggressive Indian rulers like the Mysoreans or Marathas. Lord Wellesley resorted to aggressive application of the Subsidiary Alliance System to extend British dominion in India as a defensive (counter?) measure against the imperialistic designs of France and Russia. From 1798 to 1818 the British motives were consciously imperialistic. Lord Hastings carried further the policy of Wellesley and treated India as a conquered rather than an acquired country. Thereafter the British seemed to work according to a set design to conquer the whole of India and even some neighbouring states on India's frontiers. Later Governors-General like Dalhousie annexed some states to bring them under "beneficient" British Rule.

Broadly speaking the British conquest of India was part of a world political phase when imperialistic countries of Western Europe intruded into the East in search of trade and colonies.

2

Indian Culture and Society before British Colonisation and Westernisation

Introduction

This chapter introduces, briefly, India's culture and tradition considering the social hierarchy generally and language prior to its invent and imposition of the British rule. This is quite relevant to understand the real history of India. This further demonstrates to understand the Hindu caste system by explaining in brief on each category. Furthermore, it evaluates the Indian society's perception on women both in Hindu and Muslim communities. Finally, here one can see how religion influenced education in Indian society before the British imperialism.

Historical Background

Before the British colonised India, this was the land of the Lord Buddha whose influence extended across central Asia to China; Alexandra who brought with him the age of Hellenism; Ashoka, the ruler (c. 265-238 BC) gave up hunting to be initiated as a Buddhist monk; the Gupta Empire, the Huns, the Turkish slave dynasty, the Mughal period were the beginnings of both India and Pakistan. In the sixteenth century, the charms of the Persian culture captivated the Indian autocracy and by the seventeenth century, the Maharajas (king) of the noble palaces paraded in the palanquins while the masses lived in mud huts and lived on a handful of rice a day. In this course, we will discuss the sudden rise of European domination in the eighteenth century. One can say that India's subsequent history until the coming of European colonisers was heavily influenced by Islamic groups of various nationalities.

Culture and Society

By the time India was captured by the British Company, it was not a unified nation but a geographical entity containing a number of diverse communities of different races and tribes divided by language, religion and grades of culture. Therefore, we will discuss the Indian culture and social way of life at the time of Mughal period. By this time, there were many different races in India and that was because India had often been invaded in the past and each race which settled there left its mark on its descendants to this day. Today, more than two hundred languages are spoken with around 544 dialects. In the south, a number of languages are spoken which hardly have any relation to those spoken in the north. We are now looking at two communities that existed side by side in India: the Hindus and the Muslims.

Despite political convulsions and instability in the eighteenth century, the society in general, retained most of its traditional features with some changes thrown in by new environments. At the apex of the social order was the emperor closely followed by the nobility which despite hard times led to a life of luxury and extravagance with great weakness for wine, women and music. At the lower rung of the ladder was the preponderant majority of the poor agriculturist and artisans in the village. In the middle came the small and 'frugal' middle class comprising small merchants, shopkeepers, lower cadre of employees, town artisans etc. Paucity of contemporary evidence and disparities in incomes and prices in different regions of the country makes any comparisons to standard of living a difficult exercise.

The institution of caste stands out a striking feature of Hindu society of the time. The feature of Hinduism which most strikes the observers is the caste system. Caste is so old that nobody knows quite how it began, but there no doubt that its origin was largely economical. According to the traditional Hindu theory there are four main castes in society – Brahmin, Kshatriya, Vaishya and Shudra.

It is interesting to note that teaching and priesthood belong to this high caste – Brahmin. The duty of the Brahmin is to study and teach, to sacrifice and to give and receive gifts. Kshatriya or warriors had a duty to protect the people, sacrifice and study. Vaishyas or merchants, skilled workers and some professional people's duty was also to sacrifice and to study but their chief function was to breed cattle, to till the land and to lend money.

Shudras or unskilled workers and farm peasants' duty was only to serve the three higher castes. In reality, there is also a fifth caste called the untouchables or outcastes. Gandhi called the Harijans as 'children of God' but they are on the bottom of the social ladder. Their main job was to clean dirty places. The caste system still prevails in Indian society but it has not maintained its hard and fast rules for their profession as it used to be at that time. One can say that modern caste system has taken moderate step and most people do not bother to find out someone's caste.

Caste rules prevailed in matters of marriage, dress, diet and most importantly even professions. The cast system is basically based on the idea that one's position in life is fixed by birth and rebirth. According to Hinduism, a person remains in his caste from cradle to grave. Man/woman of higher castes cannot eat or drink with one of a lower caste because according to religious laws, he would become polluted, defiled, and unclean and would have to go through many rituals to be purified. On the other hand, Muslim society has no caste system but certain form of it prevails there too and one can say is a bit different than caste system.

During the eighteenth century and even now the pillar of traditional Indian society is the family. Family ties are among the strongest in an Indian's (both in the Hindu and Muslim) family life. In fact, the Indian family has been called a "state within a state", for the decision of family bind an Indian from cradle to grave. The Indian family is often referred to as a 'joint' one. As the word 'joint' suggests, the family is thought of as being joined together into a single unit by their blood ties. It may include as many 100 persons, not only parents and children but also the wives and children of married sons, grandparents, aunties, uncles and cousins. All of these people lived together and pooled their resources. Family needs were cared for by the entire family. Sad to say that, this traditional way of life is fading day by day in modern Indian families.

Even today, Indian families are also patriarchal meaning that membership in the family is determined by the bloodline of the male family and that the eldest male member has the highest authority in the family. A girl, when she marries is no longer considered a member of her parents' family and she becomes a part of her husband's family. Men in joint family put their earnings into a common purse from which each drew an allowance.

Place of Women in Society

Women were given a place of respect in the home and society but certainly not of a quality as we understand it today. Hindu society being mainly patriarchal (except in some backward areas), the will of the male head of the family usually prevailed. Though examples can be cited of Hindu and Muslim women having played significant roles in politics, administration and scholastic fields, the common woman was denied a right place in society. The Purdah (veil) system was common among both the Hindu and Muslim women. Purdah means the seclusion of women mostly by covering their faces in front of strangers, except the immediate family. However, women from poor families could not observe this rule as they had to be outside earning a living.

Child marriages were common among both girls and boys though consummation usually took place after they attained the age of maturity. The dowry system was prevalent among the upper classes. Polygamy was common among the ruling princes, big landlords (zamindars) and men of better means among the noble (kulin) families in provinces like Uttar Pradesh and Bengal. Remarrying by widows was usually looked down upon though it prevailed in some places.

The evil practice of Sati (wife burning herself on the funeral pyre of her husband) was widely prevalent among certain Hindu classes. It is important to note here that according to the Hindu faith, a dead body is cremated rather than buried. Dependency of women on their husbands or other male relatives was a prominent feature of social life among the Hindus as well the Muslims. But they enjoyed a position of respect and were expected to observe strict fidelity in their conjugal life.

To most Hindus, an Indian woman was considered a minor (a child) in the eyes for the law regardless of her age. As a girl, she was under the authority of her parents especially that of her father. As an adult, she was under the rule of her husband, and as a widow that of her sons. No doubt, the culture of a woman varied according to the classes which she belonged to. While the ordinary village women remained at home to supervise domestic duties, those belonging to the upper classes cultivated arts and sciences.

Slavery

Another social evil practice was the prevalence of slavery. Broadly speaking, slaves could be classed into two categories, that is, the domestic slaves and the serfs tied to the land. In the latter category, the serfs were transferred with the sale of land to the new masters. European travelers and administrators have testified to the widespread prevalence of slavery in India. Economic distress, families, natural calamities, extreme poverty compelled some to sell their children at a price. The Rajputs Kshatriyas and Kayasthas (caste separate from main four castes considered to be members of literate scribe caste) usually kept slave women for domestic work. However, slaves in India were treated better than their counterparts in America and Europe. Slaves were usually treated as hereditary servants of the family than as menials, they were allowed to marry among themselves and the main offspring of such marriage considered free citizens.

Slavery and slave trade touched new dimensions with the coming of Europeans in India, particularly the Portuguese, the Dutch and the English. Traffic in slaves was abolished by a proclamation issued by 1843.

Education

The love of learning has always excised a powerful influence on both the Hindus and the Muslim minds. However, the idea of India education was culture and not literacy. Vocational education according to one's varna or family tradition assured specialisation. Both Hindu and Muslim systems of education linked learning and religion.

Centres of higher education in Sanskrit literature were called chatuspathis (a vast collection of invaluable Sanskrit and Pali manuscript) mostly situated in Bengal, Bihar, Kashi (Benaras) etc. the French traveller Bernier described Kashi as the Athens of India institutions for learning of higher education in Persian and Arabic were called Madrasas. Being the court language, Persian was taught both by the Muslims and Hindus.

Elementary education was fairly widespread. The Hindu elementary schools were called *pathshalas* (schools) and Muslim elementary schools were popularly known as *maktabs*. Here, the students were given instructions in the three Rs of reading, writing and arithmetic. Moral instructions with emphasis on truth and honesty, obedience to parents and faith in one's religion found a place in the school curriculum. Though education was mainly popular with the higher castes, there were cases of children of lower castes attending school. Female education received scant attention.

Vernacular languages like Urdu, Hindi, Bengali, Assamese, Punjabi, Marathi, Telgu and Tamil were greatly developed. It was during the eighteenth century that the Christian missionaries set up printing presses in India and brought our vernacular editors of the Bible. Ziegenbelg, Danish missionary composed a Tamil grammar and published a Tamil version of the Bible. In Bengal, the Baptist missionaries (Caray, Ward and Marahman) set up a printing press at Serampur and published a Bengali version of the Bible.

Religion

When the British came to India, it was a land of many religions. It has been the guiding principle of Indian life to let a variety of beliefs and faiths flourish together. Before the Islamic people invaded

India, it was a predominantly a Hindu country. But there were few other religions that had emerged from Hinduism like Sikhism, Buddhism and Jainism.

Emperor Ashoka in the third century B.C. and later the great Mogul emperor, Akbar in the sixteenth century told the people to respect the faith of others. It is not surprising in consequences that this long standing tradition of religious tolerance and appreciation of other people's view influenced the markers of a free and modern India. They visualised the birth a nation in which no citizen would be discriminated against because of his religion.

In general however, we notice a regrettable deterioration in the social life during the eighteenth century which forms from many points of view one of the darkest periods in the history of India. One redeeming feature in this period of all round decline was the continuity of the process of Hindu-Muslim rapprochement and an amicable contact between the members of the two communities in spite of the bitter political rivalries of several centuries. Akbar's reign (1556-1605) is remarkably important and instructive for the existence of Hindu-Muslim harmony. Aldullah Khan, one of the Sayyid brothers, observed the Basalt and *Holy* festivals and Siraj-ud-Daulah and Mir Jafar enjoyed *Holi* festivals along with their friends and relatives.

It is said that on his death bed Mir Jafar drank a few drops of water poured in libation over the idol of Kiritesware near Murshidabad. Daulat Rao Sindhia and his officers joined Muharram procession in green dress like Muhammadans. It has been observed by a modern Indian on the authority of *Jan-Jahan Nama,* a Persian weekly of the early nineteenth century how the Durga Puja was celebrated at the Delhi court so late as A.D. 1825.

Later on, admittedly difference of principle greatly separated most Hindus from Muslims. Hindus believed in many gods and worshipped many images. While Muslims are monoaithistic and rejected idols, Hindus were ranked in a hierarchy of caste. Muslims professed the equality of all true believers. The higher Hindu castes revered the cow which Muslims killed and ate. From time to time and from place to place, these differences sharply divided members of the two communities. Indeed Hinduism and Indian Islam were so heterogeneous that it might be seen that instead of discussing nineteenth century India as a home of nations, it would be more accurate to say that it was the home of none.

Europeans took advantage of the clasheds between the Hindu rulers and the Indian Muslims. How was the tiny island-nation of Great Britain situated thousands of miles away able to conquer and rule the vast Asian sub-continent of India? It must be remembered that the British were able to place all of India under their rule because they had several important advantages over the Indians: better cannons and rifles than the Indians, control of the sea with superior naval power, large trained, well equipped Indian forces which they hired to fight for them; a sense of nationalism which the Indians did not have, a policy of 'divide and conquer' which set the Indians to fight among themselves and a series of able governors and administrators who brought to India the badly needed reforms and improvements.

Reform Movements and Westernisation 1820-185

In spite of political convulsions and economic retrogression, the first British rule in India (1757-1858) is, in certain respects, a memorable epoch in history. The period witnessed a remarkable outburst of intellectual activity in India and a radical transformation of her social and religious ideas. The impetus to these changes came from the introduction of English education. Through the channel came the liberal ideas of the west which stirred the people and roused them from a slumber of ages. A critical outlook on the past and new aspirations for the future marked a new awakening. Reason and judgment took the place of faith and belief; superstition yielded to science, immobility was replaced by progress.

This great change affected at first only a small group of persons but gradually the ideas spread among the larger sections of the people and ultimately their influence reached in greater or lesser degree even to the masses. Prior to 1818, there had been little response to the western cannons and western discipline but nothing of western science or the right of man. It was in Bengal that the larger aspects of the western spirit first became known to the Indian mind. The widespread knowledge of English provided an ideological bridge. Ideas flowed over in the persons of British lawyers, officials, Missionaries and disinterested men of learning like Sir William Jones.

Educational system that prevailed in India needed few things to revisit and awakening. There is no doubt that westernisation had great impact on Indian society. Willingly or unwillingly Indians were influenced by westernisation that had both positive and negative consequences.

The Western Impact

The impact of British rule on Indian society and culture was widely different from what Indians had known it to be. Most of the earlier intruders who came to India and had settled within her frontiers were absorbed by her superior culture and had become one of the land and its people. However, British conquest was different. Eighteenth century Europe had experienced novel intellectual currents and created the Age of Enlightenment. A new spirit of rationalism and enquiry had given a new dynamism to European society. The development of science and scientific outlook had affected every aspect of activity – political, economic and even religious. In contrast to Europe which was in the vanguard of civilisation in the eighteenth century, India presented a picture of a stagnant civilisation and a static and decadent society. Thus, for the first time, India encountered an invader who considered himself racially superior and culturally more advanced.

For sometime, it seemed that India was completely bowled over by new western ideas and values. It seemed that India had lagged behind in the race for civilisation.

The new scientific outlook, the doctrine of rationalism and humanism particularly impressed the English-educated class. The Indian leaders stimulated by the new knowledge sought to reform Hinduism from within and sought to purge it of superstitious beliefs and practices. Idolatry, image worship, practice of pilgrimages came up for close scrutiny and consequent reform.

The new concept of secularisation was born. The term secularisation implies that what was previously regarded as religious was no longer regarded as such. The magic wand was moved by rationalism i.e. the emergence of a tendency to regulate individual religious and social life in accordance with the principles of reason and to discard traditional beliefs and practices which cannot stand the test of modern knowledge. This approach brought a great change in the concept of 'pollution and purity' which formed an integral part of traditional Hindu religion.

The ferment ideas gave an expansive touch to Indian culture. A spirit of renaissance pervaded the whole country. Indian intellectuals closely scrutinised the country's past and found that many beliefs and practice were no longer of any use and needed to be discarded. They also discovered that many aspects of India's cultural heritage were in intrinsic value to India's cultural awakening. The result was the birth of many socio-religious reform movements touching almost every segment of Indian society.

The Two Categories of Reform Movements

The reform movements fall into two broad categories: one, reformist movements like the *Brahmo Samaj*, the *Prarthana Samaj* and the *Aligarh* movement. Secondly, there were Revivalist movements like the Arya Samaj, the Ramakrishna mission and the *Deobandi* movement. Both the reformist and the revivalist movements depended on a varying degree on an appeal to the lost purity of the religion they sought to reform. The only difference between one reform movement to the other lay in the degree to which they relied on tradition or on reason and conscience.

Another significant aspect of all the reform movements was their emphasis on both religious and social reform. This link was primarily due to two main reasons: (a) almost every social custom and institution in India derived sustenance from religious injunctions and sanctions. This meant that no social reform could be undertaken unless the existing religious notions which sustained the social customs were also reformed. (b) Indian reformers well understood the close interrelation between different aspects of human activities. Rammohun Roy, for example believed that religious reform must precede demand for social reform or political rights.

The Brahmo Samaj (The Society of God)

The *Brahmo Samaj* (society) was the earliest reform movement of the modern type which was greatly influenced by modern western ideas. Raja Rammohun Roy (1774–1833) was the founder of Brahmo Samaj. He was a very well-read man. He studied oriental languages like Persian and Sanskrit and attained proficiency in European languages like English, Latin, Greek and Hebrew. His extensive studies freed his mind from the bigotry which characterised an average Bengali.

Rammohun Roy accepted the concept of one God as propounded by the *Upanishads* (constitute the concluding portions of the *Vedas* which is the oldest scripture of Hinduism). For him, God was shapeless, invisible, omnipresent and omnipotent, but the guiding spirit of the universe and omniscient. In August 1882, Roy founded the *Brahmo Sabha* which was later renamed *Brahmo Samaj*. The Trust Deed executed in 1830 explained the object of the *Brahmo Samaj* as "the worship and adoration of the eternal, unsearchable and immutable being who is the author and preserver of the universe." The *Samaj* declared its opposition to idol worship and "nor graven image, statute or sculpture, curving, painting, picture, portrait or the likeness of anything was to be allowed in the *Samaj* or sacrifices of any kind were allowed. The worship was performed through prayers and meditation and readings from the *Upanishads*. Great emphasis was put on "promotion of charity, morality, piety, benevolence, virtue and strengthening of the bonds of union between men of all religious persuasions and creeds."

It should be clearly understood that Ram Mohun Roy never intended to establish a new religion. He only wanted to purge Hinduism of the evil practices that had crept into it. Roy remained a devout Hindu till the end of his life and always wore the sacred thread.

The Arya Samaj

The *Arya Samaj* movement was an outcome of reaction to western influences. It was revivalist in nature though not in content. The founder, Swami Dayanand rejected western ideas and sought to revive the ancient religion of the *Aryans*.

Mulshankar (1924-83) popularly known as Dayanand was born in a Brahmin family living in the old Morvi State in Gujarat. His father, a great Vedic scholar also assumed the role of teacher and helped young Mulshankar acquire good insight into Vedic literature, logic, philosophy, ethics etc. Dayanand's quest for the truth goaded him to *yogabhyas* (contemplation of communion) and to learn yoga, it was necessary to leave home. For fifteen years (1845-60), Dayanand wandered as an ascetic in the whole of India studying yoga. In 1875, he formally organised the first *Arya Samaj* unit at Bombay. A few years later, the headquarters of the *Arya Samaj* was established at Lahore. For the rest of his life, Dayanand extensively toured India to propagate his ideas.

Dayanand's ideal was to unite India religiously, socially and nationally – *Aryan* religion to be the common religion for all, a classless and casteless society and an India free from foreign rule. He looked at the *Vedas* as India's "Rock of Ages", the true original seed of Hinduism. His motto was 'Go back to the *Vedas*'. He gave his own interpretation of the *Vedas*. He disregarded the authority of the later Hindu scriptures like the *Puranas* and described them as the work of lesser men and responsible for the evil practices of idol worship and other superstitious beliefs in Hindu religion. Dayanand condemned idol worship and preached unity of the Godhead. His views were published in his famous work *Satyartha Prakash* (The True Exposition).

The Ramakrishna Movement

The didactic rationalism of the *Brahmo Samaj* appealed more the intellectual elite in Bengal while the average *Bengali* found more emotional satisfaction in the cult of bhakti and yoga. The teachings of *Ramakrishan Mission* are based on ancient and traditional concepts amid increasing westernization and modernisation. The Ramakrishna Mission was conceived and founded by Swami Vivekananda in 1897, eleven years after the death of Ramakrishna.

Ramakrishna Paramahansa (1834-86) was a poor priest at the *Kali* temple in Dakshineswar near Calcutta. His thinking was rooted deeply in Indian thought and culture, although he recognised the truth in all religions. He considered and emphasised that Krishna, Hari, Rama, Christ, Allah are different names for the same God. Unlike the *Arya Samaj, Ramakrishna Mission* recognises the utility and value of image worship in developing spiritual fervor and worship of the eternal omnipotent God. However, Ramakrishna put his emphasis on the essential spirit, not the symbols or rituals. He stood for selfless devotion to God with a view to the ultimate absorption in Him. This spirituality and compassion for suffering humanity inspired those who listened to him.

It was left to Swami Vivekananda (Narendranath Datta) 1862–1902) to give an interpretation of the teaching of Ramakrishna and render them in an easily understandable language to the modern man.

The Theosophical Movement

The theosophical movement society was founded by Westerners who drew inspiration from Indian thought and culture. Madame H.P. Blavatsky (1831-1891) of Russo-German birth laid the foundation of the movement in the United States in 1875. Later Colonel M.S. Alcott (1932-1907) of the U.S army joined her. In 1882, they shifted their headquarters to India at Adyar, outskirts of Madras. The members of this society believe that a special relationship can be established between a person's soul and God by contemplation, prayer, revelation etc. the society accepts the Hindu beliefs in incarnation, karma and draws inspiration from the philosophy of the *Upanishads* and *Samkhya*, *yoga* and *Vedanta* school of thought. It aims to work for universal brotherhood of humanity without distinction of race, creed, sex, caste or colour. The society also seeks to investigate the unexplained laws of nature and the powers latent in man. The Theosophical Movement came to be allied with the Hindu Renaissancc.

Muslim Reform Movements

If Hindu minds had responded to Western influences with a desire to learn, the first reaction of the Muslim community was to shut them in a shell and resist the Western impact.

The earliest organised Muslim response to Western influences appeared in the form of the *Wahabi Movement* which (may more aptly be called the Walliullah movement). It was essentially a revivalist movement. Shah Walliullah (1702-62) was the first Indian Muslim leader of the eighteenth century who expressed concern at the degeneration which had set in among Indian Muslims. He voiced his anguish at the ugly departure from the purity of Islam. His contribution to the Muslim reform movement was two fold. (a) He urged the desirability of creating harmony among the four schools of Muslim jurisprudence which had divided the Indian Muslims. He sought to integrate the best elements of the four schools. (b) He emphasised the role of individual conscience in religion. He held that in cases where the *Quran* and the Hadis could be liable to conflicting interpretations, the individual could make a decision on the basis of his own judgment and conscience. The various reform movements gave the much needed confidence to educated Indians who had been demoralised and uprooted from their moorings by propaganda of western cultural superiority. These reform movements reassured Indians about the greatness of their ancient religions and their rich cultural heritage. The intelligentsia got a new identity which was badly needed.

The reform atmosphere helped Indians to discard many obsolete rites and practices and adjust their religious beliefs to the new environment of rationalist and scientific thought. Above all, a new secular and nationalist outlook also developed.

The reform movements suffered from some retrograde features. Many reformists desired and worked for social uplift within the framework of imperialism and openly preached loyalty to the British. Again, these reformists held western society as an ideal while combating inadequacies of their own. Another limitation was that most of these reform movements confined their activities to upper and middle classes in towns leaving out of purview the backward classes and countless millions living in India's villages. Still another negative aspect was the growth of religious chauvinism. The over-emphasis on superiority of one's religion and social set-up generated narrow communal outlook. The imperial rulers were quick to take advantage of this communal divide and used it to weaken the Indian national movement.

Social Reform Movements in the nineteenth and twenteeth Centuries

The same set of circumstances – the impact of modern education, rational, humanitarian and scientific approach to life which ushered in both action and reaction – reform movements in religion were largely responsible for social reform movements in the nineteenth and twentieth centuries. Rammohun Roy, a pioneer in modern religious reform movements in India was also the Morning Star of modern social reform movement in the country. Social reform became an integral part of religious reform in India and this was equally true of *Brahmo Samaj, Prarthana Samaj, Arya Samaj, Ramakrishna Mission, Theosophical Society* in Hinduism also among the Muslims, the Parsis and the Sikhs. C.H. Heimsath in an excellent analysis of the Hindu social reform movements has indicated three distinct phases in the history of social reform in India, viz-a-viz first phase of individual revolt and reform together with strong religious links from Rammohun to the early 1880s, the second phase was marked by the elevation of social reform movements to a national plane as explified by the efforts of Behramji Malabari and the Indian National Social Conference; the third stage began when social reform was identified with a regeneration of the traditional spirit of the nation and is popularly associated with the activities of 'extremist' leaders of the early twentieth century. To it may be added the fourth phase under the leadership of Mahatma Gandhi when social reform became a main plank in the all-round regeneration of Indian society.

The social reform movements in India have aimed at uprooting social evils and inculcating in men and women the spirit of sacrifice for the general good of the society. The first and biggest problem that attracted enlightened opinion was the need for a better deal for women in society, in the abolition of the cruel rites of *sati* and infanticide, in the condemnation of child marriages and polygamy and popularisation of widow remarriage, in the abolition of purdah, in provision of educational facilities for women and economic openings to make them self-supporting and finally, an equal share for women in the political life of the country by enfranchisement. Another social evil that was a major concern of the English-educated and Hindu intelligentsia was the caste restrictions in Hindu society and the degrading position of the lower castes especially the untouchables. Of these two great evils, those connected with the position of women received greater attention in the nineteenth century, while the problem of the untouchables (*Harijans*) came in sharp focus in the twentieth century because of its political overtones.

Sati or *Satti*

The term *sati* means a 'pure and virtuous woman'. It was applied in cases of a devoted wife who contemplated perpetual and uninterrupted conjugal union with her husband life after life and as proof thereof burnt herself with the dead body of her husband. Enlightened Indian rulers like Akbar and the Peshwas had imposed restrictions on its performance. Though the East India Company broadly adhered to its declared policy of non-interference with the social customs of the people, yet early Governors-general like Cornwallis, Minto and Lord Hastings had taken some steps to restrict the practice of *sati* discouraging compulsion, forbidding administration of intoxicating drugs to sorrow stricken widows, putting a ban on the *sati* of pregnant women or widows below the age of 16 years and above all, making compulsory presence of police officials at the time of sacrifice who were to see that no compulsion was used. However, these restrictions proved inadequate and achieved limited success.

Enlightened Indian reformers led by Rammohun Roy launched a frontal attack on the evil *sati.* With an eye on the coming Charter debates in the British Parliament and anxious to get a renewal of its charter for another 20 years by presenting a credible image of its activities in India, the Court of Directors encouraged William

Bentinck to enact legislation to suppress *sati.* Regulation XVIII of December 1829 declared the practice of *sati* or burning or burying alive of widows illegal and punishable by criminal courts as culpable homicide. The regulation of 1829 was applicable in the first instance to Bengal Presidency alone but was extended in slightly modified forms to Madras and Bombay Presidencies in 1830. Thus, the evil practice of *sati* on any scale was wiped out though stray cases might have occurred here and there.

Infanticide

Another horrible and cruel rite particularly common among the Bengali and the Rajputs was that of killing their infant daughters at birth, taking female to be a great economic liability. Further, their parents could not arrange marriage for these daughter as it was considered a social disgrace and a violation of religious injunctions. Some socially backward tribes followed the practice of killing their infant daughter at birth. This was done by the mother by deliberately neglecting to feed the female child or administering poisonous drugs to the child through the nipples of the mother's breast. Maharaja Dalip Singh, son of Ranjit Singh mentions that, "he had actually seen when he was a child at Lahore his sisters put into a sack and thrown into the river."

Enlightened British and Indian opinion was unanimous in condemning infanticide. When persuasion, alone, could not help the Bengal Regulations XXI of 195 and III of 1804 declared infanticide illegal and equivalent to committing a murder. Pressure was exerted through Political Residents and Agents in Indian States to eradicate this evil rite. As a precautionary measure, the Government of India passed an Act in 1870 making it compulsory for parents to register the birth of all babies and providing for verification of female children for some years after birth, particularly in areas where the custom was resorted to in utmost privacy.

Widow Remarriage and Prohibition of Child Marriage

The plight of women in society could not be improved merely by suppression of *sati* and infanticide but by positive action in popularising widow remarriage and raising the age limit for marriage of girls. The *Brahmo Samaj* debated the question of widow remarriage and popularised it among the *Brahmos*. The efforts of Ishwar Chandra Vidyasagar (1820-1891), Principal of Sanskrit College, Calcutta deserve special mention. He dug up old Sanskrit references and proved that Vedic texts sanctioned widow remarriage. He sent a petition signed by 987 persons to the Government of India urging it for legislative action. His efforts were rewarded when the Hindu Widows' Remarriage Act (Act XV of 1856) legalised marriage of widows and declared issues from such marriage as legitimate. However, in Bengal, the widow remarriage reform achieved very limited success.

In western India, Professor D.K. Karve took up the cause of widow remarriage in Madras. Veeresalingam Pantulu made Herculean efforts in the same direction. Professor Karve started his career as a teacher in a Girls school at Bombay and seven years later in 1891, he became a professor at Fergusson College. In the meantime, he became a widower and refused to marry a teenager. He instead married a Brahmin widow in 1893. Karve devoted his life to the uplifting of the Hindu widows and became the secretary of the Widow Remarriage Association. In 1899, he opened a Widows' Home in Poona with the object of giving high castes widows an interest in life by providing them openings in the profession of teachers, doctors and nurses and making them, at the same time, self-supporting. He crowned his work by setting up an Indian Women's University at Bombay in 1916.

Legislative action in prohibiting child marriages came in 1872 when the Native Marriage Act (popularly known as Civil Marriage Act) made the marriage of girls below the age of 14 years and boys below the age of 18 years forbidden. However, this Act was not applicable to Hindus, Muslims and other recognised faiths and as such had very limited impact on Indian society. B.M. Malabari, a Parsi reformer of the nineteenth century started a crusade against child marriage and his efforts were crowned by the enactment of the Age of Consent Act (1891) which forbade the marriage of girls below the age of 12. The Sharda Act (1930) further pushed up marriage age and provided for penal action in marriages of boys younger than 18 years and girls younger than 14 years of age. A further improvement was made by the Child Marriage Restraint (Amendment) Act, 1978 which raised the marriage for girls from 15 to 18 years and for boys from 18 to 21 years.

Education of Women

In the nineteenth century, the Hindu society suffered from false religious illusions that Hindu scriptures did not sanction female education and that education of girls wrought wrath of gods leading to their widowhood.

The Christian missionaries, whatever the motives, were the first to set up the Calcutta Female Juvenile Society in 1819. The celebrated name of J.E.D. Bethune, president of the Council of Education will always be remembered with respect. In 1849, he founded a Girls' School in Calcutta. Ishwar Chandra Vidyasagar also did a lot in popularising the cause of female education and was associated with no less than thirty-five girls' schools in Bengal. In Bombay, the students of Elphinstone Institute became the spear headers of the movement for women education and founded the Student's Literary and Scientific society. Charles Wood's dispatch on education (1854) laid great stress on the need for female education. In the broad perspective, women education became a part of the general campaign for amelioration of the plight of women in society.

Abolition of Slavery

Slavery of the Greek, Roman or American Negro type did not exist in India. Slavery in India was akin to what may be termed as bonded—servant, bonded-labour type and slaves in India were treated in a humane manner unknown to western countries. In this context, the observation of the Committee of Circuit deserves to be quoted. It reads, "The ideas of slavery borrowed from our American colonies will make every modification of it appear in the eyes of our countrymen in England a horrible evil. Here, slaves are treated as the children of the families to which they belong and often acquire a much happier state by their slavery that they could have hoped for by cultivating the land. Of course European slave owners in India treated their slaves in the same inhumane manner characterised by western slave owners.

Slavery was abolished in the British Empire in 1833 and a clause was inserted in the Charter Act of 1833 requiring the Governor-General- in- Council to abolish slavery in India as soon as it could be safely and conveniently carried out. Act V of 1843 declared slavery illegal in India and all existing slaves were emancipated without any compensation to the slave owners. The Penal Code of 1860 also declared trade in slavery illegal. Bonded labour in one or the other form however lingers on in India even now. There is no doubt that the above changes had a great impact on Indian society. Willingly or unwillingly, Indians were influenced by westernisation which had both negative and positive consequences.

3

The 1857 Revolt: Causes, Resistance and Aftermath

Introduction

The year 1857 stands firmly in the history of India. It witnessed the country's first gigantic anti-foreign uprising of all classes of people – the sepoy (soldiers) mutiny – with the sole objective of ejecting the alien ruling power which had become a stumbling block to many Indians' enjoyment of their economic, political, social, religious and military rights and privileges – the British East India Company. The sepoy (working under the East India Company) mutiny was the widespread and prolonged rebellion against British rule in India that began in Bengal by Indian troops (sepoys) in the service of the East India Company. Although historians have greatly emphasised the importance of the military grievances as the most potent cause of the 1857 revolt, it had many other causes which lay deeper in the history of the hundred years of Company rule. Military grievances were merely the trigger which sparked off or exploded the inflammable material which had gathered in heap on account of various causes like economic, political, social and religious.

The record of the East India Company had been of ever increasing conquest and commercial exploitation. The greed of the Company knew no limits. The cumulative effect of British expansionist policies, economic exploitation and administrative innovations over the years had adversely affected the position of all rulers of Indian States, sepoys, *zamindars* (landlords), peasants, traders, pundits and moulvies (priests) etc. excepting of course the western educated class in towns who owed their 'position' to the Company's Government. The Luck Now Proclamation pinpointed that British rule had endangered all the four things dear to Hindus and Muslims alike – religion, honour, life and property. The resentment of the Indians had found expression in a number of mutinies and insurrection from time to time in different parts of the country; to mention only a few, the mutiny of Vellore in 1806, at Barrackpore in 1824 and at Ferozepur in February 1842. The simmering discontent burst out into a violent storm in 1857 which shook the British Empire in India to its very foundation.

Historians Views

Historians have held divergent views about the nature of the outbreak of 1857. British military historians, civil servant and army officer like J.W. Kaye, G.M. Treevelyan, E. J.Lawrence and R. Holmes have painted it as a 'mutiny' confined to the army which did not command the support of the people at large. A similar view was held by many contemporary Indians like Munshi Jiwan Lal, Moinuddin (both eyewitnesses at Delhi), Durgadas Bandhopadhyaya (eye witness at Bareilly), Sir Syed Ahmad Khan (Sadr Amin at Bihjor in 1857) among many others. Others described it as a 'religious white'. Still others described it as 'a struggle between oriental and occidental civilisation and culture'. A few described it as a result of Hindu, Muslim conspiracy to overthrow the British rule. Some Indian nationalists have called it a well-planned national struggle and as \the first war of Indian independence.'

Lawrence thought it to be a Sepoys' Mutiny and nothing more. Kaye and J. R. Seeley (English historian and essayist) described the Revolt of 1857 as a 'wholly unpatriotic and selfish Sepoy Mutiny with no native leadership and no popular support.' According to him, it was a rebellion of the Indian Sepoys against the constituted government of the day. Some Indian states it is conceded also joined in the revolt but these were states which nursed a grievance because of the annexation policy of Governor—general of India, Lord

Dalhousie. The British Government as the constituted authority of the land suppressed the revolt and restored laws and order. The interpretation is unsatisfactory. Unquestioningly, the revolt began as a military uprising but it was not everywhere confined to the army. Even the army as a whole did not join the revolt and a considerable section fought on the side of the government. In fact, the rebels came from almost every section of the population. In Oudh, it enjoyed the support of the masses and so also in some districts of Bihar. In the trials of 1858-59, thousands of civilians along with the soldiers were held guilty of rebellion and punished.

Causes of Revolt

There were many reasons behind the igniting the army in 1857 to revolt against the British rulers. It sounds as if it was a revolt by the army but it included larger section of people from different groups of society. At one point it looked as if the colonial rule was over but it was suppressed ruthlessly.

The Anglo-Indian historians have greatly emphasised the importance of military grievances and the greased cartridges affair as the most potent causes which led to the great uprising of 1857. But modern Indian historians have established beyond doubt that 'the greased cartridge' was neither the only cause nor even the most important of them. The causes of the rebellion lay deeper and are to be found in the history of the hundred years of British rule from the Battle of Plassey (June 1757) to the rebellion of Mangal Pandey when March 29, 1857, he murdered an English adjutant. The greased cartridge and the mutiny of soldiers was merely the matchstick which exploded the inflammable material which had gathered in heap on account of a variety of causes – political, social, religious and economic.

Political Causes

The East India Company's policy of 'effective control' and gradual extinction of the Indian native states took a definite shape with the perfection of the Subsidiary Alliance System under Lord Wellesley. Its social culmination was reached under Dalhousie who

Plate 2

Mangal Pandey

threw all codes of morality and political conduct to the winds and perfected the infamous doctrine of Lapse. Dalhousie's annexations and the Doctrine of lapse had caused suspicion and uneasiness in the minds of almost all ruling princes in India. The right of succession was denied to the Hindu Princes. The guarantee of adoption to the throne "did not extend to any person in whose veins the blood of the founders of the dynasty did not run." Distinction between 'dependent states and "protected allies" was very thin that looked more like hair splitting. Oudh was annexed on the pretext of "the good of the governed". Legal titles of the Nawabs of Carnatic and Tanjore were abolished and the pension of Peshwa Baji Rao II's adopted son was stopped. The Indians held that the existence of all states was threatened and absorption of all states was just a question of time. King of Jhansi's adopted son was not recognised after his death, by the Company rulers by applying the Doctrine of Lapse, which was not tolerated by the widow of king, Rani(queen) Laxmibai and consequently she supported the mutiny but was killed in battle with British soldier under Field Martial Hugh Ross. As such, the dominant belief then was that annexations were not because of the Doctrine of Lapse but due to the 'lapse of morals' on the part of the East Indian Company.

The Muslim feelings had been grievously hurt. Bahadur Shah II, the Mughal Emperor, was an old man and might die any moment. Lord Dalhousie was not in favour of retaining an *imperium in imperia* and recognised the succession of Prince Faquire-ud-Din but imposed many strict conditions on him.

Administrative and Economic Causes

The annexation of Indian states produced startling economic and social effects. The Indian aristocracy was deprived of power and position. It found little chance to gain the same old position in the new administrative set-up as under the British rule all high post, civil and military were reserved for Europeans.

The administrative machinery of the East India Company was 'inefficient and insufficient.' The land revenue policy was most unpopular. Many districts in the newly-annexed states were in permanent revolt and the military had to be sent to collect land revenue. In the district of Panipat, for example, 136 horsemen were maintained for the collection of land revenue while only 22 were employed for the performance of police duties. At the outbreak of the rebellion, Sir Henry Lawrence (British soldier and statesman) is reported to have remarked: "It was the A.M. T. Jackson (the district magistrate of Nasik), G. Thomason (appointed to command of the levy raised for the protection of the lines at Peshawar) G.F. Edmonstone (Agent to the governor general in central India) brought India to this." In the land revenue settlement of newly acquired territories, the English administration had eliminated the middleman by establishing direct contact with the peasants. The land revenue settlement of North-Western Province was described as "a fearful experiment….calculated to flatten the whole surface of society." Many *Talukdars* (tax collector for the Government), the hereditary landlords were deprived of their positions and gains. Many holders of rent free tenures were disposed by the use of a quo-warrantor requiring the holders of such lands to produce evidence like title deed by which they held that land. Large estates were confiscated and sold by public auction to the highest bidders. Such estates were usually purchased by speculators who did not understand the tenants and fully exploited them. It was Coverly Jackson's (Chief Commissioner of Oudh) policy of disbanding the native soldiers and of strict inquiry into the titles of the *Talukdars* of Oudh that made Oudh the chief centre of rebellion. The Land Commission appointed in 1852 in Bombay confiscated as many as 20,000 estates.

Thus, the new land settlements made by the East India Company in the newly-annexed states drove poverty in the ranks of the aristocracy without benefiting the peasantry which groaned under the weight of heavy assessments and excessive duties. The peasants whose welfare was the chief motive of the new revenue policy did not like the passing of old ways. They fell in the clutches of unprincipled money lenders; they often visited their disposed landlords and with tears in their eyes expressed sympathy for them. The *Taluqdars* of Oudh were the hardest hit. In the words of Asoka Mehta: "out of the 20,543 villages included in their estates at the time of the annexation of the kingdom, 13,640 paying a revenue of Rs 35,065,19 were settled with *Taluqdars*, while 11,903 villages paying Rs. 32,08,319 were settled with persons other than *Taluqdars*. The *Taluqdars* had lost half their villages, some had lost their all." The ruthless manner in which the Thomason Ian system was carried into effect may be clear from the resumption of the revenue of free villages granted for the temple of Lakshmi in Jhansi. British economic policies in India worked against the interests of Indian trade and industry. The East India Company used its political power to destroy Indian handicrafts and industry and developed it into an appendage of a foreign exploitative system. Writing in 1853, Karl Marx a very shrewd observer very aptly remarked: "it was the British intruder who broke up the Indian handloom and destroyed the spinning wheel." England began with depriving the Indian cottons on the European market. It then introduced twist into Hindustan and in the end inundated the very mother of cotton with cottons. The ruining of the Indian market increased the pressure on agriculture and land which lopsided development in turn resulted in the pauperisation of the country in general.

Social and Religious Causes

Like all conquering people, the English rulers of India were rude and arrogant towards the subject people. However, the English were infected with the spirit of racialism. The rulers followed a policy of contempt towards the Indians and described the Hindus as barbarians with hardly any trace of culture and civilisation while the Muslims were dubbed as bigots and faithless.

European officers and European soldiers on their hunting sprees were often guilty of indiscriminate criminal assaults on Indians. The European juries which alone could try such cases, acquitted European criminals with light or no punishment. Such discrimination rankled in the Indian mind like a festering sore.

It may be easy to withstand the physical and political injustices but religious persecution touches tender conscience and forms complexes that are not easy to eradicate. That one of the aims of the English in India was to convert the Indians to Christianity is clear from the speech of Mr Mangles, the Chairman of the Directors of the East India Company, in the House of Commons: "Providence has entrusted the extensive empire of Hindustan to England in order that the banner of Christ should wave triumphant from one end of India to the other. Everyone must exert all his strength that there may be no dilatoriness on any account in continuing the grand work of making all Indians Christians." Major Edwards had openly declared that "the Christianisation of India was to be the ultimate end of our continued possession of it." Vir Savarkar (fearless freedom fighter) has pointed that the superior military and civil officers used to abuse the very names of Ram and Mohammad and prevail upon the sepoys and the civilians to embrace the Christian faith. Sepoys were promised promotions if they accepted the True Faith. The missionaries were given ample facilities and the American Missionary Society at Agra had set up an extensive printing press. Idolatry was denounced, Hindu gods and goddesses ridiculed and Hindu superstitions dubbed as ignorance.

The Religious Disabilities Act of 1850 modified Hindu customs. A change of religion did not debar son from inheriting the property of his heathen father. Strange rumours were rampant in India that Lord Canning had been specially selected and charged with the duty of converting the Indians to Christianity. In this surcharged atmosphere, even the railways and steamships began to be looked upon as indirect instruments for changing their faith. The telegraph was regarded as 'the accursed string' and the rebels once said that "it was this accursed string that strangled them."

The Indian mind was getting increasingly convinced that he English were conspiring to convert them to Christianity. The activities of Christian Padris (priest) and efforts of Dalhousie and Bethune towards women's education made Indians feel that through education, the British were going to conquer their civilisation.

Military Causes

Since the Afghan adventure of Lord Auckland, the discipline in the army had suffered a serious setback. Lord Dalhousie had written to the Home authorities that "the discipline of the army from top to bottom, officers and men alike, is scandalous." The Bengal army was "a great brotherhood in which all the members felt and acted in union," and service in the army was hereditary. Three-fifths of the recruits of the Bengal Army were drawn from Oudh and the North-Western Provinces and most of them came from high caste Brahmin and Rajput families who were averse to accepting that part of the army discipline which treated them at par with the low caste recruits. Sir Charles Napier(General of the British Empire and the British Army's Commander- in- Chief, notable for conquering Sindh, in 1843) had no confidence in the allegiance of 'high caste mercenaries.' During the Governor-generalship of Lord Dalhousie, three mutinies had occurred in the army- the mutiny of the 22nd N. I. (Native Infantry)) in 1849; of the 66th N. I. in 1850 and the 38th N. I. in 1852.

The Bengal Army sepoys reflected all the feelings of the civil population of Oudh. In the opinion of Maulana Azad (revolutionist and journalist), the annexation of Oudh "marked the beginning of a rebellious mood in the army generally and in the Bengal Army in particular…. It gave a rude shock to the people….they suddenly realised that the power which the Company had acquired through their service and sacrifice was utilised to liquidate their own king."

The extension of British dominion in India had adversely affected the service condition of the sepoys. They were required to serve in areas far away from their homes without extra payment (*bhatta*). The sepoys yearned for the good old days when the Indian rulers used to crown their meritorious deeds by bestowing *jagirs* and other prizes upon them whereas their victories in Sind and the Punjab had brought worse days for them. In 1824, the sepoys at Barrackpore refused to serve across the seas in Burma and the 47th Regiment was disbanded. In 1844, the Four Bengal Regiments refused to move to Sind till extra *bhatta* was sanctioned.

In 1856, Governor-general Charles Canning's (shown on next page) passed the General Service Enlistment Act which decreed that all future recruits for the Bengal army would have to give an undertaking to serve anywhere their service might be required by the Government. The Act did not affect old incumbents, but was unpopular because service in the Bengal army was usually hereditary. Moreover, those soldiers who had been sent in the army of invasion of Afghanistan during the 1839-1843 war had not been taken back in the folds of the caste. Sepoys declared unfit for Foreign Service were allowed to retire with a pension but were to be posted for duty at cantonments.

The privilege of free postage so long enjoyed by the sepoys was withdrawn with the passing of the Post Office Act of 1854. Besides, the disparity in numbers between the European and Indian troops had been growing bigger. In 1856, the Company's army consisted of

Plate 3

Governor General Charles Canning (1856–1862)

238,000 natives and 45,322 British soldiers. This disproportion was rendered more serious by the deficiency of good officers in the army, most of whom were employed in administrative posts in the newly annexed states and frontiers. The distribution of the troops was also faulty. Moreover, disasters in the Crimean war had lowered the general morale of the British soldiers. All these factors made the Indian soldiers feel that if they struck at that hour, they had reasonable chances at success. Therefore, they were only waiting for an occasion which was provided by the 'greased cartridge' incident. The greased cartridges did not create a new cause for discontent in the army but supplied the occasion when the underground discontent came out in the open. In 1858, the Government decided to replace the old fashioned musket 'Brown Bess' by the 'Enfield rifle'. The training for the use of the new weapon was to be imparted at Dum, Ambala and Sialkot. The loading process of the Enfield rifle involved bringing the cartridge to the mouth and biting off the top paper. In January 1857, a story got currency in Bengal regiments that the greased cartridge contained the fat of pigs and cows. At once, a denial was issued by the military authorities without investigating into the matter. Subsequent enquiries proved that "the fat of cattle really had been used at Woolwich arsenal". Assurances of superior officers and slight concessions proved of no avail. The sepoys became convinced that the introduction of greased cartridges was a deliberate move to defile their religion. It was argued that the East India Company was playing the part of Aurangzeb and it was but natural that sepoys should play the part of Shivaji (also known as Chhatrapati Shivaji Maharaj, 1827–1680, was an Indian warrior).

The Beginning and Spread of the Mutiny

The refusal of the sepoys to use the greased cartridges was regarded by the authorities as an act of insubordination and punished accordingly. On 29th March 1857 the sepoys at Barraokpore refused to use the greased cartridge and one Brahmin sepoy, Mangal Pandey, attacked and fired at the Adjutant. The 34 N.I. regiment was disbanded and sepoys guilty of rebellion punished. At Meerut, in May 1857, 85 sepoys of the 3rd Cavalry regiment on their refusal to use the cartridge were court-martialed and sentenced to long terms of imprisonment. On 10th May, the sepoys broke out in open rebellion, shot their officers, released their fellow sepoys and headed towards Delhi. General Hewitt, the Officer Commanding at Meerut, had 2,200 European soldiers at his disposal but did nothing to stem the rising tide.

Delhi was seized by the rebel on 12th May 1857. Lieutenant Willoughby, the officer-in-charge of the magazine at Delhi, offered some resistance but was overcome. The palace and the city were occupied. Some European inhabitants of Delhi were shot dead. Bahadur Shah II was proclaimed the emperor of India. The loss of Delhi was a serious loss of prestige to the English.

Very soon the rebellion spread throughout Northern and Central India at Lucknow, Allahabad, Kanpur, Bareilly, Banaras, in parts of

Bihar, Jhansi and other places. Fortunately for the English, the Indian rulers remained loyal and rendered valuable services in the suppression of the rebellion. India, south of the Narbada remained practically undisturbed.

Descriptive Notes on the Spread of Mutiny and the Civil Rebellion in the Period 1857-1858

2nd February 1857	- Mutiny of the 19th Native Infantry at Berhampur
10th May 1857	- Mutiny of sepoys at Meerut
11-30th May 1857	- Outbreaks in Delhi, Ferozepur, Bombay, Aligarh, Etawah, Bulandshahar, Nasirabad, Bareilly, Moradabad, Shahjehanpur and other stations in U.P.
	- The Mughal Emperor proclaimed as the Emperor of India
June 1857	- Mutinies at Gwalior, Bharatpur, Jhansi, Allahabad, Faizabad, Sultanpur, Lukhnow etc.
	- The civil rebellion spreads through the Indo-Gangetic plain, Rajputana, central India and some parts of Bengal.
July 1857	- Mutinies at Indore, Mhow, Saugor and certain places in the Punjab like Jhelum, Sialkot etc.
August 1857	- Civil rebellion spreads throughout Saugor and Nerbudda districts.
September 1857	- The English recapture Delhi: further outbreaks in central India.
October 1857	- Revolt spreads to Kotah State
November 1857	- The rebels defeat General Windham outside Kanpur.
December 1557	- Sir Colin Campbell wins the battle of Kanpur.
	- Tantia Tope escapes.

March 1858	- Lucknow recaptured by the English
April 1858	- Jhansi falls to the English fresh rising in Bihar led by Kunwar Singh
May 1858	- The English recapture Batreilly, Jagdishpur and Kalpi.
	- Indian rebels begin guerilla warfare in Rohilkhand.
July- Dec 1858	- English authority re-established in India.

The recapture of Delhi could be of great psychological importance and English efforts were directed towards that end. Troops from the Punjab were rushed and took their position to the north of Delhi. Tough resistance was offered by the Indian soldiers. In September 1857 Delhi was recaptured by the English but John Nicholson, the hero of the siege was badly wounded during the operations and succumbed to his injuries. The emperor was arrested. Terrible venegeance was wrecked on the inhabitants of Delhi. Two sons and a grandson of the emperor were publicly shot by Lieut Hodson himself.

The rebellion broke out at Lucknow on 4th June. Henry Lawrence, the British Resident, the European inhabitants and a few hundred loyal sepoys took shelter in the residency. The residency was besieged by the Indian rebels and Sir Henry was killed during the siege. The command of the besieged garrison devolved on Brigadier Ingles who held out against heavy odds. The early attempts of Havelock and Outram to recover Lucknow met with no success. Some relief came in November 1857 when Sir Colin Campbell, the new Commander-in-Chief sent from England entered the city with the help of Gorkha regiments and evacuated the Europeans. In March 1858, the city was finally reduced but guerilla activity continued till September the same year.

Kanpur was lost to the British on 5th June 1857. Nana Sahib was proclaimed the Peshwa. General Sir Hugh Wheeler commanding the station surrendered on June 27. Some Europeans men, women and children were murdered. At Kanpur Nana Sahib was joined by his able and experienced Lieutenant, Tantia Tope. The military operations for the recapture of Kanpur were closely associated with the recovery of Lucknow. Sir Campbell occupied Kanpur on December 6. Tantia Tope escaped and joined the Rani of Jhansi.

In the beginning of June 1857, the troops at Jhansi mutinied. Rani Lakshami Bai, the widow of the late Raja Gangadhar Rao, was proclaimed the ruler of the state. After the loss of Kanpur, Tantia Tope joined the Rani. Sir Hugh Rose recaptured Jhansi by assault on 3rd April 1858.

The Rani of Jhansi and Tantia Tope marched towards Gwalior where they were hailed by the Indian soldiers. The Sindhia however decided to remain loyal to the English and took shelter at Agra. Nana Sahib was proclaimed the Peshwa and plans were chalked out for a march to the south. Gwalior was recaptured by the English in June 1858, the Rani of Jhansi died fighting clad in soldier's uniform on the ramparts of the fort. Tantia Tope escaped southward in April 1859. He was captured by one of Sindhia's feudatory who handed him over to the British to be hanged.

At bareilly Khan Bahadur Khan had proclaimed himself the Nawab Nazim. In Bihar a local zamindar Kunwar Singh of Jagdishpur raised the banner of revolt. At Banaras a rebellion had been organised which was mercilessly suppressed by Colonel Neill who put to death all rebels, suspected and even disorderly boys. By July 1858 the rebellion had been almost completely suppressed.

Reasons for Failure of the Revolt

1. The Revolt of 1857 localised and lacked support from other states. The Bombay and the Madras armies remained loyal. India south of the Narbada was hardly disturbed. Sind and Rajasthan remained quiet and Nepal's help proved to be of great avail in the suppression of the Revolt. The ruler of Afghanistan, Dost Muhammad remained friendly with the British. The Punjab was effectively controlled by John Lawrence. The worst affected areas were western Bihar, Oudh, Rohitkhand, Delhi and the territory between the

Chamal and the Narbada and did not get enough support from other states.

2. The resources of the British Empire were far more superior than those of the rebels. Luckily for the British, the Crimean and the Chinese wars had been concluded by 1856 and British troops numbering 1,12,000 poured into India from all parts of the world. About 3,10,000 additional Indian soldiers were recruited in India. The Indian soldiers had very few guns and muskets and mostly fought with swords and spears. On the other hand, the European soldiers were equipped with the latest weapons of war like the Enfield rifle about which Nana Sahib said: "The blue caps kill before they fire." The electric telegraph kept the Commander-in-chief informed about the movements of the Indian rebels and their strategy. A concerted plan was formed to suppress the rebellion. Russell the correspondent of *The Times of London* summed up the advantages of the electric telegraph thus, "Never since its discovery has the telegraph played so important and daring a role as it now does in India. Without it, the Commander-in-Chief would lose the effect of half his force. It has served him better than his 'right arm.'" Considering the vast resources of the British Empire and her naval superiority, it may be said that even if the English had been driven back to the coastal areas or into the sea, before long, she would have reconquered India by her superior military strength.

3. The Revolt of 1857 was mainly feudal in character carrying with it some nationalistic elements. The feudal elements of Oudh Rohilkhand and some other parts of northern India led the rebellion. Other feudal princes like the Raja of Patiala, Jhind, Gwalior, Hyderabad helped in its suppression. European historians have greatly praised Sir Dinkar Rao, the Minister of Gwalior and Salar Jang, the Wazir-Hyderabad for their loyalty. In the moment of crisis, Canning said: "if the Sindhia joins the mutiny I shall have packed off tomorrow." Canning acted very wisely when he gave solemn

assurances to the Indian princes and thus won over their support. The Indian princes were amply rewarded after the suppression of the rebellion. The districts of Berar were restored to the Nizam and his debts remitted. Nepal was rewarded with the cessation of some Oudh territory. The Sindhia, the Gaikwad and the Rajput princes also received some rewards or concessions.

4. The Revolt was poorly organised. The leaders were not lacking in bravery but were deficient in experience, organising ability and concerted operations. Surprise attacks and guerrilla tactics could not win them their lost independence. The various commissions and boards appointed by the Government of India after the suppression of the rebellion could not find any plan behind the rebellion or any scheme on which the Revolt was launched. The trial of Bahadur Shah II rather proved that the rebellion was as much a surprise to him as to the British.
5. The rebels had no common ideal before them except the anti-foreign sentiments. Bahadur Shah II was declared the Emperor at Delhi while at Kanpur and Gwalior Nana Sahib was proclaimed the Peshwa. Hindu-Muslim differences lay dormant against the common enemy but were not dead. The peasants and the inferior castes showed no active sympathy and the soldiers in the Bombay and Madras armies were mostly recruited from the lower castes and they remained loyal.
6. The East India Company was fortunate in having the services of men of exceptional abilities in the Lawrence brothers, Nicholson, Outram, Havelock, Edwards etc. they fought the toughest battles in the initial stages of the Revolt and controlled the situation till reinforcement came from abroad.

It has been argued by the nationalist historians that whatever might have been its original character, it soon became a symbol of challenge to the mighty power of the British in India. It remained a thriving example before nascent nationalism in India in its struggle for freedom from the British yoke and was invested with the full glory of the first national war of independence against the British rule.

The Transfer of Power in 1858: From Company to the Crown

The Revolt of 1857 though completely suppressed had shaken the British rule in India from its very foundations. Lord Cromer once remarked: "I wish the young generation of the English would read, mark, learn and inwardly digest the history of the Indian Mutiny; it abounds in lessons and warnings." The techniques of controlling India though well established by 1857 were confirmed and uniformly acted upon thereafter. The reactionary and vested interests were well protected and encouraged and became pillars of British rule in India. The policy of divide and rule was deliberately pursued and made the main prop of British control. Tight European control over key positions both in the civil and military administration were maintained. It is important to know that the mutiny failed at that time but brought a lot of changes. It let the change of the master and India was taken by the British Crown from the Company rulers. Crown re-organised certain sectors but for Indians positives were still far away.

New Administrative Set Up

All sections of political opinion in England came to the conclusion that the East India Company's economic and administrative policies were largely responsible for the widespread discontent among different segments of Indian society which had erupted in the revolt of 1857. The British Government also got alarmed and took the decision to end the Company's rule in India. The Government also decided to put Indian administration under the direct rule of the Crown.

The British Parliament passed the Government of India Act, 1858 which transferred the government, territories and revenue from the Company to the Crown. The Act also declared that India was to be governed by and in the name of the Sovereign Queen and also authorised the appointment of an additional Principal Secretary of State and created the Council of India. Immediately after Queen Victoria issued a proclamation to the princes, chiefs and people of

India notifying them that she had taken upon herself the government earlier administered in trust for her by the Company. The Queen appointed George (Lord Canning) to be the first Viceroy.

A further development about the Crown's position in India was made in 1876 when the Sovereign was empowered by an act of parliament to assume the title of Empress of India (or Kaiser-i-Hind) and a proclamation to that effect was made in a Durbar held at Delhi on 1st January 1877. Since that time, it became customary in India to use the title 'Queen Empress' and 'King Emperor'.

The Secretary of State and the Indian Office

Under the Act of 1858, the Secretary of State (a British Minister of Indian Affairs) became the Constitutional advisor of the Crown in all matters relating to India. The Secretary of State was to be assisted by the Indian Council consisting of fifteen members appointed at first for life but later for periods of 10 to 15 years. The establishment of the Secretary of State-in-Council was commonly known as the Indian office. The Council divided Committees each under a Secretary, an Assistant Under Secretary with a staff of clerks. The other Departments of the Indian Office were those of the Accountant General, The Registrar, Superintendent of Records and the Director of Funds. The Medical Board, the Legal Advisor and Solicitor to the Secretary of State may also be mentioned. It should be noted that the salary of the auditor and his assistants as well as the salaries, pensions and other charges of the entire establishment of the Indian office were paid out of the revenue of the Government of India.

The Government of India

The Act of 1858 did not make any important changes in the administration of India but the Governor-general as representing the Crown became known as the Viceroy. The designation 'Viceroy' though most frequently used in ordinary parlance had no statutory authority and had never been used by parliament. This title of Viceroy was frequently employed in Warrants of Precedence in the statutes of Indian Orders and in public notifications, appeared to be one ceremony and was most appropriately used in connection with the State and social functions of the Sovereign's representative for the Governor general was the sole representative of the Crown in India. The salary of the Viceroy was fixed at Rupees 2 ½ lakhs per annum.

The Executive Council of the Governor-general consisted of four members. A fifth member was added in 1861 and permission for appointment of the sixth member made in 1874. For legislative purposes only, the Indian Council Act, 1861 expanded the Viceroy's Executive Council by addition of 'not less than six or more than twelve additional members'. The Indian Councils Act, 1892 carried this system further by increasing the strength of "additional" members from not less than 10 or not more than 16 members. The Indian Councils Act, 1909, the Government of India Act, 1919 and 1935 further expanded the Legislative Council but the real powers remained in the hands of the Governor-general.

The laying of direct cable line between England and India in 1870 and the introduction of steam vessels and the opening of the Suez Canal enabled the Secretary of State to tighten his control over Indian affairs. An offshoot of the centralisation of all effective authority in London was an indirect increase in the hold of British industrialists, merchants and bankers over the economic policy of India. In reality, the new administrative set-up after 1858 remained as before 1858, a foreign despotism. This was not a chance development but the result of a deliberate conviction and policy as is evident form the speech of Charles Wood at the time of moving the Indian Council's bill, 1861 in the British Parliament when he said: "All experience teaches us that where a dominant race rules, the other – a mild form of government is a despotism."

Reorganization of the Army

As the sepoy revolt at Meerut on 10th May had heralded the Mutiny and Revolt of 1857 and shook the very foundations of British rule in India, the reorganisation of the army received the maximum attention of the Home authorities. Sir, John Lawrence, the Chief Commissioner of the Punjab who had organised the English recapture of Delhi in September 1857 wrote, "among the defects of pre-mutiny army, unquestionably the worst and one that operated most fatally against us was the brotherhood and homogeneity of the Bengal army and for this purpose, the remedy is counterpoise of the Europeans and secondly of native races."

Another factor which brought the army in great focus was the fact that in the second half of the ninteenth century, Britain was spreading its tentacles over the whole of Africa and Asia and in reality emerged as the biggest imperial power in the whole "where the sun never set." Britain had perforce to fight against other imperial powers like France, Germany, Russia, Italy etc. thus the Indian army was strengthened and used: (a) for the defense of India's borders as also; and (b) for the defense and expansion of the British empire elsewhere in the world (e.g. the Indian army was sent to Crimea, China, New Zealand for defense of British imperial interests). The major changes introduced were:

(a) The East India Company's European forces were amalgamated with those of the Crown. The infantry became regiments of the line; the Bengal, Madras and Bombay artillery and the corresponding corps of Indian Engineers were amalgamated with the Royal Artillery and Royal Engineers.

(b) The strength of the European troops in India was increased from the pre-1857 figure of 45,000 to 65,000 and the number of Indian troops reduced from the pre-mutiny figure of 238,000 to 140,000.

(c) In Bengal presidency, the proportion between the European and Indian troops was at 1:2 while for Bombay and Madras presidencies, it was 1:3.

(d) A distinction between martial and non-martial races was made. The native troops from Punjab, Nepal and the North-West were declared as martial races and soldiers from these areas were recruited in large numbers.

(e) Various steps were taken to encourage regional loyalties among the soldiers so that they could not unite on national considerations.

As a result of the army reorganisation, defense expenditure increased and accounted for 25 per cent_30 per cent of the total central and provincial government's revenue in India.

Administrative Decentralisation

The Charter Act of 1833 passed by the British Parliament had brought about legislative centralisation in the Company's territories in India. The governments of Bombay and Madras were drastically deprived of their powers of legislation and left only with the right of proposing to the Governor-general-in-Council projects of law which they thought expedient.

The Indian Council Act, 1861 reversed the trend of legislative decentralisation when the Act restored legislative powers making and amending laws to provinces of Bombay and Madras with the reservation that in certain matters the Governor-General's prior approval had to be obtained. Legislative Councils were set up in Bengal and Bombay in 1862, in D.P. in 1886, in the Punjab in 1894, western Bengal and Assam in 1905 and the process was continued as and when new provinces were created. The powers of provincial Legislative Councils were enlarged by the Indian Councils Act, 1892. The process so begun was carried further by the Indian Councils Act, 1909. The Government of India Act, 1919 introduced 'Dyarchy' in the provinces and the Act of 1935 introduced 'provincial autonomy.'

The policy of financial devolution was initiated by Lord Mayo and continued further by Lord Lytton and Lord Ripon. In 1877, the provincial governments were given the control of expenditure on financial services like excise, land revenue reforms, law and justice etc. and also handed over some specified sources of revenue (e.g. licence fees) from their respective provinces. In 1882, the system of giving fixed grants to the provinces was stopped and instead, the system of 'Divided Heads' was introduced i.e. income from subjects like excise, stamps, forest. Registration was divided in equal proportion among the central provincial governments. The system of 'Divided Heads' remained operative till it was modified by the Government of India Act, 1919.

Local Bodies

The policy of legislative and financial decentralisation inaugurated in 1861 made possible the development of local self-government in the form of Municipalities and District Boards. The need for municipal-measures was recognised and Acts were passed for Bengal in 1864 and 1868 for Madras, in 1865 for the Punjab in 1867 and the North-western provinces (modern U.P) in 1868.

In 1870, Lord Mayo's Government while introducing the system of provincial finance emphasised the need for development of self-government and strengthening of municipal institutions. As a follow-up measure new municipal acts were passed for Madras in 1871; for Bombay, Bengal and the North-western provinces, the Punjab and the Central Province since 1873, and for Burma (then a part of India) in 1874. These Acts widened the sphere of municipal usefulness and extended the elective principle. However, the election procedure was not brought into practical operation in many places. It was Lord Ripon's government which through a Resolution in 1882 extended the election principle and local self-government acts were passed in 1883-1884 which greatly altered the Constitution, power and functions of municipal bodies. Even a private citizen was eligible for contesting the office of the chairman of a municipality, a position which had hitherto been filled by the executive officer. The Decentralisation Commission Report, 1908 recommended development of District Boards, Sub-Boards and Village Panchayats (group of five people). The Montfort Report, 1918 recommended, "There should be as far as possible complete popular control in local bodies and the largest possible independence for them of outside control." The Government of India Act, 1935 which introduced provincial autonomy gave a further impetus to development of local institutions.

The unfortunate part of the development of local self-institutions was the racial bias of the Anglo-Indian bureaucracy and their distrust about the competence of Indians to manage their own affairs even in local bodies. Lord Curzon's Government passed the Calcutta Corporation Act, 1899 which reduced the strength of elected members in the Calcutta Corporation. Even on the eve of Indian independence, the local bodies functioned more as departments of the Government rather than any local self-government bodies.

Economic Policy

The economic policy under the British Crown rule in India was subservient to the larger interests of Great Britain. In other words, Great Britain used her political control over India through economic exploitation of India's vast resources. However, the *modus-operandi* for economic exploitation changed with changing times. The character of 'drain of wealth' from India which operated on Mercantilist principles under the East India Company underwent a change under the Crown and took the form of exploitation through the policy of forced *laissez-faire*, that is free trade. At a later stage it took the form of British India Finance Capitalism.

In the latter half of the nineteenth century, many European countries imposed high custom duties to protect their indigenous industries against dumping of British industrial products. To compensate British industries for its loss of markets in Europe, the British Government forced the Government of India to adopt the policy of free trade and open Indian markets for unlimited sale of British industrial goods. Later, British Finance Capital entered India in a big way and made an iron grip over Indian industry, trade and commerce. Under the slogan of modernisation of India, British Capital was employed in the extension of railway lines (more for strategic defense purposes and also for better infiltration of British products into remote areas of India), development of iron and coal mines and intensive cultivation of plantation industry of tea, coffee, jute, indigo etc. the ports were developed and British owned steam companies carried on India's international trade. In short, Britain's financial, economic and industrial activities were interlocked in the race for thorough economic exploitation of India's resources.

Every section of Indian society barring the small comprador class was hard hit by Britain's economic policies.

The Land Tenure and Land Revenue policy of the British Indian Government divided the agricultural class into two rival camps-the *zamindar* class versus the tenant and agricultural labour. Further, the Government's excessive land revenue demand strengthened the money-lending class which emerged as the new parasite class in rural India. The new judicial system introduced by the British also became an instrument of exploitation of the poor and illiterate classes. In short, the rural masses were pushed below the poverty line.

The fate of the industrial worker was no better under the Crown rule. Unable to compete with the British industrial products available in the Indian market, the Indian industrialist tried to economise which took the form of payment of inadequate wages to the worker, long hours of work and even employment of child labour in factories. No doubt, the Trade Union Movement began in India with two organisations of the All India Trade Union Congress (AITUC) in 1920 and the All India Trade Union Federation in 1929, but these organisations functioned as appendages of national and international political parties.

The educated middle class faced racial discrimination in the sphere of higher civil and military services. The facilities for higher technical education remained inadequate.

For the country in general, the situation –whether it was in the field of industrial development or modernisation of agriculture was that of underdevelopment. Indian nationalist leaders like Dadabhai Naoroji, M.G. Ranade, G.V. Joshi and R.C. Dutt strongly criticised the economic policies of the Indian Government. Naoroji's famous book *Indian Poverty* and *un-British Rule in India* held British policies responsible for the '*growing poverty of India*' and accused Britain of "bleeding India White." J.L. Nehru used more blunt language when he wrote, "British and Indian economic interests conflict all along the line." The logical corollary of this statement was that only India's freedom from British colonial rule could improve the economic position of India.

Civil Services

Lord Cornwallis began the process of Europeanisation of higher services in India. Since the Court of Directors made all appointments to the Indian Civil Services (ICS) through nominations, no Indian ever got a chance. The Charter Act of 1833 under Section 87, provided that no Indian subject of the Company in India was to be debarred from holding any office under the Company "by 'reason of his religion,' place of birth, descent and colour." In actual practice, no Indian ever got appointment to the C.C.S. later renamed I.C.S.

In 1853, an Act of Parliament threw appointments to the I.C.S. through open competition. The first competitive examination was held in 1855. Though the doors were open to India aspirants, very few Indians got the chance because of numerous handicaps.

(a) The Indian Civil Service (I.C.S) examination was held in London only with no examination centre anywhere in India.

(b) The syllabus for the exam of Greek, Latin and England.

(c) The maximum limit for candidates was lowered from 23 years to 22 years in 1860, further lowered to 21 years in 1866 and later lowered to 19 years. After considerable agitation by Indian nationalists, the age limit was fixed between 22 to 24 years in 1906.

Not only were the higher services virtually closed to Indians even in the higher grades of minor services Indians were discriminated against. In the later category the competitors were the Eurasians popularly known as Anglo-Indians. In some services like the Survey of India, the Indian Salt Department, the Excise and Post Office Departments, the educational qualifications required from Anglo-Indian and domiciled Europeans were fixed lower than required from Indian candidates. For a long time, the P.W.D. Railways (Engineering), telegraph (engineering), the Railway (Stores) Departments were considered to be the close preserve of the Anglo-Indian community.

Relations with Princely States

The Indian princes like many other feudal elements in Indian society stood by the British Government during the Revolt of 1857.

Lord Canning openly recognised their pro-British role when he remarked, "if Gwalior, Hyderabad greatly helped the Government in the suppression of the Revolt.

After 1857, the British Government and the Government of India identified the Indian princes and the *zamindars* as the vested interests who benefited from the continuation of British rule in India. Thus, these elements became the main prop of British rule under the Crown.

The Queen's proclamation of 1858 promised "to respect the rights, dignity and honour of native princes as their own." The princes were amply rewarded when the Government abandoned the policy of the Doctrine of Lapse and the annexation of Indian states. Henceforth, the new policy was to punish the princely rulers for mismanagement but not to annex their state. For example, in 1874 Malhar Rao Gaekwad of Baroda was accused of misrule and attempts to poison the British resident. He was deposed from the *gaddi (throne)* after a mock trial but the state was not annexed. Instead, another member of the Gaekwad family was put on the *gaddi*. The immunity from annexation was given to the Indian States but various measures brought about the complete subordination of the Indian princes to the Paramount Power. Lord Canning declared in 1862 in unambiguous language, "The Crown of England stood forth as the unquestioned ruler and Paramount Power in all India." Lord Canning granted 140 sanads or 'instrument of grant adoption' to Hindu and Muslim princely rulers. By the Royal Title Act, 1876 passed by the British Parliament, Queen Victoria assumed the title of Empress of India-British India and Princely India. A Government notification in August 1891 read, "The Paramount Supremacy of the former (the Crown) presupposed and implies the subordination of the latter (Indian princes)." Under the Crown rule, the British Crown regulated the status and salutes of Indian princes in all matters of ceremonial. The Government of India also encroached upon the internal sovereignty of the Indian princes in matters of extension of railways, irrigation canals, telegraphs, construction of strategic railways etc. the Indian princes lost their international status. None of them enjoyed even an iota of external sovereignty. Lord Curzon, the die-hard imperialist even put restrictions on the foreign trips of Indian princes. During World War I and II, the

Indian princes stood by the Government of India and placed all their resources at the disposal of the Crown. In the last decade of India's Freedom Struggle the British Government used the Indian princes as a counterpoise to nationalist aspirations. However, for all their loyalty to the British Crown, Prime Minister Attlee's announcement of 20th February 1947 and Mountbatten Plan of 3rd June 1947 simply emphasised the lapse of British paramouncy in India and the Indian states were left to face the new scenario of Free India and Free Pakistan.

In spite of al the tall claims made by the British politicians and imperial school of British historians that Great Britain ushered in India a new era of progress and modernisation through consolidation fo political unity, establishment of peace and internal stability, organisation of an all-India administrative system, development of economic infrastructure by developing rapid means of transport and communications, inflow of foreign Finance Capital etc in 1947 presented the picture of an under-developed country. Rather, it will be more correct to say that many of our present day problems politically loaded casteism, regional chauvinism, religious, fundamentalism, communalism, reservation quotas in legislative bodies, government and university service for Scheduled Castes, Scheduled Tribes and the O.B.Cs. – have their roots in the divide and rule policies followed by the Government India during a century of Crown Rule in India.

It is worth noting that although the causes of the 1857 revolt might be economic, political, social, religious and military by distinct, they were all a clear demonstration of Indians' dissatisfaction against Company rule. Although, the revolt might have started as a fight for religion, it soon assumed a national character, became a symbol of protest against foreign domination and exploitation, and ended up as a war of independence. In view of the fact that the participants were moved by patriotic considerations and wanted to liberate themselves from foreign rule, it is logical to assert that the 1857 uprising was India's first nationalist movement; it became the mother of all nationalist movements in India's struggle for independence because it gave inspiration and hope to the country's future freedom fighters/ young nationalists for independence.

4

British Policy towards Indian Princely States and its Neighbouring Countries

Introduction

The Indian states numbered no fewer than 562 and covered a total area of 71,508 square miles. These states included some big states like Hyderabad (as large as Italy) with a population of 14 million and an annual revenue of 8½ Crores of Rupees and tiny states like Bilbari with a population of 27 persons and an annual income of Rs 8 only. It has been estimated that 202 states had each an area of less than 10 miles, 139 less than 5 square miles each while 70 states had each an area of not exceeding one square mile. Generally speaking, the Indian states were "the inaccessible and less fertile tracts of the Indian peninsula." In the process of conquest, the East India Company acquired important coastal tracts, the valleys of the great navigable rivers accessible from the sea and such tracts which were rich in agriculture products and densely populated by prosperous people.

The making of Indian states was largely governed by the same circumstances which led to the growth of the East India Company's power in India. Many Indian states as independent or semi-independent principalities came into existence in the later Mughal period. The East India Company became a political power during the same period, profiting from the weakness of the Mughal central authority. Many states notably the Rajput states of Central India had for centuries resisted the Mughals and later the Marathas and were saved from extinction by British intervention. Some states were created by the British in the process of the overthrow of Maratha Confederacy.

The princely states got relieved from further annexation when Crown took over India. They were even assured that there will be less interference from the British rulers. But, they exercised their complete and undisputed control over princely state's military and economic expansion. This chapter highlights the British policy towards the Indian princely states and identifies specific policies that were put in place, such as, the policy of subordinate union of 1857–1935, Queen's Proclamation of 1858 and the Policy of Equal Federation of 1935-1947. It examines the status of princely states under the British colonial rule in India and looks into social, political and economic changes for Princely states that were brought by the crown, after the mutiny.

The Policy of Subordinate Union, 1857–1935

The assumption of direct responsibility by the British Crown in 1858 provided an occasion for better definition of the relations between the Government of India and the Indian states. The Queen's proclamation however confirmed the existed anomalies:

> "We hereby announce to the native of India, that all treaties and engagements made with them by or under the authority of the East India Company are by us accepted and will be scrupulously maintained and we look for the like observance on their part."

Yet the years following the Proclamation of 1858 marked a vital transformation in the relations between the Indian states and the Government of India.

The Queen's Proclamation announced the abandonment of the policy of annexation. The Doctrine of Lapse was buried deep in the soil. An assurance was given that the Crown desired "no extension of present territorial possessions." The change in policy was due to the loyal attitude of the ruling princes during the Revolt of 1857-1858 which had amply demonstrated that the princes could be used as breakwaters to future possible storms of India. Lord Canning gave practical shape to the new trend by granting 140 *sanads* (deeds) or 'instruments or grants of adoption' to Hindu and Muslim princes. Lord Lansdowne issued seventeen more *sanads*. The new policy was to punish the ruler for misgoverning and if necessary to depose him but not to annex the state [e.g. in 1874, the Gaikward was removed from the *gaddi* (throne) for charges of misgovernment abut he state was not annexed). The change in policy was welcomed by the princes.

This immunity from the policy of annexation was obtained at great cost and lowering of the status of Indian princes. Under the East India Company, the sanction of the Governor-General was necessary only in case of failure of 'natural heirs'. After 1858, the fiction of the authority of Mughal Emperor came to an end and the Crown stood forth as the unquestioned ruler and paramount power in India. As such, all successions had to regularly seek the sanction of the Crown. The Central Government wrote to the Chief Commissioner of Central Provinces in 1884, "The succession to the native state is invalid until it receives in some form the sanction of the British authorities." The ruler did not inherit the *gaddi* as of right but as a gift from the Paramount Power. The Indian prince was granted possession and administration not sovereignty and his continuation as ruler was conditional on his loyalty to the British Crown. Normally every ruler was formally installed on the *gaddi* by the British Agent. The British Government also acted as the guardian of a minor prince and arranged for administration of the state during minority.

Further, the friction of the Indian princes standing on a status of equality with the Crown as sovereign independent states finally came to an end. Canning referred to the rulers of Indian states as "feudatories and vassals" and to the Crown as "the unquestioned ruler and Paramount Power in India." Again, he wrote: "There is a reality in the suzerainty of the sovereign of England which has never existed before and which is not only felt but eagerly acknowledged by the chiefs." Paramouncy was not only a historical fact but a legal principle capable of interpretation and expansion. The Royal Titles Act of 1876 put the final seal on the new relationship by proclaiming the Queen as *Kaiser-i-Hind*, i.e. Queen Empress of India. At the time of rendition of Mysore in 1881, the position of the new prince was made conditional on his remaining "unfaithful in allegiance and subordination to the Crown" the conditions on which the Indian prince was restored in Mysore became a set of principles which were applied in cases of all Indian states. A Government notification dated 21st August, 1891 declared: "The paramount supremacy of the former (the Crown) presupposed and implies the subordination of the later (Indian princes).

The Crown also excised the right to regulate the status and salutes of the Indian princes in all matters of ceremonials. Just as the Mughal Emperor before 1858 granted titles and honours, the Crown awarded titles and decorations to Indian princes.

The Government of India exercises the right to interfere in the internal sphere of India states, partly in the interests of the princes himself, partly in the interests of the welfare of the people of the state and partly to secure proper conditions for British subjects or foreigners in the state and partly in the interests of India as a whole. In a minute of 1860, Canning wrote: "The Government as may threaten any part of the country neither with anarchy or disturbance nor from assuming temporary charge of a native state when there will be sufficient reason to do so. Of this necessity the Governor-General-in-Council is the judge subject to the control of Parliament." In 1867, the *Nawab* (ruler) *of Tonk*, Mohammad Ali Khan was charged with complicity in an attack on the relations of his tributary, the Thakur of Lawa. The *Nawab* had to resign in favour of his son. Similarly, in 1870 the ruler of Alwar was deposed and a Council of Regency was set up. In 1875, the Gaekward of Baroda was charged with an attempt to poison the British Resident. In addition, the Gaekward had refused to introduce changes in administration on the lines suggested b the British Resident. A Commission of Enquiry was appointed. Although the charges against the ruler could not be proved yet the Gaekward was removed from the *gaddi* on the score of mal-administration. In 1881, a British Resident was forced on the *Maharaja of Kashmire* and in 1889 the *Maharaja* was forced to resign in favour of a Council of Regency. Again, in 1891 the Government of India interfered in the turbulent affairs of Manipur. The ruler and the *Senapati*

(Commander-in-Chief) were exiled. The removal, trial and sentence of *Jubraj* (crown prince) of Manipur Sydney Low (British writer), was not an 'unquestioned right' as Administrator Lee Warner puts it, but "an act of prerogative justified by necessity than a legal power vested in the Government of India." In 1892, the *Khan of Kalat* (Baluchistan) was also deposed for mismanagement of the state.

The British were further helped in their encroachments on the internal sovereignty of the Indian princes by the pressure of irresistible current of history and by force of circumstances. Developments of an all Indian character compelled the rulers of Indian states to fall in line with the Government of Indian policy. The development of modern means of transport and communications of a public press and all Indian public opinion all worked in that direction. The rulers were required to aid economic schemes for the welfare of the whole country to cede land and jurisdiction thereto for extension of railways, irrigation canals, telegraphs, post offices, construction of strategic roads. Further, the states were required to assist in military plans and provide all facilities for movement of the Indian army.

The Government of India exercised complete and undisputed control over the external and international affairs of the Indian states. The Government of India could declare war, neutrality or peace for the Indian states. The Butler Committee remarked, "For international purposes, state territory is in the same position as British territory and state subjects are in the same position as British subjects."

The period also saw the growth of 'political practice' and 'usage' which further circumscribed the rights of Indian princes. Under the impress of changing circumstances, the Crown exercised powers which exceeded the most liberal interpretation of treaties. Rather than abrogate the old treaties or seed for revision of those, the Government resorted to the less provocative devise of 'constructive interpretation' of old treaties. In the words of N.D. Varadachariar (advocate Madras High Court), "the treaties began to be regarded as guides of political conduct rather than sources of legal right." Thus grew up the Political Department under the Viceroy. In other words, a body of case law grew up.

Viceroy Lord Curzon and the Indian States

Lord Curzon stretched the interpretation of old treaties to mean that the Indian princes in their capacity as servants of the people should work side by side with the Governor-General in the scheme of Indian Government. He adopted a policy of patronage and "intrusive surveillance." He issued a circular, desiring Indian princes to devote their energies not in pursuit of pleasures but "in the welfare of their subjects and administration." He put restrictions on their trips to Europe. Long absence from India was to be regarded as dereliction of duty. Curzon went to the extent of declaring at Bhawalpur in 1903 that the relationship between Indian states and the Government of India "was neither federal nor feudal but tended to be a type not based on treaty. It represents a series of relationships that have grown up between the Crown and the Indian princes under widely differing historical conditions but in the process of time had gradually conformed to a single type."

The new trend seemed to reduce all the Indian states to conform to a single type whether they were treaty states or enjoying varying degrees of authority. All the states were uniformly dependent on the British Government and were considered as having become integral parts of the India political system. Lord Reading removed the misconceptions of the Nizam when he wrote to the latter that "the title Faithful Ally which was your Exalted Highness enjoys has not the effect of putting your government in a category separate from that of other states, under the paramountcy of the British Crown."

Policy of Subordinate Union – The Chamber of Princes

From 1905 onward, the Government of India followed a policy of cordial co-operation towards the Indian states. The growth of political unrest in British India put the Government of Indian on the defensive and the Government thought it expedient and prudent to utilise the support of Indian princes to counter progressive and revolutionary developments. The Government of India and the Indian princes formed a "common front to preserve their positions and privileges." The Government of India no longer feared the India princes individually or jointly. Thus, the policy of Subordinate Isolation gave place to the policy of Subordinate Union.

As early as 1876, Lytton had suggested the formation of an Indian Privy Council of Chiefs of great Indian states to confer with the Governor-General on matters of common interest. The idea did not find favour with the authorities in England. Similar schemes of Lord Curzon for a Council of Ruling Princes and of Minto for an Imperial Advisory Council proved abortive. During the First World War, Lord Hardinge often called the Indian Princes for joint consultations on matters of Imperial Defence. Lord Chelmsford carried the scheme of conferences further by utilising them for the purpose of discussing general questions affecting the states as a whole. The authors of Montagu-Chelmsford Reforms favoured the formation of a council of princes and made definite suggestions in the matter. These recommendations formed the nucleus for the formation of the Chamber of Princes formally inaugurated in February 1921.

For purposes of representation in the Chamber of Princes, the Indian states were divided into three categories:

(i) 109 states which enjoyed full legislative and jurisdictional powers were represented directly.

(ii) 127 states which enjoyed limited legislative and jurisdictional powers were represented by 12 members chosen from among themselves.

(iii) Remaining 326 states which could better be classed as *jagirs* or estates or feudal holdings.

The chamber of princes was merely an advisory and consultative body. It had no concern with the internal affairs of individual states nor could it discuss matters concerning the existing rights of states or their freedom of action.

Working of the Chamber of Princes

The Indian Princes thus became the favourite children of British Imperialism and in fact were "collectively recognised as an independent constituent of the Empire." The princes however were worried about the uninterrupted and continuous growth of 'political practice' and the concept of paramountcy. On the request of the princes, a Codification Committee was appointed as early as September 1919 to codify 'political practice and define limits of the concept of paramountcy. While accord was reached on minor issues like settlement of boundary disputes, payment of compensation to states for land taken for railways, irrigation, navigation, defence and other purposes, the larger problem of the extent of the sovereignty of Paramount Power could not be settled.

Lord Reading's statement that extension of paramountcy was based "not only upon treaties and engagements but existed independently of them" further alarmed the princes. At a time when proposals for the future constitutional reforms of India were being discussed, the Indian princes urged Lord Irwin of having the nature of relationship between the states and the supreme power properly examined and clearly defined. In 1927, the Government appointed the Indian States Committee popularly known as the Butler Committee (from the name of its chairman Sir Harcourt Butler) to investigate the relationship between the Paramount Power and the Indian states. The Indian Princes engaged a distinguished lawyer, Sir Leslie Scott, to present their viewpoint before the Committee. Scott argued that as each state was originally independent so each remained independent except to the extent to which any part of the ruler's sovereignty was transferred to the Crown. In other words, Scott pleaded that residuary powers rested with the Indian states.

The Butler Committee made the following points:

On the question of paramountcy and development of political practice, the Committee reported: "Paramountcy must remain paramount. It must fulfill its obligations by defining and adopting itself according to the shifting necessities of the time and the progressive development of states" and further that "usage lights up the dark corners of treaties."

(1) The states were bound by treaties with the Crown and the states should not be handed over without the ruler's prior

consent to an Indian Government in British India responsible to an Indian legislature.

(2) The Viceroy, not the Governor-General-in-Council was to be the Crown agent in dealing with the states.

The Indian princes were surprised at the concept of paramountcy being left undefined. Nevertheless, the hydra-headed creature was fed on usage and Crown prerogative and the implied consent of the princes.

Policy of Equal Federation, 1935–1947

The Indian princes were invited at the Round Table Conferences during 1930–1932. In the Federal structure proposed for the whole of India by Government of India Act 1935, the Indian states were to be allotted 125 out of 375 seats in the Federal Assembly and 104 out of 260 seats in the Council of States. The Federation of India was to come into existence only when rulers of states representing not less than one half of the total population of the states and entitled to not less than half of the seats (i.e. 52) allotted to the states in the upper chamber of the Federal Legislature agreed to join the Federation.

The Solicitor-General explained the position thus, "the whole principle of the Federation is that the ruler shall remain ruler of his state and his subjects shall therefore 'remain his subjects' the Ruler undertakes to see that the provisions of the Act are enforced in that state."

Professor Rushbrook William, the Chief Advisor of the Indian princes at the Round Table Conference wrote in 1930, " the rulers of the Native states are very loyal to their British connection...the situation of these feudatory states check boarding all India as they do are a great safeguard. It is like establishing a vast network of friendly fortresses in debatable territory. It would be difficult for a general rebellion against the British to sweep India because of this network of powerful loyal native states." Lee-Warner wrote about 'the steadying influence' of the Indian princes in the proposed Federal set-up. He wrote: "What is it we have most to fear? There are those who agitate for independence for India, the right to secede from the

Empire altogether....it becomes important, therefore that we should get what steadying influence we can against this view.... There will be approximately thirty three per cent of the princes who will be members of the Legislature with 40 per cent in the Upper Chamber... with that influence in the federated legislature I am not afraid in the slightest degree of anything that may happen even if the congress managed to get the largest proportion of votes."

The federation never came into existence or the requisite number of states did not agree to join it.

The Congress successes in the elections of 1937 had repercussions on the states where agitation started for civil liberties and responsible governments. On December 3, 1938, Mahatma Gandhi declared that the awakening in the states was due to the 'time spirit' and that there could be no half way house between total extinction of the states and full responsible government. The outbreak of the Second World War in September 1919 finally shelved the federal scheme.

Integration and Merger of States

During the Second World War, India witnessed hectic political activity. The Indian National Congress adopted the policy of non co-operation. The British Government made various efforts to break the deadlock-Cripps' Proposal (1942), Wavell's Plan (1945), the Cabinet Mission Plan (1946) and finally Attlee's announcement (20 February 1947). The future of the Indian states figured in all constitutional discussions. Cripps declared that the British Government did not contemplate transferring the paramouncy of the Crown to any other party in India. The princes worked on various schemes to form a union of their own with full sovereign status a Third Force in the Indian political set-up. The *Nawab* of Bhopal as Chancellor of the Chamber of Indian Princes, expressed the hope that the British Government would not leave the states 'as a sort of no man's child and would treat their problem on the same basis as a major communal issue. Attlee's announcement of 20th February 1947 and Mountbatten's Plan of 3rd June 1947, however emphasised that with the lapse of paramouncy, Indian states would be free to join any dominion they liked, India or Pakistan. Lord Mountbatten refused to recognise any state or combination of states as separate dominions.

British Captured Afghanistan, Burma,Nepal and Tibet

This section assess the British Indian foreign policy with Nepal, Afghanistan, Burma and Tibet and the role of the British ruler on India's neighbouring countries. After having strong and firm footing in India, Britain gradually captured her neighbouring country for its economic and political interest. Countries like Afghanistan, Burma, Nepal and Tibet lies in North West, east, north east and north respectively. It is clear that Britain wanted to save India from all sides. They had no fear from the southern side as India is covered by the sea there.

Was the capture of neighbouring countries of India was necessary? Most of these countries were not as rich as India was at that time neither it were threat for the British Empire in India. As if British colonisers were trying to secure Indian territories from all the sides and they made it possible by capturing its neighbouring countries.

The Nepal War, 1814-1816

The first problem Hastings had to face in India was a war with the *Gurkhas* of Nepal. The *Gurkhas* from western Himalayas had wrested the control of Nepal form the successors of Ranjit Malla of Bhatgaon in 1768. A hardy people, the *Gurkhas* began to expand their dominion beyond the mountains. Checked in the north by the Chinese, they pushed forward towards the ill-defined frontiers of Bengal and Oudh. The English occupation of Gorakhpore district in 1801 had brought the Company's frontier co-terminous with the territory of the *Gurkhas*. The dispute between the Company and the Nepalese arose out of the latter's occupation of the districts of Butwal (north of Basti district) and Sheoraj (further east of Butwal). The English reoccupied the district without an open conflict.

Hastings who also held the office of the Commander-in-Chief of the army planned the campaign. A large army of 34,000 soldiers was marched against the *Gurkha* army of 12,000. The campaigns of 1814-1815 were a dismal failure. The General Gillespie's attack on the mountain fortress of Kalanga failed, the General losing his life in action. Gillespie's successor, Major General Martindell also suffered an ignominies defeat before the stronghold of Jaitak. The English prestige suffered a great set back.

The fall of Fort Malaon in 1815 induced the *Gurhkas* to open negotiations for peace. However, Hasting's exorbitant demands hardened the attitude of the Gurkhas and the war party came in ascendancy in Nepal. Hostilities commenced again. David Ochterlony now in supreme command advanced into the heart of Nepal and inflicted a defeat on the Nepalese at Makwanpur on 28th February 1816. Finding further resistance difficult, the Gurkhas accepted the Treaty of Sagauli in March 1816.

The Treaty of Sangauli – 1816

The Company's gains were not unimportant. The Gurkhas surrendered to the Company the districts of Garhwal and Kumaon, including, including a great portion of the Tarai. The Tarai boundary was marked by pillars of masonry. The *Gurkhas* agreed accept a British Resident at Kathmandu and permanently withdrew from Sikkim.

The north-west frontier of the Company was pushed up to the mountains. The English obtained the sites for the hill stations and summer capitals of India-Simla, Missoorie, Ranikhet, Landour and Naini Tal. Besides the route for communications, with the most remote regions of Central Asia was opened. This gave the Company an effective barrier on the eastern frontier of Nepal.

The friendship between Nepal and the English subsisted till the British rule lasted in India. The *Gurkhas*, one of the finest classes of soldiers in the world were too glad to serve as mercenaries for the English army. Actually, three battalions of the *Gurkhas* soldiers were formed by Ochterlony even before the end of the war. The *Gurkhas* were ready to fight for any side capable of giving them a good living considerably strengthened the Company's army and helped in the expansion of its dominion in India.

Tibet

As regards the relations of the Government of India with Tibet, it was Warren Hastings who sent in 1774 Mr George Bolgle to Lhasa. In 1783, Samuel Turner was sent. In 1811-1812 Manning went to Lhasa and met the Dalai Lama. In 1885-1886 the Chinese Government gave permission for a British commercial mission to Tibet. In 1886, the Tibetans invaded Sikkim but they were beaten back. In 1890, a convention settled the frontier between Sikkim and Tibet. In 1893, a trade mart was established at Yatung. In spite of all this, the Tibetans were not willing to have free intercourse with India "except through fear to something which they regarded as a greater calamity."

When Lord Curzon became the Governor General some new factors made their appearance. The people of Tibet began to show a strong desire to become independent of China. The new Dalai Lama proved himself to be a strong ruler. He was influenced by Dorjieff who was a Russian subject by birth. Dorjieff had gone to Russia to collect money from the Buddhists in the territory of the Czar. In 1900 and 1901, Dorjieff was received by the Czar of Russia. The Russian press gave a lot of importance to the visit of Dorjieff to their country. No wonder, there was a lot of uneasiness in the Government of India. Lord Curzon was not prepared to tolerate the increase of Russian influence at the capital of Tibet. It is true that the Russian Foreign Minister categorically stated that the visit of Dorjief has absolutely no political importance but that did not remove the suspicion of the Government of India. It could not be denied that the new Dalai Lama was himself in favour of increasing the Russian influence in his country with a view to oust the Chinese influence.

Lord Curzon was in favour of sending a mission to Tibet. He contended that the isolation of the Government of Tibet "is not compatible either with proximity to the territories of a great civilised power at whose hands the Tibetan Government enjoys the fullest opportunities both for intercourse and trade or that due respect for the treaty stipulations into which the Chinese Government had entered on its behalf." The Home Government was not in favour of sending a mission to Tibet. It was thinking more in terms of establishing friendly relations with Russia than to antagonise her by sending a mission to Tibet. The Government of India pressed hard but the Home Government followed delaying tactics. Ultimately, the Home Government agreed to dispatch a mission under Army officer and Commissioner F. Younghusband. Once the mission started, it went on till it reached Lhasa itself. Resistance by the Tibetans was futile.

Younghusband entered into a treaty with the Dalai Lama and that treaty was known as the Treaty of Lhasa (1904). According to this treaty, the Chumbi Valley was to be occupied by the British troops till the whole of the war indemnity was paid. The amount of indemnity was fixed at Rs 75 lakhs and it was to be paid in 75 installments. Trade marts were to be established at Yatung, Gyantse and Guttok. A British commercial agent was to be stationed at Gyantse but he was given the power to go to Lhasa if circumstances required. Great Britain was given complete control over the foreign policy of Tibet. No agent of any foreign power was to be allowed in Tibet. No part of Tibetan territory was to be given to any other country. No concessions were to be granted to any foreign power in form of railways, roads, telegraphs, etc. If such concession were given to any power, similar concessions had to be given to the British Government.

Younghusband had gone beyond the powers given to him and no wonder the Home Government refused to accept the Treaty of Lhasa. The Russian Government protested. Ultimately, in spite of the opposition of Lord Curzon, the Treaty of Lhasa was revised. The war indemnity was reduced from Rs 75 lakhs to Rs 25 lakhs. It was also provided that after 3 annual installments were paid, the British troops were to withdraw from the Chumbi Valley. The British Agent at Gyantse was not to be allowed to go to Lhasa.

There has been a lot of controversy with regard to the Tibetan policy of Lord Curzon. Lord Curzon complained of the uncalled for interference of the Home Government. It is pointed out that it was not proper for the Home Government and the Government of India to differ. Either, the Home Government should not have allowed the mission of Younghusband and if it did so, it should not have revised the Treaty of Lhasa. The justification of the Home Government was that the higher interests of the British Empire demanded that friendly relations must be established with Russia. The danger of Germany was so great that all other considerations could be set aside. It was under these circumstances that the Home Government had to overrule Lord Curzon. After all has been said, it cannot be denied that the expedition of Lhasa was successful undoubtedly. It was triumph of organisation and daring.

Burma (now Myanamar)

The First and Second Burmese war (1826)

The First war was in 1826 where the Treaty of Yandboo was signed. The real cause of the Second Burmese War was the determination of Dalhousie to exclude all European powers from Burma. He could not tolerate the idea of France or any other country capturing any part of Burma. However, he got an excuse to interfere into the affairs of Burma.

The imperialist character of Dalhousie encouraged the English traders to appeal to him for the removal of their grievances. They sent him a long petition in which they narrated all the wrongs suffered by them. Dalhousie welcomed the petition as God-sent. He declared that the Treaty of Yandaboo had been violated and the Burmese Government must pay damage for the wrongs done to the Englishmen. Coomodore Lambert was sent to Rangoon for this purpose. On account of the behavior of Lambert, the Burmese Government could not satisfy the demands of the Government of India. The result was that there was the exchange of guns and the Second Burmese War started. Even before the declaration of war, a British force was sent under General Godwin. Martaban was taken; Rangoon and Bassein also fell into the hands of the English. Later on, Prome was occupied. Thus, the British were able to bring the whole of lower Burma under their control. Negotiations were started but no treaty was signed. Lord Dalhousie declared the annexation of Pegu by a proclamation issued in 1852. According to Arnold, "The second Burmese War was neither just in its origin nor marked by strict equity in its conduct or issue." Dalhousie's view was that the annexation of Pegu was "unavoidably demanded by sound views of general policy."

The Third Burmese War (1885)

The real cause of the third Burmese War was the attempt of King Theebaw of Burma to secure French help against the British giving them special privilege and concessions. The Burmese mission visited Paris in 1883 and in 1885, a French envoy went to Mandalay. King Theebaw was a savage and cruel despot and he imposed a heavy fine upon the Bombay and Burma Trading Company and ordered the arrest of its officials. Lord Dufferin insisted on an enquiry to be made into the matter. King Theebaw refused to reopen the question. Lord Dufferin sent an ultimatum demanding that King Theebaw should admit a British envoy have no external relations with foreign countries except on advise of the Government of India and grant the British the right to trade with the Chinese through his dominions. King Theebaw refused to accept the terms of the ultimatum and consequently, war was declared. The Burmese could not stand before the British armies and surrendered. King Theebaw was sent to India and Upper Burma was annexed to India in 1886.

British interference in Upper Burma has been the subject of criticism from many quarters. It is contended that it was no business of the British Government to interfere in Upper Burma even if its ruler was a despot and a savage. The British Government had no justification to interfere into the internal affairs of a neighbouring country whose ruler was absolutely independent to follow any policy he liked. If King Theebaw wanted to have friendly relations with France, it was no business of the British to intervene. It seems that the British Government was determined to check the advance of France into Upper Burma.

Afghanistan

The problem of imperial defence and search for a scientific frontier towards the north-west brought the English into contact and clash with the Afghans. The Napoleonic fear in the early years of the nineteenth century and later Russian designs and advances in central Asia kept the Government of India in a state of disquietude. The Russophobia gives the clue to the nature and character of Anglo-Afghans relations in the nineteenth and twentieth centuries. The increased Russian influence in Persia alarmed the English about possible Russian designs in India. Experts in England raised the cry of 'India in danger.'

Amir (ruler) of Afghanistan Dost Muhammed was anxious for English friendship and sent a congratulatory letter to Lord Auckland on his appointment as Governor General for which he had a cold response from him. Because of this, Dost Muhammed turned to Russia and Persia for friendship to recover Peshawar. Circumstances changed and Auckland invaded Afghanistan in 1839 and Dost Muhammed surrendered in 1840.

The Afghan policy of Auckland has been subjected to universal condemnation and been called as the most qualified blunder committed in the whole history of the British in India.

With the arrival of Lytton as Viceroy of India in 1876, a change in the policy towards Afghanistan was perceptible. Sher Ali the then *Amir* in Afghanistan was very friendly with Russia and he allowed the Russian envoy at Kabul but objected for the English to do the same. Lytton decided on the invasion of Afghanistan and sent a large army on 20th November 1878. All opposition by Sher Ali crumbled very soon and he fled into Turkistan where he died on 21st February 1879. A peace treaty was signed with Yakub Khan, the eldest son of Ali Sher on 26th May 1879. Yakub had to agree to admit a British Resident at Kabul and agents at Heart and certain other places and committed himself to conduct his foreign relations only with the advice of the British. The Afghan policy of Lord Lytton has been universally condemned both on moral and political ground.

Now Ayub Khan, another son of Sher Ali who had been in the occupation of Hevat marched from that placc to Kandhar to avenge the insult and death of his father and to recover power for himself. In the battle of Kandhar inflicted a complete defeat upon him. Kabul and Kandhar thus reunited under Abdur Rahman (An Amir who was a nephew of Sher Ali) and the British thereby won his complete loyalty.

After the death of Abdur Rahman in 1901 his son Habib Ullah became the Amir of Afghanistan but was murdered in 1919 by a group of fanatic people. His son and successor Amanullah was forced by Chelmsford (Governor General) to sign the treaty of Rawalphin India in 1921 where Afghan ruler was given freedom to pursue an independent foreign policy.

5

The Rise of Nationalist Movements by 1914 and World War One

Introduction

The year 1885 marks the beginning of a new epoch in Indian history. In that year, an all Indian political organisation was set on foot under the name of the Indian National Congress. It is important to note that harsh and prolonged rule by the British in India propelled the formation of Indian National Congress and it is interesting to note that the main initiator was an English man called Mr Hume. He was a retired government officer who called the Indians to form their own nationalist group to demand their rights; freedom from the British colonisers.

The Indian mind became increasingly conscious of its political position. A retrospective examination of the National Movement suggests three broad stages in its development. In the first stage of its existence (1885–1905), the vision of the Indian National Congress was dim, vague and confused. The movement was confined to a handful of the educated middle class intelligentsia who drew inspiration from western Liberal and Radical thought. During the second stage (1905–1918), the Congress came of age and its aim and scope were considerably extended. It aimed at an all-round uplift of the people-social, cultural, economic and political. *Swaraj* or self-government was the goal on the political front. Some progressive elements within the Congress adopted western revolutionary methods to liquidate Western imperialism. The final stage (1919–1947) was dominated by the objective of *Purna Swaraj* or complete independence to be achieved under the leadership of Mahtama Gandhi by the characteristically Indian method of non-violent non-cooperation.

As such, this chapter explains the rise and development of the nationalist movement in India up to 1914 and identifies on the factors that favoured the growth of Indian nationalism. It even shows the existence of the various political associations as evidence of growth of modern political ideas in India and finally the reasons behind the formation of the Indian National Congress and also assesses the causes behind its split. Finally, it shows the reasons behind the differences between the moderates and the extremist wings of the congress.

Factors Favouring Growth of Indian Nationalism

Stimulus-Response Debate

Traditional Indian historiography explains rise and growth of Indian nationalism in terms of Indian response to stimulus generated by the British Raj through the creation of new institutions, new opportunities, resources, etc. in other words, Indian nationalism grew partly as a result of and partly as a reaction to colonial policies.

The growth of the Indian national consciousness in the later half of the nineteenth century was not to the liking of British colonial rulers. At first, British scholars and administrators denied the existence of any felling of nationality in India. R. Coupland in a more forthright language wrote "Indian nationalism" was the child or the British Raj." Coupland forgot to mention that Indian nationalism was an unwanted child of the Raj whom it refused to feed at birth and sought to strangle it. It would be more correct to say that Indian nationalism was partly the product of a worldwide upsurge of the concept of nationalism and right of self-determination initiated by the French Revolution, partly the result of Indian Renaissance party, the offshoot of modernisation initiated by the British in India and partly developed as a strong reaction to the British imperial policies in India.

1. Impact of British Rule. The British colonial rulers followed modern methods–political, military, economic and intellectual to establish and continue their stronghold over India and for further economic exploitation of India's resources. A dose of modernisation was an essential conmitant of the colonial scheme of administration and this modernisation distorted though it generated some developments and one of these was growth of the Indian nationalism.

2. Political Unity of India. Imperial Britain conquered the whole of India from the Himalayas in the north to the Cape of Comorin in the south and from Assam in the east to Khyber Pass in the west. They created a larger state than that of the Mauryas or the great Mughals. While Indian provinces were under "direct" British rule, Indian states were under "indirect" British rule. The British sword imposed political unity in India. Common subjection, common institutions, common laws began to shape India in a common mould. Despite imperial efforts to sow communal, regional and linguistic dissensions, pan Indianism grew. The establishment of political unity fostered the spirit of one-mindedness.

3. Establishment of Peace and Administrative Unification of India. After the chaotic conditions of the eighteenth century (partly created by the aggressive wars waged by European trading companies), British rulers established peace and orderly government in India. British scholars take pride for brining prolonged peace and order for the first time in India.

The British also established a highly centralised administrative system in India. Percival Griffiths refers to the impersonality of British administration to be its most important characteristic i.e. the fundamental character of administration did not change with the changes of top administrators like Secretaries of State and Viceroys (as had been the case with all previous empires in India). Further, administrative unification had important effects in many other fields. A highly trained professional Indian Civil Service managed the district administration in all parts of India. A unified judicial setup, codified civil and criminal law rigorously enforced throughout the length and breadth of the country imparted a new dimension of political unity to the hitherto cultural unity that had existed in India for centuries.

4. Development of Rapid Means of Transport and Communication. The necessities of administrative convenience consideration of military defence and urge for economic penetration and commercial exploitation were the drives behind planned development of modern means of transport. A network of roads linked one province with another and the metropolitan centres with mofussil (small) areas.

For more than anything else the development of railways unified the country. The construction of railways began in India in the 1850s and by 1880, some 850 miles of rail track had been built, extending to 25000 miles by 1900. Apart from many other advantages, the railways facilitated the growth of nationalism.

The development of the modern postal system and the introduction of telegraph in the 1850s helped unify the country.

5. Introduction of Modern Education. The introduction of modern system of education unfolded opportunities for assimilation of modern western ideas which in turn gave a new direction to Indian political thinking. Sir Charles E. Trevelyan, T.B. Macaulay and Lord William Bentinck (then Governor General) took a momentous decision in 1835 when they inaugurated the system of English education in India.

The English system of education though conceived by the rulers in the interest of efficient administration opened to the newly educated Indians the flood gates of liberal European thought. The liberal and radical thought of European writers like Milton, Shelley, Bentham, Mill, Spencer, Rousseau and Voltaire inspired the Indian intelligentsia with the ideals of liberty, nationality and self-government and made clear to them the anachronism of British rule in India.

The newly-educated class usually adopted the profession of junior administrators, lawyers, doctors, teachers etc. some of them visited England to receive higher education. While in England, they saw with their own eyes the working for political institutions in a free country. On the return to India, these persons found the atmosphere cringing and slavish with the total denial of basic rights to citizens.

These 'vilayat-returned' (UK return) Indians with the ever expanding English educated class formed the middle class intelligentsia.

The spread and the popularity of the English language in all parts of India gave to the educated Indians a common language a lingua franca-through the media of which they could communicate with one another and transact their conferences and congresses. In the absence of such a lingua franca it would have been very difficult for the Bengalis, the Tamilians, the Maharastrians etc., to come to a common platform or organise a movement of an all-India character.

6. Emergence of a Modern Press. The emergence of modern presses both English and vernacular was another offshoot of British rule in India. It was the Europeans who set up printing presses in India and published newspapers and other cheap literature. Gradually, the vernacular press came into existence and developed on the western pattern. In spite of the numerous restrictions imposed on the press by the colonial rulers from time to time, Indian journalism made rapid strides. The latter half of the nineteenth century saw an unprecedented growth of Indian-owned English and vernacular newspapers. In 1877, there were about 169 newspapers published in vernacular languages and their circulation reached a neighbourhood of 100, 000.

The Indian press had played a notable role in mobilising public opinion, organising political movements, fighting out public controversy and promoting nationalism.

7. Rise of the Middle Class Intelligentsia. British administrative and economic innovations gave rise to a new urban middle class in towns. The new class readily learnt English for it promoted employment and gave a sense of prestige. This class, prominent because of its education, new positions and its close ties with the ruling class came to the forefront. P. Spear writes, "the middle class was a well-integrated all-India class with varied backgrounds but a common foreground of knowledge, ideas, and values....it was a minority of Indian society, but dynamic minority....it had a sense of unity of purpose and of hope." This middle class proved to be a new soul of modern India and in due course infused the whole of India with its spirit. This class provided leadership to the Indian National Congress.

8. Influence of Historical Researchers. Historical researches in ancient Indian history conducted mostly by European scholars like Max Muller, Monier Williams, Roth, Sassoon, etc. opened new vistas of India's rich cultural heritage. In particular, the excavations conducted by archaeologists like Marshall and Cunningham created a new picture of India's past glory and greatness no less impressive than that of ancient civilisations of Greece and Rome. The scholars praised the *Vedas* and the *Upanishads* for their literary merit and excellent analysis of the human mind. The theory put forward by the European scholars that the Indo-Aryans belonged to the ethnic group of mankind from which stemmed all the nations of Europe gave a psychological boost to educated Indians. All these gave a new sense of confidence to the educated Indians and inspired them with a new spirit of patriotism and nationalism.

9. Impact of Contemporary European Movements. Contemporary strong current of nationalist ideas which pervaded the whole of Europe and South America did stimulate Indian nationalism. A number of national states came into existence in South America on the ruins of the Spanish and the Portuguese Empires. In Europe, the national Liberation Movements, of Italy in general and *Ireland* in particular deeply stirred the emotions of Indians. Educated Indians touring Europe were impressed by these nationalist movements.

10. Progressive Character of Socio-Religious Reform Movements. In the nineteenth century, educated Indians began to examine afresh their religious beliefs and customs and their social practices in the light of new knowledge of western science and philosophy which they had acquired. The result was that various religious and social reform movements in Hindu religion like the *Brahmo Samaj*, the *Prahma Samaj*, the *Arya Samj*, the *Ramakrishna Mission*, the *Theosophical Society*. Similar movements reformed Muslim, Sikh and Parsi societies also.

Most of the religious societies had no political mission, all the same whosoever came under their influence rapidly developed a sense of self respect and a spirit of patriotism, since many reform movements drew their inspiration from India's rich cultural heritage, these prompted pan-Indian feeling and spirit of nationalism.

11. Racialism. One unfortunate legacy of the rebellion of 1857 was the feeling of racial bitterness between the rulers and the ruled. The Anglo-Indian bureaucracy developed an attitude of arrogance and contempt towards the Indians. They somehow came to the conclusion that the only argument that worked effectively with the Indians was superior force. Thus, Europeans developed their own social code of ethics and worked out the theory of the superior race. The Indians were dubbed as belonging to an inferior race and no longer worthy. The narrow approach evoked a reaction in the Indian mind and put the educated Indians on the defence.

12. Economic Exploitation. The impact of British rule on the Indian economy was disastrous. Jawaharlal Nehru has summed up the Indian viewpoint when he writes: "The economy of India had... advanced to as it could reached prior to the industrial revolution" but "foreign political domination...led to a rapid destruction of the economy she had built up, without anything positive or constructive taking its place," the net result being "poverty and degradation beyond measure." The general object of British policies –even though claimed to be social welfare by some British scholars – was a systematic destruction of traditional Indian economy.

The sharp reaction to discriminatory British economic and fiscal policies gave rise to economic nationalism in India. In the first half of the nineteenth century, Britain was in the vanguard of industrial revolution and needed cheap raw material and a market for her industrial products. Interests in imperial Britain required that the Indian economy be developed on the classical colonial model. Thus, the economic policies of India in all fields-agricultural, heavy industry, finance, tariffs, foreign capital investment, foreign trade, and banking – were all geared to the preservation of the colonial economy.

The extravagant civil and military administration, the denial of high posts to Indians, the ever mounting "home charges", the continuous drain of wealth from India resulted in stagnation of Indian economy. The cumulative effect was increasing misery for the people. Periodic famines became a regular feature of Indian economic life. During the second half of the nineteenth century, 24 famines visited various parts of India taking an estimated toll of 28.5 million souls. What is worse is that during the famine times, export of food grains from India continued.

Growth of Modern Political Ideas and Political Associations

Western domination of India generated certain forces – some as a result of its impact and others as a reaction to it – which ultimately challenged western imperialism. As early as 1833, Lord Macaulay in the course of a speech before the House of Commons had explained the implications of his educational policy: "it may be that the public mind of India may expand under our system until it has outgrown that system, that by good government we may educate our subjects into a capacity for better government; that having become instructed in European language they may in some future age demand European institutions." One important effect of the introduction of western culture in India was the growth of modern political concepts like nationalism, nationality, political rights etc. the Indian sub-continent witnessed the growth of political ideas and political organisation hitherto unknown to the Indian world, and it was political associations that heralded nineteenth century India into modern politics.

Political Association in Bengal Presidency. Raja Ram Mohun Roy was a pioneer of political movement in India. He was greatly influenced by western ideas. He was a widely-read man. His extensive studies had freed his mind from bigotry that characterised an average Bengali. His sympathies in the domain of politics were cosmopolitan and his heart went in sympathy for popular movements all over the world. In 1821, the Raja celebrated in Calcutta the establishment of a constitutional government in Spain.

Ram Mohun Roy was the first Indian to focus the attention of the Englishmen on the grievances of India an to ask for remedial measures. He demanded liberty of the press, appointment of Indians in civil courts and other higher posts, codification of law etc. It was generally believed that some of the beneficent provisions in the Charter Act of 1833 were due to his lobbying in England.

Political Associations in Bombay Presidency. While to the Bengali Hindus the English might have appeared as deliverers from the tyrannical rule of the Muslim *Nawabs*, in Maharashtra the British were looked upon as foreign tyrants who had displaced indigenous rulers.

On the lines of the British India. Association of Calcutta on 26th August 1852 was founded the Bombay Association with the object of 'memorialising from time to time the Government authorities in India or in England for the removal of existing evils and for the prevention of proposed measures which may be deemed injurious or for the introduction of enactments which may tend to promote the general interests of all connected with this country." The Bombay Association sent a petition to the British Parliament urging the formation of new legislative councils to which Indians should also be represented. It also condemned the policy of exclusion of Indians from all higher services, lavish expenditure on secure posts given to European. However, the Bombay Association did not survive for long.

Political Association in Madras Presidency. A branch of the British Indian Association of Calcutta was set up at Madras under the name of the Madras Native Association. The Madras Association also sent petitions to Parliament on the eve of the passing of the Charter Act of 1853 making demands similar to that of the British Indian Association and the Bombay Association. However, the Madras Native Association right from its inception was worked by some officials; possessed very little vitality, had hardly any hold upon the public mind and languished into obscurity after 1857.

Foundation of the Indian National Congress. It will not be correct to trace the genesis of the Indian National Congress to the efforts of a single individual like A.O. Hume or assume that it appeared as a sudden efflorescence. The various political organisations in different parts of India and the ferment of ideas had prepared the ground and the foundation of the Indian National Congress in 1885 was only a visible embodiment of that national awakening.

The efforts of the Indian Association of Calcutta and its leader Surrendranath Banerjee in organising the Indian National Conference, deserve special mention. In December 1883 met the first Indian National Conference to which representatives drawn from all the major towns of India were invited. Shri Ananda Mohan Bose, the president expressed the hope that the Conference would prove to be the first stage in the formation of a national parliament. The second National Conference met at Calcutta during the Christmas week of 1885. However, the Indian National Conference was soon eclipsed by the more popular and more representative Indian National Congress.

It was left to Mr Hume, a retired official of the Government of India to give a practical and definite shape to an organisation of all India character. W.C. Banerjee popularised the view that the idea of the Indian National Congress was a product of Viceroy Lord Dufferin's brain that he suggested it to Mr Hume who undertook to work it out. Dufferin's idea was to have a political organisation through which the Government could ascertain the real wishes of the people and thus save the administration from any possible political outburst in the country.

Whatever might have been the motive of Dufferin and Mr Hume, it cannot be denied that Mr. Hume was a true liberal and a 'deadly earnest' about the necessity and desirability of a political organisation. Mr Hume's open letter to the graduates of Calcutta University is revealing. He wrote: "Scattered individuals however capable and well-meaning are powerless singly. What is needed is union, organisation and a well-defined line of action and to secure these, an association is required." Hume asked for fifty volunteers to join in a movement to promote the mental, moral, social and political regeneration of the people of India. Mr Hume secured the sympathy of Government officials and public men in India and England for the Indian National Congress. Thus, the movement was a child born of England and India.

Recent researches have proved that Allan Hume was an enlightened imperialist. He was alarmed at the growing gulf between the rulers and the ruled. Hume saw with considerable misgivings the establishment of the Indian National Conference in 1883 by S.N. Banerjee, 'a dismissed government servant' of 'advanced political views' who had done much to popularise the ideas and teachings of Italian nationalists like Mazzini and Garibaldi. Hume decided to bypass this Indian National Conference and instead organised a 'loyal and innocuous' political organisation. Hume did succeed in organising the Indian National Congress and made it at least in the beginning, a forum for pro-British and anti-Russian propaganda.

In 1885, he met the first Indian National Congress at Bombay under the presidency of Shri Womesh Chandra Banerjee.

First Phase, 1885 – 1905 (Period of Moderate Politics)

The national leaders like Dadabhai Naoroji, P.M. Mehta, D.E. Wacha, W.C. Banerjee, S.N. Banerjee who dominated the Congress policies during this period were staunch believers in liberalism and 'moderate' political and came to be labelled as moderates to distinguish them from the neo-nationalists of the early twentieth century who were referred to as extremists. The moderate leaders explained their political outlook as a happy combination a of liberalism and moderation. Believes in the spirit of liberalism, they worked to procure for Indian freedom from race and creed prejudices, equality between man and man, equality before the law, extension of civil liberties, extension of representative institutions etc.

During this period the Congress was dominated by the affluent middle class intelligentsia, men of legal, medical, engineering, literary pursuits and journalists. The ideas and methods of this middle class held the field and governed the character of the national struggle. The educated middle class was enamoured of titles and services under the state and by its training and culture had isolated itself from the masses. The delegates at the Congress sessions were mostly drawn from the cities and had hardly any real contact with the masses.

As we have seen, the Congress was founded by A.O. Hume after consultation with Lord Dufferin (Viceory 1884-1888). The Congress leaders were full of admiration for British history and culture and spoke of the British connection as 'providential'. It was their cardinal faith that British rule in India was in the interest of the Indians. As such, they looked upon the British Government not as an antagonist but as an ally. In the course of time, they believed, Britain would help them to acquire the capacity to govern themselves in accordance with the highest standards of the west. In 1886, Dadabhai Naoroji (educator, social reformer and nationalist leader) presiding over the Calcutta session of the Congress dwelt at length on the "Blessings of British rule' and his remarks were cheered by the audience.

The moderate leaders stood for the maintenance rather than strengthening of the British empire. This approach was the outcome of their apprehension that anarchy and disorder would reappear in India if the British Government was superseded. In their eyes, British rule was the embodiment of peace and order in the country and as such, British rule was indispensable in India for a long time to come.

Most of the Congress leaders of the period believed that the British people were just, righteous and freedom –loving. They were further convinced that the British people meant justice to be done in India. If Indians had certain grievances, these were only due to the reactionary policy of the British bureaucracy in India or ignorance of the British people about these grievances. As such, the nationalist leaders believed that all they had to do was to prepare their case and present and plead it before the British Parliament and nation and their grievances would be redressed and justice done. As a natural corollary, the Congress leaders put great emphasis on Congress propaganda in England. A British committee of the Indian National Congress was set up in London which published a weekly journal in India to present India's case before the British public.

Thus, with a view to educating the English people about the real needs of India, in 1890 a decision was taken to hold a session of the Indian National Congress in London in 1892 but owing to the British elections of 1891, the proposal was postponed and afterwards never revived.

During the period under review, the Congress demanded a few concessions and not freedom for the nations True, Lokamanya Tilak was one of the first and strongest advocater for independence, used the word *Swaraj* for self-government towards the last decade of the nineteenth century but it did not become popular nor did it figure in the official resolutions of the Congress. Congress resolutions generally demanded expansion of Legislative Councils with enlarged powers and more representation of Indians in them; representation of Indians in the Secretary of State's Council, Viceroy's Executive Council and Governors' Executive Councils more opportunities for Indians in the Civil Service holding of simultaneous examinations in India as well as England. These demands were always worded in prayerful and apologetic language and the Congress was worded to the use of constitutional methods.

Official Attitude Towards the Congress. Despite its moderate methods and its emphasis on loyalty to the British Crown, the Indian National Congress failed to evoke sympathetic responses from the Government. In the beginning however, the official attitude was outward neutrality. It was in this spirit that Lord Dufferin gave a garden party to the delegates attending the second Congress Session (1886) at Calcutta taking care to explain that the invitation was not to representatives of the Congress but to 'distinguished visitors to the capital.' In 18871, the Governor of Madras gave facilities to the organisers of the third session of the Congress at Madras. However, the official attitude stiffened after 1887. The publication of Congress pamphlets which condemned despotic system of government and absentee landlordism brought about the open hostility of the Government. The officials encouraged reactionary elements like Sir Syed Ahmed Khan and Raja Shoo Prasad of Benares to organise the United Indian Patriotic Association to counter Congress propaganda. Further, Lord Dufferin challenged the very national character of the Congress and dubbed it as representing only 'a microscopic minority' and Congress demands as 'a big jump into the unknown.' In 1890, Government employees were forbidden from participating in its deliberations or attending its meetings. Lord Curzon was categorical in his pronouncements when he said that the Congress was tottering to its fall' and one of his greatest ambitions in India was to 'assist it to a peaceful demise.'

Second Phase, 1905 – 1919 (Rise of Extremism or Radical Politics)

The closing decade of the nineteenth century and early years of the twentieth century witnessed the emergence of a new and younger group within the Indian National Congress which was sharply critical of the ideology and methods of the old leadership. These 'angry young men' advocated the adoption of *Swaraj* as the goal of the Congress to be achieved by more self-reliant and independent methods. The new group came to be called the Extremist Party in contrast to the older one which began to be referred to as the Moderate Party.

The process of splitting in the Congress Party began when Tilak clashed with the Moderates (also called *Sudharaka*) over the question of Social Reform. There was no love between Tilak and Gokhale. Tilak (supporter of extremist) and G.K.Gokhale (Nationalist leader and supporter of moderate) from national politics over the 'apology affair' and Gokhale was labelled a *Kacha* (weak) reed i.e. spineless fellow who could be blow beaten by the Government. And, by 1907 Indian National Congress was split in two parts; as Moderate and Extremists.

Tilak was made of a different stuff from most of the Congress leaders. He was forthright in his criticism of the Government and its policies and was prepared to make sacrifices to get wrongs redressed. He was the first Congress leader to suffer several terms of imprisonment for the sake of the country. As early as 1882, the Government tried and sentenced Tilak to four months imprisonment for criticising in strong language the treatment meted out to the Maharaja of Kolhapur. Again in 1897, Tilak was charged with 'exciting feelings of disaffection to the British Government and sent to jail for 18 months. At the Congress session at Amraoti (Dec. 1897) the supporters of Tilak made an attempt to push a resolution demanding the release of Tilak. The Moderate leaders who controlled the Congress did not permit it. Similarly, the Moderates foiled the attempt of Tilak's admirers to move a resolution praising his spirit of martyrdom at the Congress session at Madras (Dec. 1898). At the Lucknow session of the Congress (Dec. 1899) Tilak's attempt to move a resolution condemning Governor Sandhurst's administration of Bombay was also blocked by the Moderate leaders on the plea that the matter was of provincial interest and could not be discussed at the National Congress. It was because of ideological differences with Tilak and his group that the Moderate leaders were determined to keep Tilak and Congressmen of his line of thinking out of all positions of power and responsibility in the Congress and never gave him a chance to become the Congress President. Tilak's saying '*Swaraj* is our birth right and we shall have it' became very popular among the youths.

Indian National Congress experienced a split in 1907 (Moderate and Extremist) followed their own ways to demand for independence from the British colonisers.

World War One and Its Effects on India

In August 1914, Viceroy Lord Harding announced his government's entry into World War One. The outbreak of the war called forth an outburst of legal sentiment among both the political classes and the princes. All believed that the war would be short and that Britain would emerge on the winning side. For the princes, it was an opportunity for action while popular leaders more soberly calculated that present service would mean future rewards.

The Indian National Congress was under the control of the Moderate who decided to support the British war efforts both as a matter of duty and in a spirit of bargaining to get concessions. Some historians have argued that India had no choice. They were never asked whether they would like to fight or not. Nonetheless, national pride was stirred by the dispatch of an Indian army corps to France in the autumn of 1914 and later of troops to East Africa (Tanzania) and Egypt (for the defense of the *Suez* Canal) and to the Persian Gulf. In all some 800,000 men were recruited to the fighting force together with some 400,000 noncombatants.

India participated in the World war One both with money and man power. In fact this war was not for their cause but they wanted to show their loyalty to their master and had a feeling that they will be rewarded. For them the best and the only reward at that time was 'freedom'. During war India lost both man and money but never was been appreciated even.

One can examine the role played by India in the Great War and identify the contributions that were offered by the Indians. This chapter further assesses the social, economic and political impacts of the war on India. It also examines the reasons that compelled both Indian National Congress and Indians' in general to participation in the war.

India's Contribution to the War Effort

The initial response to Lord Harding's announcement was for the most part enthusiastically supported throughout India. Indian princes volunteered their men, money and personal service while leaders of the Congress – from Tilak, who had just been released from the Mandalay jail and had wired the king-emperor vowing his patriotic support to Gandhi who toured Indian villages urging peasants to join the British army –were allied in backing the war effort. Support from the Congress was primarily offered on the assumption that Britain would repay such loyal assistance with substantial political concessions – if not immediate independence or at least dominion status following the war, then surely its promise soon after the Allies achieved victory. The government of India's immediate military support was of vital importance in bolstering the western front, and an expeditionary force including two fully manned infantry divisions and one cavalry division left India in late August and early September 1914. The Indian Corps sustained extraordinarily heavy losses during the winter campaigns of 1914-1915 on the western front. The myth of Indian racial inferiority especially with respect to courage in battle was thus dissolved in sepoy blood on Flanders fields. In 1917, Indians were at last admitted to the final bastion of British Indian racial discrimination – the ranks of royal commissioned officers.

Seventy million rounds of small arms and ammunition, 60,000 rifles, latest guns and other war materials were sent from India. The contribution in terms of money too was stupendous. Apart from the expenditure on the books, there was a gift of one hundred million pounds, an amount which exceeded the annual revenue of the Government of India and raised her national debt by 30 per cent. Total expenditure of the Government of India up to 31st March 1918 was about two million one hundred pounds. As the war dragged on, India became a vital supply base for vast quantities of small arms and ammunition, clothing and food supplies to allied armies in the Middle East.

The so called voluntary war contribution of India was more of an exaction. The amount of money to be raised and the number of man drafted was fixed for each district and woe betide any officer who did not fulfill his target. Even then, Lloyd George (then Prime Minister of Britain) commented that India did not spend an extra paise on the war.

We have seen that when the war started, there was great enthusiasm and the people of India were willing to serve the Government in every possible way. When Turkey joined the central power in October 1914, Indian troops fought through the long campaign of Macedonia and German East Africa. They played an important part in the Iraq campaign leading to the capture of Bagdad in 1917. In this way, they helped to found the present state of Iraq. They were the allied army which took Jerusalem in 1917. All this involved a great effort on India itself. Indian self-confidence grew when the magnitude of their efforts and to which extent it depended upon Indians themselves were realised.

The Impacts

History reveals that Great War had both positive and negative impact on India. Among the impacts far more significant were the economic and social consequences like drain of wealth, the decline of handicrafts, revenue pressures and obstacles to indigenous capital growth.

Economic Sphere: Industries

The First World War proved a boon for Indian industries and gave them some sort of protection against foreign competition. Foreign imports fell to a very low level while there was increase in Government purchases for war purposes. Further, exports of raw material became less which kept down their prices to the advantages of Indian industrialists. Again, wages did not rise much. All these advantages made possible fabulous profits during the war.

It can be said that in the economic sphere, the effect to the war was one of stimulus. The industrial development of modern India owes a great deal to the demands of World War One. However, increasing demand and expenditure led to the rise in prices and ultimately, enthusiasm was turned into discontent. Englishmen could be expected to put up with inconveniences because they felt that they were fighting for their very existence and their victory was likely to add to their glory. The same could not be said about the Indians for whom the war was merely an external affliction. No doubt, they became not only exhausted and war weary but also discontented and resentful.

Political Awakening

Another impact of the war was the quickening in the pace of political awakening and the Indian demand for protection of Indian industries out of patriotic considerations. The Government response was somewhat favourable though mainly guided by the twin objectives of: (a) search for more revenue; and (b) strategic necessity for development of some degree of economic self-sufficiency. In 1915, Lord Hardinge announced, "After the war, India will consider herself entitled to demand the utmost help which her Government can afford to enable her to take place so far as circumstances permit as a manufacturing country." As a first step, the Government appointed an Industrial Commission in 1916 to report on possible openings for Indian capital enterprises in industry and commerce and to suggest the manner in which Government could help industrial development.

Indian Munitions' Board

As a conciliatory gesture, in April 1917, the Government established the Indian Munitions Board which recommended a policy of purchase of stores for the army inside India and of setting up new plants in India for production of such stores.

Administrative Sphere

In the administration sphere, the British Government made a mistake in allowing the British civilian officers to serve the force during the war. Many of them never returned and those who did found themselves in a strange new mental world to which it was difficult to adapt themselves. When time grew difficult towards the end of the war, the Government had only an aging and tired cadre of officers to rely upon.

Attitude towards the Europeans

The attitude of India towards Europe and its people was altered radically and permanently. No longer were they seen as the possessors of a culture which was morally as well as superiorly superior to their own. Their moral prestige vanished in conflict and they were regarded at best as more powerful, the possessors of useful machines and processors and the inventors of some useful institutions such as British law and democratic machinery. Previously, it was assumed that Europeans in the main held together like the members of some loose confederacy. Now it was realised that they were as divided as the Indians.

Russian Revolution

The Russian Revolution of 1917 also had a profound influence on the minds of the Indians. They felt that if the people of Russia could overthrow an imperialist regime, the same could be done by the Indians in their own country. Indians themselves came to realise what an asset their country was to the empire and felt a sense of pride that Indian sepoys were fighting shoulder to shoulder with British soldiers. The myth of the invincibility of the British arms and the superiority of the white man exploded. Ideas of equality of races and partnerships in a free empire began to be entertained as practical issues.

Wilson's Fourteen Points

The fourteen points of President Wilson had great influence on the Indians. They also demanded the rights of national freedom and self-determination of people. By the end of the war, Tilak had come back from jail and had become a leader of all India importance. Tilak was opposed to the old policy of making prayers to the British Government. He laid the foundation for the great anti-Government movement that was led by Gandhi in the following years. According to Tilak, every Indian had the birth right to be free. No wonder the Indian demanded self-government in the name of the fundamental principles accepted by the Allied powers.

As regards the effect of war on Muslims, they were very unhappy. After the war, the Turkish Empire was reduced to a small size. When Allies stripped her of her territory to create a new nation, they hurt the feelings of the young Turks. Some of the territories of the Ottoman Empire were coded to Greece on the Turkish mainland. However, when the Greeks wanted to occupy the same land, the Turkish Nationalist forces led by a young officer, Mustapha Kemal Pasha drove them out. Mustapha Kemal Pasha subsequently deposed the sultan and declared himself as the President of the Turkish Republic. Muslims did not approve of the dismemberment of Turkey, which was regarded as the second sword of Islam.

6

Mahatma Gandhi and Emergence of Mass Politics and Muslim India

Introduction

Present chapter discusses Indians' participation, with Mahatma Gandhi, in the nationalist movement and analyse the role of Indian women in the participation of their freedom struggle which and justifies the various revolutionary political movements i.e. non-violence, civil disobedience and non-cooperation; that were introduced by Mahatma Gandhi in a bid to enhance Indian nationalist struggles.

History has placed India and its people in a privileged position that they can proudly count on for generations to come as a result of *Mahatma* (great soul) Gandhi – an Indian revolutionary of phenomenal magnitude who was not only the pioneer or prime mover in the struggle for Indian independence but who also immensely inspired African nationalist movements for civil rights and freedom during the continent's struggle against colonial oppression and exploitation. Historians have argued that the Indian National Congress, was dominated for almost thirty years (1919–1948) by Gandhi.

Gandhi was called *Mahatma* by a famous poet from Bengal Rabindranath Tagore (a Nobel Laureate for Literature in 1913). He came back from South Africa in 1915 and took some time to follow the Indian Nationalist movement. While he was in South Africa, he had already experienced the British attitude towards the colonised people, hence took a different approach to defeat them and that was passive resistance. He also encouraged the women to give their hands towards struggle for independence.

Early Life of Mahatma

Gandhi was born on 2nd October 1869 at Porbander in northwest India, Gujarat. His full name was Mohandas Karamchand Gandhi. His father Karamchand Gandhi was the *diwan* (chief minister) of Porbander, the capital of a principality in Gujarat under the British. As a child he learnt from his mother, Putlibai, the idea of *ahimsha (*non-injury to all living things or non-violence). She also taught him to value of *satyagraha* (insistence on truth or clinging to truth) which he later defined as 'the force which is born of truth and love'. Gandhi practiced both ideas throughout his life and set an example for all of India and for the rest of the world. He was married to Kasturba, at the age of thirteen. He loved to go out on long walks when he was not nursing his ailing father or helping his mother with her household chores.

At the age of nineteen, he left for England to pursue law at the University College in London. After successfully completing his studies, he returned to India in 1891 and attempted to establish a law firm in Bombay (now Mumbai) and Rajkot but without much success. Two years later, he went to South Africa after an Indian firm with interests there hired him as a legal advisor. His stay in South Africa proved to be the formative period of his political life because it was while there that Gandhi put into practice his weapon of s*atyagraha* and developed self-confidence to lead a struggle.

In South Africa

In South Africa, Gandhi not only found himself treated as a member of an inferior race but was also appalled at the widespread denial of civil liberties and political rights to the Indian immigrants to that country. In a Durban court, he was asked by the European magistrate to take off his turban. He refused and left the courtroom. A few days later while traveling to Pretoria, he was unceremoniously thrown out of a first class railway compartment and left shivering at the station. In the further course of his journey, he was beaten by a white driver of a stagecoach as he blocked room for a European passenger and finally, he was barred from a hotel reserved for Europeans only.

Gandhi, on the outbreak of Boers war in 1899 between the British and Boers, argued that the Indians, who claimed the full rights of citizenship in the British crown colony of Natal, were must support to defend it. He, then raised the an ambulance corps of 1,100 volunteers, out of whom there were about 300 free Indians and rest of them were indentured labourers. Gandhi protested against carrying an identity card, many other discriminatory remarks and regulation which were parted to Indians. By 1913 he had several followers who went with him to jail. He had called his place of residence as Tolstoy (Rusian writer and philosopher) farm. When he was almost leaving Africa, gifted a pair of sandal made by himself while in jail, to General Jan Smut (a prominent South African and British commonwealth statesman, military leader and philosopher, served as prime minister of union of South Africa from 1919 to 1924) saying that it was from Tolstoy's farm. The sandal was returned to Gandhi on his 70 birthday and Smuts remarked that "I have worn these sandal for many summer even though I may feel that I am not worthy to stand in the shoes of so great man. It was my fate to be antagonist of a man for whom ever then I had the highest respect". Gandhi's relation with Smut was difficult one but both men maintained a degree of respect for each other. Same Smuts told a press Conference in London in 1942, that to talk to Mahatma was as fifth columnist and as one of the great men of the world.

Gandhi tirelessly protested against the economic, political and social discriminatory treatment meted out to Indians through the Asiatic and Transvaal Immigration Act. Realising his undying determination and dedication to ensuring national dignity for his people the South African Government had no option but to heed the voice of reason by making important concessions to Gandhi's demand by 1914 and for this was even sent to jail there. Gandhi's achievements in South Africa made him known throughout the world, but especially in India.

They repealed most of the oppressive acts directed against Indians. When Gandhi left South Africa in 1914, the annual poll taxes had been abolished, Indian marriages were validated and the Government had agreed to stop indentured labour from India. Thus, although he had come to South Africa as a lawyer, he left it for India as a liberator. When President Mandela of South Africa visited India to receive the most prestigious and highest reward of India *Bharat Ratna* (jewel of India), he acknowledged Gandhi's contribution in his country. He even addressed the people of India by commenting about Gandhi that 'you sent him to South Africa as a lawyer but we returned him to you as a nationalist'.

Gandhi in India

Upon his return, Gandhi spent some time in studying the Indian situation and then he hurled himself in the mainstream of Indian politics. There existed the Indian National Congress for about thirty years. The Congress had aroused national consciousness to a certain extent but the awakening was confined largely to urban areas and to the English educated middle class who were not in touch with the masses of India. But upon assuming direct control of the party, Gandhi brought about a revolution in the nature of the nationalist movement.

From 1915 to 1918, Gandhi seemed to hover uncertainly on the periphery of Indian politics declining to join any political agitation, supporting the British war effort in World War One and even recruiting soldiers for the British Indian Army. At the same time, he criticised British officials for any acts of high handedness and took up the grievances of the long-suffering peasantry in Bihar and Gujarat. In February 1919, he protested against the British over the Rowlett Acts which gave the authorities the power to imprison without trial. He announced a *satyagraha* struggle. The result was a virtual political earthquake that shook the subcontinent in the spring of 1919.

On 13th April 1919, one religious meeting led to the Jallianwala Bagh (in Amritsar, Punjab) massacre in which General R.E.H. Dyer ordered around 400 *Gurkha* and *Baluchi* troops to fire 1650 rounds of live ammunition at point blank range on some ten thousand or more unarmed men, women and children, mostly peasants who had gathered in a grove to celebrate the Sikh Festival of *Baisakhi*. According the official estimates, nearly 400 civilians were killed, and another 1,200 were left wounded with no medical attention. Dyer called that meeting as a protest meeting, despite a ban on public assembling and argued his action was necessary to produce a 'moral and widespread effect', admitted that the firing would have continued had more ammunition been available.

As the news spread, a wave of horror spread among Indians. General Dyre was relieved of his command on the Secretary of State's instruction but in England, he got a hero's reception and was presented with a costly jeweled sword inscribed 'Saviour of the Punjab.' Atrocities continued in Punjab. In defense of realm British officers flogged Indians, made them crawl and undergo all kinds of unthinkable indignities. Rabindranth Tagore surrendered the Knighthood which was conferred to him, after he won the Nobel Prize for Literature in 1913. When Gandhi was about to visit Punjab, he was not allowed to enter by the British Government. Millions of others, estranged because of the atrocities joined the popular movement to get rid of the British yoke. Only a few days after the announcement of the Montagu-Chelmsford (Secretary of States and Viceroy of India respectively) for India Reform in 1919, Motilal Nehru (father of Jawaharlal Nehru), presiding over the Amritsar Congress, in December 1919 said that if the ordinary rights of human beings are denied to us then all talk of reform was a mockery.

By the autumn of 1920, Gandhi was the dominant figure on the political stage commanding an influence never attained by any political leader in India or perhaps in any other country. He refashioned the 35 year old Indian National Congress into an effective political instrument of Indian nationalism. He emerged as a new messiah in Indian politics in 1919 and completely dominated Indian politics down to 1947. Gandhi was in favour of united India's independence and did not participate in the freedom celebration on 15th August 1947. He was busy on his spinning wheel when whole of India was celebrating. A messiah of non-violence was assassinated violently on 30th January 1948 by a phonetic Hindu who didn't approve his desire to visit Pakistan. Gandhi was planning to visit Pakistan to meet his Muslim brothers there.

Gandhi as Leader of Nationalism in India

During this period, the object of the congress was the attainment of *Swaraj* (self-rule) by all regime legitimate means within the Empire. The period was dominated by the personality of Mahatma Gandhi who introduced new ideas into Indian politics. Gandhi deprecated the policy of violence and underground plots but preached open and active resistance to injustice. He advocated the adoption of the policy of *Satyagraha* (literally persistence in Truth), i.e. non-violent non-cooperation towards a government which did not look to the interests of the governed and was high handed and oppressive. The Congress movement gradually became a mass movement. The Congress organisation was considerably strengthened and its constitution made more democratic. The aim of the Congress was the all-round improvement of Indian society. Gandhi used to explain his programme for strengthening India by pointing to the five fingers of his hand, exhorting the people to practice five virtues-spinning, removal of untouchables, sobriety (non-consumption of alcohol or opium), Hindu-Muslim amity and equality for women. The five virtues were to be achieved through non-violent methods.

Gandhi lovingly called *Bapu* (father) so completely dominated the Indian scene from 1914 to 1947 that this period is rightly called the Gandhian Era in Indian history, while across the world, Mahatma's place in humanity is measured not in terms of the twentieth century but in terms of history. His greatest contribution to India's national movement and to the suffering humanities across the world did not in fact lie that he was able to make the masses of India politically self-conscience but in the unique methods that he prescribed and employed for fighting against colonialism.

The Non-Cooperation Movement

The events of the year 1919 greatly disillusioned Gandhi and from a cooperator, he turned into a non-cooperator. The passing of the Rowlatt Acts (abridgement of court procedure in trial of political cases and giving the Executive extensive powers to arrest and detain persons without trial), the Jallianwalla Bagh tragedy and the *Khilafat* movements (Pan-Islamic movement) gave a new turn to Indian politics.

As to the non-cooperation cause of action, the *Khalifat* Committee in its *6th June 1920* meeting outlined four stages of non-cooperation viz, resignation of titles and honorary posts, resignation from the civil service under the Government, resignation from police and army services and finally, non-payment of taxes. The Indian National Congress outlined a seven –term programme of non-cooperation viz,: (1) Surrender of titles and honorary offices, (2) Refusal to attend Government *durbars* and official functions, (3) a boycott of government aided schools and colleges, (4) boycott of British courts, (5) refusal of all classes to offer themselves for service in Mesopotamia, (6) boycott of elections to provincial and central assembly elections, and (7) the boycott of foreign goods. On the constructive side, people were urged to develop a spirit of discipline and self-sacrifice, set up national educational institutions, decide their disputes through mutual arbitration, take to hand spinning, and hand-weaving and use of *swadeshi* (homemade) goods. Gandhi toured the whole country to whip up enthusiasm of the people. Wherever Gandhi went, he gave an impression to each individual that unless he non-cooperated with the Government, he would delay *Swaraj.*

In support of the *Khilaft* Movement, Gandhi inaugurated the Non-cooperation campaign with a bang on 1st *August* 1920. At its Nagpur session (*December* 1920) the Congress approved and ratified the policy of Non-violence non-cooperation towards the unjust Government. The Nagpur session is also memorable for the new Congress Constitution that was adopted. The Congress' aim of *Swaraj* was reaffirmed but now explained to mean "self-government within the empire if possible and outside if necessary." Further, the earlier emphasis on the use of "constitutional means" was substituted by "all peaceful and legitimate methods." The Congress party was organised on modern lines with local Congress Committees at the grass-root village level through sub-divisional, district and provincial committees with the All India Congress Committee of 350 members at the apex; a working committee of 15 was to act as the chief executive. The new Congress Constitution really marked the beginning of Gandhian era in Indian politics.The *Khalifat* Committee and the Congress agreed upon the triple purposed of Non-cooperation satisfactory solution of the *Khilafat* question, re-addresses of the Punjab wrongs and attainments of *Swaraj*.

Lord Reading who became Viceroy in 1920 was, in some respect, fairer that his predecessors in regards to his Indian subjects. But, in his opposition to the Indian nationalist, however, Reading was uncompromising on any other governor generals. Reading invited Gandhi on *March* 1921 to win his support in organising a suitable reception to the British prince who was due to arrive on 17 *November* 1921. But the meeting did not come off well and while appreciating the gesture Gandhi said that he did not see any change of heart. Gandhi announced that the civil disobedience movement would begin on 17th *November* on the date of arrival of Prince of Wales. The Prince's landing in Bombay was marked by riots and closure of shops. Much to Gandhi's disappointment the violence led to many deaths through police firing and many more were arrested. Gandhi immediately put off civil disobedience and went on a self purificatory fast and warned his followers that if the movement was not peaceful he would withdraw it. The Prince fared no better in Calcutta and Delhi where *hartal* (strike), boycott and hostile demonstrators greeted him.

In 1921, about 30,000 person courted arrest on different occasions. Much against the wishes and instructions of Gandhi, the movement led to serious mob violence at *Chaurai-chaura* in Uttar Pradesh where a police station was burnt and a number of police officials were killed. Gandhi at once suspended the non-cooperation movement in February 1922 and declared that *Swaraj* had "stink" in his nostrils and that without adequate discipline and restraint on the part of the people, the Movement had proven to be a 'Himalayan blunder.' Gandhi advised constructive work to the people.

Dissatisfied with Gandhi's policies, C.R. Das and Motilal Nehru founded the *Swaraj Party*. The *Swaraj Party* advocated the programme of 'council entry.' They hoped to wreck the functioning of legislative council by a policy of uniform, continuous and consistent obstruction. In the election of 1923, the *Swarajists* (people demanding for self-government) secured an absolute majority in Bengal Fond the central provinces and by their tactics made it impossible for the ministers to function. On Das's death on 16th June 1925 Gandhi hurried to Calcutta to attend the funeral and won over the Bengali's by his sympathetic utterance. In gratefulness they decided to popularise hand made *Khadi* and spinning. Gradually, the *Swarajists* drew towards Gandhi and his policy of direct action.

To report on the working of the constitution set up by the Government of India Act, 1919, the British Government announced the appointment of the Simon Commission of in 1927. Lord Birkenhead (Secretary of States for India) had justified the exclusion of Indians from the Simon Commission (1927–1939) on the plea that they were vital differences among the various Indian political parties and challenged them to produce an agreed constitution and submit it to Parliament for consideration. The Indians accepted the challenge and the All Parties Conference which met in 1928 appointed a sub-committee presided over by Motilal Nehru to draft a constitution. The Committee produced the famous Nehru Report which advocated a constitution based on the principle of responsible government for India on the lines of self-governing dominions within the British Empire. At its Lahore session (29-31st December 1929), the Congress adopted the resolution of complete independence for India as its goal. The Nehru hoisted the tricolour flag of Indian independence on *1st January 1930.*

The Civil-Disobedience Movement to Government of India Act of 1935

Gandhi who had re-entered active politics in 1928 gave the call for a Civil Disobedience Movement (C.D.M.) in 1930. The C.D.M.

differed from the earlier Non-Cooperation Movement (1921-1922) in that while the Non–Cooperation Movement (N.C.M.) sought to bring the working of the Government to a standstill by not cooperating with the administration, the C.D.M. aimed at paralysing the administration by performance of specific illegal acts. The Mahatma himself started the C.D.M. by breaking the obnoxious Salt laws. On March 12 1930, Gandhi led by 78 followers started from Sabarmati Ashram on the famous Salt March to Dandi Beach to manufacture illegal salt. Subash Bose, compared the Salt March to Napoleon's March to Paris, on his return from Elba. Mr Brailsford and English journalist described the Dandi March as 'the kindergarten stage of revolution' and ridiculed the notion that 'the King Emperor can be unseated by boiling salt water in a kettle.' The statesman of Calcutta sarcastically commented that Gandhi could go on boiling sea water till Dominion Status was attained. The imperialists however had miscalculated the moral effects of the Civil Disobedience Movement. Soon, the number of volunteers offering *Satyagraha* increased and the number reached 60,000 or even more.

Gandhi was invited by the Prime Minister R. MacDonald to London in 1929 for consultation. Upon his return from there Gandhi, Nehru and other prominent Congress members went to seek a definite assurance from the Viceroy Irwin about the national issue of India's constitutional progress but the Viceroy could not give such assurance. This shattered Gandhi's faith in British promises. The first Round Table Conference was inaugurated by the British king on *12th November* 1930. The Indian states and various parties in British India were represented, the notable exception being the Congress.

Rapprochement was effect by the famous Gandhi-Irwin Pact (*5th March 1931*) and the Viceroy declared that Dominion Status was the goal of India's constitutional development. The Civil Disobedience Movement (CDM)was provisionally suspended and Gandhi attended the Second Round Table Conference to discuss the scheme of constitutional reform for India. He returned home towards the end of 1931 greatly disappointed and talked of resuming the Civil Disobedience Movement. In January 1932, the Government struck again, arrested Gandhi and other Congress leaders and declared the

Congress an illegal organisation. However, the C.D.M. gained more popularity and more than 100,000 persons courted arrest. In 1933, Gandhi confessed failure of the Movement and resigned his membership of the Congress and confined his work to the uplifting of the *Harijans.* Nevertheless, the year 1928–1934 had greatly changed the Congress movement by giving it greater unity, self-confidence, pride and determination. Above all, the Congress became a Movement of the masses and village oriented where *Charkha* (wooden spinning wheel) became its symbol.

After lots of ups and down in 1935 Britain offered home rule to India under the Government of India Act of 1935, with Britain still controlling finance, defence, and foreign policies and day to day administration of land. This mainly provided a Federation of Indian consisting of the British Indian Provinces and the Indian states. The British Governor was to remain as the head of the executive with overriding and emergency power. The provincial part of the constitution was implemented in 1937, the Federal part was never. This act provided autonomy to the British provinces and installed a diarchy at the centre. The Congress was not happy at the way the Act sought to establish a federal set up. What desired was a new constitution to be drafted by a truly representative Constituent Assembly. Congress formed ministries in seven provinces in United Province, Bombay, Madras, Central Province, Orissa, Bihar and North West Front Province and joined the coalition ministries in Sindh and Assam. The Muslim League failed to secured a majority in any province (in fact initially they wanted to keep reserved their seats in certain provinces). Muslim League secured 110 seats out of 482. As Congress had Hindu members in majority, the Muslim League began to have their own apprehension at the prospect of Muslim minority coming under the Congress rule in many states. It issued statements regarding the atrocities committed by the Hindus everywhere and about the bias of Congress. However, Congress practically ruled the whole country with the exception of the Punjab and Bengal.

World War Two and the Constitutional Deadlock

The outbreak of the Second World War in September 1939 and the Allied Powers declaration that they were fighting to save the world for democracy greatly raised the hopes of Indian nationalists. The Congress urged the Government to declare their war aims in clear terms. The British Prime Minister declared that the war aim was self-preservation while another minister announced that Britain's aims in joining the war was to win it. The British Government involved India into war without consulting the people of the country. The Viceroy assumed emergency powers under the Defense of India rules. Unsatisfied with the Government of India's policies, the Congress part executive immediately ordered the Congress ministers in all states to resign in October 1939, as a mark of protest. This day was called by the Muslim League supporters as the Day of Deliverance which was even celebrated by them.

Cultural and Social Division

Looking upon the communal problem in India merely as the Hindu-Muslim question or of religious antagonism between the Hindus and the Muslims is misleading. The communal problem at its base was more politically motivated than religiously oriented. Apart from the Hindus and Muslims, there was a third party in the communal triangle, the British rulers who interposed themselves between the Hindus and the Muslims and thus created a communal triangle of which they remained at the base.

The strongest arm of the communal triangle was the British rulers. They were neither the true friends of Muslims nor the foes of the Hindus. They were the true friends of British Imperialism and acted on the tested and tried maxim of Divide *et Imperia*. Until the seventies of the nineteenth century it suited the Imperial interest to support the Hindus more than the Muslims. The British looked upon the Muslims as chief conspirators in the Revolt of 1857. The British Government deliberately adopted the policy of suppressing the Muslims. However, a change in British policy is perceptible towards the 1870s. The Hindus, politically more advanced than the Muslims, demanded more share for Indians in higher services, agitated for grant of political rights, introduction of representative government, etc. The Hindu posed a serious menace to the stability of British rule in India than the politically, economically and educationally backward Muslims.

This marked the beginning of a change in British policy towards the two communities. The Anglo-Indian bureaucracy who worked at the grassroots of British administration in India worked for a change in British policy.

Muslim communities in India formed their communal party in 1906, called Muslim League and it is interesting to note that the initiator behind it again was an English retired principle of Aligarh Muslim College, Mr Theodore Beck, the first British Principle of the newly-started Muslim college at Aligarh, played a notable role in mobilising Muslim opinion and influencing British policy towards the Muslims. This was a communal body established to look after the political rights and interest of the Muslim community alone which ultimately led to the partition of India at the time of independence.

The chapter examines the cultural and social division which consequently led to the emergence of Muslim League (nationalist party) in India and analyses the causes of the differences between the Muslims and Hindus who had been living together for long period. Finally, it exposes the demands made by Jinnah for the Muslim community which widened the gap between them.

Sir Syed Ahmad Khan: Drift from Nationalism to Communalism

The utterances and changing policies of Sir Syed Ahmad Khan (teacher, politician and founder of a school which later became the Aligarh Muslim University) clearly indicates the strong political undertones of the communal problem. Syed Ahmad started as an advocate of the united Indian nation and preached Hindu-Muslim unity, but later changed his views to become a staunch opponent of the Indian National Congress; he fell into line with British imperialists.

Syed Ahmad Khan started his political career as an advocate of Hindu-Muslim amity. He described the Hindus and Muslims as "two eyes of a beautiful bride, i.e. India." In a speech delivered in 1884 he said, "Do you not inhabit the same land?...remember that the words Hindu and Mahomedan (Muslims) are only meant for religious distinction-otherwise all persons, whether Hindu or Mahomedan, even the Christians who reside in this country, are all in this particular respect belonging to one and the same nation."

Contrast with this Syed speech at Meerut on *16th March 1888* where he maintained that the Hindus and Muslims were not only two nations, but as two warring nations who could never lead a common political life should the British ever quit India. Why this sudden change in Syed's outlook and policy. The Muslim demand for separate electorates almost synchronised with the introduction of the system of election in the constitution of local bodies. Speaking in the central legislature in January 1888 on Ripon's bill for establishment of local self-government in the central province, Syed A. Khan referred to the vital difference between different Indian races and different religions, the unequal or disproportionate progress of education among different sections of the population and expressed the fear that any system of election, pure and simple, would result in the larger community overriding the interest of the smaller community. A true devotee of the Muslim cause, Syed was fully aware of Muslim backwardness in the fields of education and politics and came to the conclusion that India was not fit for the introduction of western political institutions like representative or responsible governments, for his community could not get its due share in it. This fear took the form of Indophobia and loomed large in all subsequent Muslim political thinking. The Anglo-Indian administrators were quick to work on Muslim apprehensions and strove to drive a wage between the Hindus and the Muslims. The three English principles of the Mao College, Beck, Morrison and Archibald, gave the pro-British and anti-Hindu bias to the Aligarh Movement. The Aligarh Movement worked to instill into the minds of the Muslims a spirit of loyalty towards the British Crown and worked consciously and deliberately to keep them away from the main stream of Indian political life.

Colonialism in Writing of Indian History

British writers on Indian history also served the imperial cause by initiating, developing and emphasising the Hindu-Muslim approach in their study of Indian history and development of Indian culture.

This communal approach to Indian history, also imitated by Indian scholars, fostered the communal way of thinking. For example, the ancient period of Indian history was described as Hindu period and the medieval period labeled as 'Muslim period of Indian history,' implying thereby that religion was the guiding force behind politics during the whole of medieval period. True, both the rulers and the ruled not often used religious slogans to suit their material and political ambitions, but it was certainly a distortion of history to infer-as was done by these writers that all Muslims were the rulers and all Hindus were the ruled.

Communal Side Effects of Religious Reform Movements

The religious reform and revival movements – both Hindu and Muslim of the nineteenth century contained some mutually contradictory aspects. These movements were launched to purge Hinduism and Islam of irrational and obscurantist tendencies but these generated some unhealthy tendencies. The Wahabis' Crusade against all non-Muslims and aim to establish *dar-ul-islam* (the world of Islam) was as odious to Hindus and Dayanand's slogan of aryanisation of India and to aim to study (conversion of non-Hindus to Hinduism) were unpalatable to Muslims. Even Vivekananda's references to ancient Indian achievements as constituting the real Indian spirit – popularised to give a sense of pride and national identity to a demoralised nation – created a reaction in the Muslim mind that turned to western Asian history for a tradition and identity.

Myths and Communal Overtones

Similarly, the militant nationalists of the early twentieth century in their search for 'national heroes' and 'hero-myth' referred to Maharana Pratap, Shivaji and Guru Gobind Singh as national heroes and the Muslim rulers like Akbar, Shajahan and Aurangzeb as 'foreigners.' The straight logic was that Pratap, Shivaji or Gobind Singh were nationalists because they were Hindus, and Mughal emperors were foreigners because they were Muslims. Besides, it was too much to assume that nationalism of the modern type existed in the medieval period of Indian history.

True, Tilak, Lajpat Rai, Aurobindo and later Gandhi were strong believers in Hindu-Muslim unity. But in their writings and speeches, they often employed a language, imagery and symbolism derived exclusively from Hindu sources (e.g. the slogan of *Ram Rajya* popularised by Gandhi) had a religious tinge and did create a reaction in the Muslim mind. True, the references to Hindu theology were intended to involve the politically inert masses into the nationalist struggle by explaining to them nationalism couched in a language within their comprehension, i.e. religious phraseology but it did have the undesired effect of rousing Muslim communal susceptibility-feelings cleverly exploited by the British rulers.

Patronage in Government in Services Used to Foster Colonialism

In the absence of any avenues of gainful employment in trade and industry, the British-Indian Government remained the biggest employer to which the educated youth hopefully looked for their means of livelihood. This enormous patronage – in higher and subordinate services – was cleverly used by the rulers to promote rivalry and discord among different sections of society. Our nationalist leaders were fully aware of the mischievous character of this bait, but the hunger –rather compulsion – for loaves and fishes rather blinded them to eat dangerous potentialities.

The Simla Deputation (*1st October 1906*) and Acceptance of the Principle of Communal Electorate

The imperial administrators, right from the Secretary of State in England to the District officer in India, all were convinced that adequate "counter-poises" to the growing strength of the Indian National Congress must be found, if the British rule in India was to be stable. One such counter poise thought about was the official acceptance of the principle of separate Muslim electorates i.e. reservation of seats for the Muslim community and election to such seats to be made by separate Muslim electorates. The opportunity presented itself because a new scheme of constitutional reform was being considered.

Inspired by Principal Archibald of M.A.O. College, Aligarh, H.H. the Aga Khan waited in a deputation on Lord Minto at Simla on *1st October 1906*. The deputation as described by Maulana Mohammad Ali was a 'command performance.' Mr Archibald prepared the draft of the Muslim Address, acted as a liaison between the Government and Muslim leaders and saw to it the success of the deputation to the last detail. The deputationists expressed sentiments of loyalty to the British Crown, showed grateful appreciation of the Government's policy of introducing further reforms but expressed apprehension that if the principle of 'election' was introduced without conceding reservation of seats for the Muslims, it would prove detrimental to their interest. The deputationist demanded the reservation of seats for the Muslim community not only on the basis of their population but on the basis of their political importance and their services in the defense of the Empire. Lord Minto gladly accepted the Muslim demand for separate communal electorates.

Foundation of the Muslim League, *30th December 1906*

In the wake of the fateful Simla Deputation the Muslim leader mooted the idea of a Central Muhammadan Association to look exclusively after the interests of the Muslim community. The All India Muslim League was formerly inaugurated on *30th December 1906* with the following aims and objectives:

(a) To promote among Indian Muslims feelings of loyalty towards the British Government and to remove any misconception that could arise as to the intentions of the Government with regard to any of its measures.

(b) To protect the political and other rights of the Indian Muslims and to place their needs and aspirations before the Government in temperate language.

(c) So far as possible without prejudice to the objects mentioned under (a) and (b) to promote friendly relations between Muslims and other communities of India.

Thus from its very inception, the Muslim League was a communal body established to look after the political rights and interests of the

Muslim community alone. This character more or less retained till 1947.

The true political ideas of the league are apparent from Nawab Waqar-ul-Mulk's speech delivered at Aligarh. The Nawab said, "God forbid, if the British rule disappears from India Hindus will Lord over it and we will be in constant danger of our life, property and honour. The only way for the Muslims to escape this danger is to help in the continuance of the British rule.

For about a decade after 1913, the Muslim League came under the influence of progressive Muslim leaders like Maulana Muhammad Ali, Maulana Mazhar-ul-Huq, Syed Wazir Hussein, Hassan Imam and M.A. Jinnah (then a nationalist). From 1920 to 1923, the activities of the Muslim League remained suspended. However, the appointment of the Simon Commission (1927–1930) and the Round Table Conferences at London (1930–1932) that followed again brought the Muslim League into activity. By 1934, M.A. Jinnah now a communalist became its undisputed leader. The Communal Award (1932) of the British Government further widened the gulf between the Hindus and the Muslims.

Congress Ministries and the Muslim League, 1937 – 1939

The first elections for the provincial legislative councils under the Government of India Act were held in 1937. The Muslim League contested the elections to various legislative bodies but achieved moderate success. Out of the 485 reserved Muslim seats, the League could capture only 110 seats. Even in the Muslim majority provinces of the Panjab, the North-West Frontier Province, Bengal and Sind, the League was trounced by rival Muslim parties. The Congress Party gained an absolute majority in Bombay, Madras, U.P, Bihar, Orissa and the Central Provinces like Bengal, Assam and the Panjab and desired the Congress to take Muslim League ministers in U.P. and Bihar. The Congress, consistent with its principles and policies – liberation of the country and amelioration of the condition of the masses – advised the Muslim League members to sign the Congress pledge and become its members, if they desired to accept responsibilities of the office.

Mr Jinnah interpreted these moves by the Congress as a calculated policy against the Muslim League. He leveled 'sweeping and fantastic' allegations against the Congress ministers and dubbed the Congress a Hindu organisation out to crush all minorities. He came to the conclusion that the Muslims could expect neither justice nor fair play from the Congress ministries. In 1938, the Muslim League appointed a committee under the Chairmanship of the Raja of Pirpur to report on the oppressions of the Muslims in what it called "Hindu Congress Provinces." The Pirpur Report fabricated cases of alleged horrible atrocities perpetrated on the Muslims by the Hindus.

The Muslim League observed a 'Day of Deliverance and Thanksgiving' when the Congress ministers resigned in 1939 over the war issue.

The Two-Nation Theory and the Pakistan Movement

The poet and political thinker Mohammad Iqbal is thought to be the originator of the idea of a separate Muslim State for the India Muslims and is believed to have given the necessary emotional content to the movement. The idea of a separate homeland for Muslims to be called Pakistan took a definite shape in the mind of a young undergraduate at Cambridge, Rahmat Ali. He visualised the Panjab, North West Frontier Province (also called Afghan Province), Kashmire, Sind and Baluchistan as the national home of the Indian Muslims and he coined the word Pakistan in 1933. The word Pakistan was formed by taking the initials of the first four and the last of the fifth. Rahmat Ali maintained that the Hindus and Muslims were fundamentally distinct nations.

The most unequivocal declaration of the Hindus and the Muslims as separate nationalities was made by M.A. Jinnah at the Lahore session of the League in March 1940, "They (Hindus and Muslims) are not religious in the strict sense of the word but are in fact different and distinct social orders and it is a dream that Hindus and Muslims can ever evolve a common nationality. The Hindus and Muslims belong to two different religious philosophies, social customs, literature...to yoke together two such nations under a single state, one a numerical minority and the other as a majority must lead to growing discontent and final destruction of any fabric that may be so built up of the Government of such a state."

Demanding the partition of India, the Muslim League passed the resolution: "It is the considered view of this session of the All-India Muslim League that no constitutional plan would be workable in this country or acceptable to the Muslims unless it is designed on the following basic principle, viz, that geographically contagious units are demarcated into regions which should be so constituted with such territorial readjustments as may be necessary that the areas in which the Muslims are numerically in the majority as in the North-Western and eastern zones of India should be grouped to constitute 'independent states' in which the constituent units shall be autonomous and sovereign.." in 1942, Mr Jinnah explained to Professor Coupland that Pakistan would be 'a Muslim State or States comprising N.W.F.P, the Panjab and Sind on the one side of India and Bengal on the other." He did not mention Baluchistan and Assam, nor did he claim Kahmir and Hyderadad.

Thus, the Lahore session of the Muslim League gave it an ambition and a programme. Henceforth, the demand for Pakistan became as much an article of faith for the Indian Muslims as their holy book, the *Quran*.

The Hindu Mahasabha

British imperial policies in India provided a congenial climate for the emergence, growth and popularity of communal organisations. A communal organisation through primarily organised to promote the interest of a particular community also indirectly promoted British imperial interests apart from serving the personal ambition of opportunistic leadership. This was not only true of the *Hindu Mahasabha* but also of the *Muslim League*, the *Akali Dal* and the *All-Indida Depressed Classes Federation*.

The genesis and early history of the *Hindu Mahasabha* are clouded in obscurity. In 1910, the leading Hindu of Allahabad decided to organise an *All-India Hindu Mahasabha*. In 1911, the *Panjab Hindu*

Mahasabha organised a Hindu Conference at Amritsar. The Hindu Conference at Hardwar on the occasion of important Hindu fairs.

The communal riots particularly in the Malabar Coast and Multan that followed the suspension of the first Non-cooperation movement in 1922 caused heavy losses to the Hindus both in human life and property. A section of the Hindus decided to organise the Hindus in self-defence.

The tall claims of the *Hindu Mahasabha* as a socio-cultural organisation were hardly less hypocritical than similar claims put up by the *Muslim League*, the *Akali Dal* and other communal organisations. Under the leadership of V.D. Savarkar who became the President of the *Hindu Mahasabha* in 1938 and was re-elected again and again, the *Mahasabha* developed a political programme.

Sore at the Muslim appeasement policy of the Indian National Congress, Savarkar popularised the concept of *Hindu Rashtra.* He maintained that India was a land of Hindus having only one nation i.e. Hindu nation. The Muslims must accept their position as a minority community in a single Indian State, of course being promised just treatment and equal political rights on the basis of 'one man one vote.' On the question of a national language, Savarkar upheld that according to democratic practices, the language of the majority must prevail.

The *Hindu Mahasabha* never gained that popularity with the Hindu masses as the Muslim League did with the Muslims in India. All the same, against the Muslim League's demand for Pakistan, it raised the slogan of *Akhand Hindustan.*

The Second World War and Furtherance of the Pakistan Plan

The August Offer, 1940

In response to the Congress' offer for co-operation with the British Government conditional on its declaration of "the full independence of India" and formation of a Provisional National Government at the centre, Lord Linlithgow in August 1940 offered the plan of setting up a constitution making body after the war but assured the minorities that the British Government would not agree to any system of government whose authority was directly denied by large and powerful elements in India's national life. The Muslim League welcomed this part of the August offer and passed the resolution, "The partition of India is the only solution of the most difficult problem of India's future constitution."

7

World War Two and Struggle for Freedom

Introduction

The outbreak of war in September 1939 found India even more unprepared in a material sense than Britain and with a much more divided mind. Britain was anxious to utilise India's abundant resources for the prosecution of the war.

During the World war Two Indians leaders tried to patch up their differences with the Muslim League leaders which could not work out. Under Mahatma Gandhi *Quit India Movement* was called which could not maintain its nonviolence policy; hence Gandhi called off this movement. Even Gandhi was arrested and whole country was fallen in chaos. The chapter investigates the reasons behind the non-participation by the Indian nationalists in the World War Two.

World War Two

When war broke out, there was a general approval of the cause couple with a wide spread reluctance to do very much about it. It was 'Britain's affair, not India's.' The two great political parties in India, the Congress and the Muslim Leagues refused to cooperate with the Government in its war effort. The Indian princes however stood solidly behind the Government which had also no difficulty in securing sufficient recruits without any compulsion.

At home, Congress viewed the situation as national crises. Nehru begged Jinnah to join in protesting against the Government's policy but he did not respond. Congress which was in partnership with Government protested this war and on *23rd October 1939* its minister resigned. This action by Congress minister was rejoiced by the Muslim League by celebrating as 'Day of Deliverance' on 22nd December 1939 also as a day of thanksgiving.

On *1st September 1939*, the Second World War began. On *3rd September 1939*, the Viceroy of India declared war against Germany without consulting or taking into confidence the Indian leaders. Indian troops were sent to the various theatres of war for the defense of the British Empire. After having done all this, the Viceroy started consultations with the Indian leaders. The Working Committee of the Congress met at Wardha in September 1939 and after prolonged deliberation, a resolution was adopted in which it was declared that if the war was "to defend the *status quo*, imperialist possessions, colonies, vested interests and privileges then India can have nothing to do with it. If however the issue is democracy and a world based on democracy, then India is intensely interested in it, if Great Britain was fighting for the maintenance and extension of democracy in India." The British Government was called upon to declare its war aims "in regard to democracy and imperialism" and also to declare whether those aims were "going to apply to India and to be given effect to at present."

On *27th July 1940*, resolution was passed by the Congress in which an offer of co-operation in the war was made provided India's demand for independence was conceded and a provisional National government responsible to the then Central Assembly was formed at the Centre. On *8th August 1940*, the Viceroy issued a statement in which it was declared that the new Constitution of India would primarily be the responsibility of the Indians themselves. However, it was made clear that Great Britain "could not contemplate transfer of their present responsibilities of the peace and welfare of India to any system of Government whose authority is directly denied by large and powerful elements in India's national life nor could they be parties to the coercion of such elements into submission of such a Government." It was also declared that after the war, a "representative Indian constitution-making body would be set up and the Indian proposals as its form and operation would at any time be welcome." The Congress was wholly disappointed with the August offer.

It was in the month of *March 1942* that S. Cripps (A senior left-wing politician and government minister in the War Cabint of Prime Minister (W. Churchill) was sent to India with certain proposals with a view to seek the co-operation and support of the Congress in the prosecution of the war. To begin with, the response of the Congressmen was favourable. Cripps is stated to have assured the Congress leaders that under the proposed scheme, the Governor-General would function as a constitutional head. It appears that the offer was made without consulting the Viceroy and consequently, the Viceroy complained to Prime Minister Churchill and the latter informed Cripps that he would be repudiated if he "went too far." Fresh instructions were sent to Cripps and the latter told the Congress President that the position of the Viceroy could not be changed without a change in the law. On *11th April, 1942*, a resolution was passed by the Congress working Committee rejecting Cripps' proposal. It was pointed out that only a free and independent India could undertake the defence of the country on a national basis.

An effective stress after the failure of the Cripps Mission, there were differences of opinion among the Congress leadership regarding the future course of action to be adopted. The view of Maulana Azad who at that time was the Congress President was that negotiations should be resumed with Great Britain and full co-operation should be extended to the United Nations if the American President or the United Nations gave a guarantee that the promise will be fulfilled. Nehru's view was that the British Government must make a formal declaration of India's independence at once. The Provisional Government must make a formal declaration of India's independence at once. The Provisional government then formed should negotiate with Great Britain the terms of co-operation. The Commander-in-Chief of the Allied Forces was to be given full support in all decisions relating to military matters and the Japanese must be resisted by the Indians at all costs. Mahatma Gandhi advocated mass action to drive the British out of India.

Meeting of the Congress Working Committee was held at Wardha and after a lot of discussion, a resolution was passed on *14th July 1942* which stated that the failure of the Cripps Mission and the attitude of the British Government towards India "has resulted in a rapid and widespread increase of ill-will against the British and a growing satisfaction at the influence of Japanese arms." It was stated that the Congress desired "to build up resistance to any aggression or invasion of India by the Japanese or any foreign power" and the Congress would change the ill will against Great Britain into good will, "if India feels the glow of freedom." It was made clear that in making the proposal for the withdrawal of the British rule from India, the Congress had no desire whatsoever to embarrass Great Britain or the Allied Powers in their prosecution of the war or in any way to encourage aggression on India or increased pressure on China by the Japanese or any other power associated with the Axis Group." It was hoped that this "very reasonable and just proposal" would be accepted by Great Britain, "not only in the interest of India but also that of Britain and of the cause of freedom to which the United Nations proclaimed their allegiance." It was made clear in the resolution that in case India's appeal was not accepted, the Congress would "the be reluctantly compelled to utilise all the non-violent strength it might have gathered since 1920 when it adopted non-violence as part of its policy, for the vindication of political rights and liberty." The final decision was to be taken by the All India Congress Committee whose meeting was fixed from 4th to 7th August, 1942 at Bombay.

The Congress gave 24 days to the Government to make a favourable response. On 15th July 1942, Mahatma Gandhi told the foreign press that if the movement had to be launched it would be a non-violent one. *On 25th July 1942,* President Chiang Kai-shek (Chinese political and military leader who served as the leader of the Republic of China between 1928 and 1975, was President of China from 1948 to 1949). wrote to President Roosevelt to intervene so that the Congress was not forced to launch the movement. The letter was forwarded to Churchill but nothing came out of it.

Last Great Struggle of the Congress to Oust the Imperialism

Under Gandhi

A meeting of the All India Congress Committee was held in Bombay on *7th August 1942* as scheduled. The general feeling was that an attempt be made to come to terms with the Government and for that purpose, Mahatma Gandhi expressed the wish to meet the Viceroy. However, on *8th August 1942*, the famous **"Quit India"** resolution was moved by Jawaharlal Nehru and passed by an overwhelming majority. It was declared in that resolution that the immediate ending of the British rule in India was an urgent necessity, both for the sake of India and for the success of the cause of the United Nations. India had become the crux of the question. Britain and the United Nations will be judged by the independence of India. Addressing the Congress delegates on the night of *8th August 1942*, Gandhi said, "I, therefore want freedom immediately, this very night before dawn if it can be had. You may take it from me that I am not going to strike a bargain with the Viceroy for ministers and the like. I am not going to be satisfied with anything short of complete freedom. Here is a *mantra,* a short one that I give you. You may imprint it on your hearts and let every breath of yours give expression to it. The *Mantra* is: 'Do or die.' We shall either free India or die in the attempt; we shall not live to see the perpetuation of our slavery."

When the resolution was passed, an appeal was made to Great Britain and the United Nations to respond to the "call of reason and justice," it was also decided that all efforts should be made to come to a settlement with the Government and it was only when those efforts failed that the movement was to be started after Mahatma Gandhi had given his sanction. Mahatma Gandhi and Maulana Azad (president of the Indian National Congress in 1924 and then from 1940-46) openly declared that they would approached the Viceroy again and the heads of the various Governments for an honourable settlement.

It was decided that Jawaharlal Nehru was to explain on *9th August 1942* to the United States the scope and contents of the 'Quit India' resolution.

It appears that the Government had already finalised their plans to arrest the Congress leaders and crush their movement and consequently in the early hours of *9th August 1942*, Mahatma Gandhi, Jawaharlal Nehru, Maulana Azad, Sadar Patel (one of the leader of the Indian National Congress during the struggle for indian independence), Rajendra Prasad (active member of Indian National Congress, president of the Congress party in 1934, 1939 and 1947, later became the First President of India), Acharya Kriplani (politician, noted particularly for holding the presidency of the Indian National Congress during the transfer of power in 1947), etc. were arrested. As many as 148 Congress leaders were arrested and interned along with their followers. The people were stunned as their leaders were arrested and all of a sudden, they did not know what to do. The result is that they carried on the movement in any way they could. All over the country, there were '*hartals' (*strikes) in factories, schools and colleges and public demonstrations. Angered by repeated firings and lathi-charges, the people took to violence in many places. They attacked police stations, post offices, railway stations etc. they cut off telegraph and telephone wires and railway lines. They burnt Government buildings and railway carriages were put on fire. Even military vehicles were destroyed. Madras and Bengal were the most affected in this respect. In many places, the Indians got temporary control over towns, citizens and villagers. British authority disappeared in parts of Uttar Pradesh, Bihar, Orissa, West Bengal, Maharashtra, Andhra and Madras. In some places, the people set up parallel governments. To quote Jawaharlal Nehru, "for the first time since the great Revolt of 1957, vast numbers of people rose to challenge by force (but a force without arms) the fabric of British rule in India.

The Government used all its machinery to suppress the movement. Hundreds of people were arrested and imprisoned. A large number of them were killed chiefly by the firing of the military and the police.

The people were insulted, assaulted and injured regardless of their position and status. Whipping was inflicted on many and heavy collective fines were imposed and recovered. K.C. Neogy (member of of the Indian National Congress and was elected as a member of the Central Legislative Assembly in 1920 representing Bengal, later became the member of the United Nations on Human Rights) called those fines as communal fines as those were realised only from the Hindus. There was machine gunning of mobs from the air in five places: Patna, Bhagalpur and Monghyr in Bihar, Nadia in Bengal and Talchar city. According to the official figures, the civilian casualties from August to December 1942 were 940 killed and many more injured. Nehru's view was that figures of the dead varied between 4,000 and 10,000. More than 60,000 people were arrested up to the end of 1942. Twenty six thousand people were convicted and 18,000 were detained under the Defense of India Rules.

Many reasons have been advanced for the beginning of the "Quit India" movement. The first was the threat of Japanese invasion of India. Mahatma Gandhi wanted to save India from that attack and his view was that if the British Government withdrew from India, the Japanese might not attack India. Another reason was the defenselessness of the British position in India and their easy defeat in Singapore. Gandhi's view was that India would meet the same fate if the British did not withdraw from India. Another reason was the alarming growth of Axis propaganda which was having its effect on the minds of the people of India. This was particularly so on account of the broadcasts of Subhash Chandra Bose (separately highlighted after assessment of Quite India movement), from Berlin in the Indian languages. Another cause was that the mind of Mahatma Gandhi was revolting against the racial discrimination shown in the process of evacuation from Burma. The British provided separate routes for the evacuation of Europeans and Indians. The White road was meant for Europeans and the Black road for Indians. The result was that the Indian evacuees had to undergo too many hardships on the way. There was a a lot of resentment in the country when the people heard of the suffering of the Indians and that contributed to the decision by Mahatma Gandhi to start the "Quit India" movement. Another reason was the suffering of the people on account of the 'Scorched Earth' policy followed by the British Government in India. The land belonging to the people of India was taken for military purposes and they were not given adequate compensation. They were deprived of their means of livelihood. A lot of harshness was used by the Government while getting the houses of peasants evacuated for the military. The inefficient and ineffective controls and transportation muddles added to the suffering of the people. Prices rose in those months and the people lost faith in the paper currency issued by the Government. There was a lot of discontentment among the people and Mahatma Gandhi decided to take advantage of it.

Assessment of Quit India Movement

The failure of the "Quit India" movement was due to many causes. The first was the tactical mistake of organisation and planning. The arrest of Gandhi and the Congress leaders left the people without any leadership or guidance. There was no coordination and no strategy. Those who led the movement were divided in their views on the course of action. Nobody knew what to do. The loyalty of the services and superior physical strength of the Government succeeded in crushing the revolt. The movement did not have the support of the upper classes of India consisting of rich merchants, landlords and princes and also a pat of the labour force. On the whole, the Muslims remained aloof from the movement. They were told by the Muslim League that the movement was directed to coerce the British Government to hand over to the Hindus the administration of the country.

As regards the gains of the revolt of 1942, Dr Amba Prasad (popularly known as Sufi Amba Prasad, an indian nationalist and pan-Islamist leader) says that although the revolt failed, it prepared the ground for independence in 1947. This was because there was no more doubt in the minds of the British rulers that the days of British dominion of India were numbered. It was only a question of time. The revolt marked the culmination of the Indian freedom movement. It gave utterance to India's anger against imperialism and her determination to be free. It is true that there were many political developments and much parleying and bargaining between the revolt of August 1942 and the independence of India in August 1947 but there was no doubt about the fact that the freedom struggle was bound to win.

Two important events took place in 1945. One was that general elections took place in England and the Labour Party came to power. The other was the surrender of Japan on 14th August 1945 and the termination of hostilities in the Far East. Unlike Churchill, the new Labour Government was sympathetically inclined towards the Indian demand for freedom. As the pre-occupation with war was over the Labour Government tried to solve the Indian problem, the Viceroy of India was summoned to London. After prolonged discussions, the Viceroy came back to India and declared on *19th September 1945* that the Government had decided to convene a constitution making body in the near future. It was declared that elections to the Central Assembly and the Provincial Legislatures would be held "during the coming cold weather."

Elections to the Central Assembly were held in November and December 1945. In the first week of January 1946, the Parliamentary Delegation came to India to meet the Indian leaders. On 15th March 1946, Prime Minister Attlee declared in the House of Commons that India herself must decide her future constitution and no minority will in India would be allowed to place a veto on the advance of the majority. The Cabinet Mission reached Delhi on *24 March 1946* and on *15 March 1946*, it gave its own solution of the problem known as the Cabinet Mission Scheme. On *2 September 1946*, Jawaharlal Nehru formed the Interim Government. The Constituent Assembly met on 9 December 1946 but was boycotted by the Muslim League. On *20 February 1946*, the British Government declared that it would transfer power into the hands of the Indians by a date not later than *June 1948*. Lord Mountbatten gave his *3 June* Plan for the partition of India. The Indian Independence Act was passed in *July 1947* and India became Independent on *15th August 1947*.

Under Bose

Subhash, son of a wealthy Bengali family, returned home in 1921 from England after passing Indian Civil Service examination and joined Gandhi's movement. He was expelled in 1916 from Presidency College in Calcutta due to his nationalist activities. Gradually, he became youth leader, journalist and commandant of Bengal Congress volunteers.

Plate 4

Subhash Chandra Bose

He was advised by Gandhi to work under Chittranjan Das, an active politician in Bengal. His nationalist activities led to his imprisonment in *December 1921.* In 1924 he was appointed chief executive officer of the corporation of Calcutta, with das as mayor.. Bose was soon deported to Burma (now Myanmar) due to his association with secret revolutionary movements. He was released in 1927, returned to find Bengal Congress affairs in disarray after the death of Das. Das had died at a very crucial juncture in Indian politics. Bose was in sympathy with the Bengal tradition of the national revolutionaries who preferred violent action to Gandhi's non-violence. When the Civil Disobedience Movement was called in 1930, Bose was in detention. He was released and again arrested but was allowed to proceed to Europe after a year's detention. In his enforced exile he wrote a book "The Indian struggle, 1920-1934" and pleaded the Indian cause with European leaders. After return from exile in 1936 again he was arrested for one year. In 1938 he was elected president of the Indian National Congress and formed a a national planning committee, which formulated a policy of industrialisation. His idea of industrialisation did not harmonise with Gandhian economic thought, which clung to the spinning wheel as symbol. Bose's vindication came in 1939, when he defeated a Gandhian rival for re-election but resigned due to internal conflict. He founded the Forward Block, hoping to rally radical elements, but was again put in jail July 1940. British government was forced to release him from jail due to his determination to go on fast unto death. On January 1941, he escaped from Calcutta residence in disguise and reached Germany in April via Kabul and Moscow.

In Nazi Germany Bose came under the guardianship of a newly created Special Bureau for India, guided by Adom von Trott su solz (lawyer and diplomat who was involved in the conservative opposition to the Nazi regime). He with other Indians made regular broadcasts from the German-sponsored Azad Hind Radio beginning in January 1942, speaking in English, Hindi, Bengali, Tamil, Telgu, Gujrati, and Pashto.

After the invasion of Southeast Asia, Bose left Germany, travelling by German and Japanese submarine and plane arrived in *May 1943* in Tokyo. In July he assumed leadership of the Indian independence in East asia and proceeded, with Japanese aid and influence, to form a trained army of about 40,000 Indian men and women, rounded up in Japanese-occupied Southeastern Asia. Bose proclaimed the establishment of a provisional independent Indian government, in October 1943, and his Indian National Army (*Azad Hind Fauz*), alongside Japanese troops, advanced to Rangoon (now Yangon) and reached India on March 1944.

Subhash Chandra Bose wanted to free India from the Eastern front. He had taken care the Japanese interference was not present from any angle. Army leadership, administration and communications were managed by Indians only. These troops were determined to drive out the British and their cry was for *Delhi Chalo* (Let's march to

Delhi). The Bombing of Hiroshima and Nagasaki and surrender of Japan not only changed the history of mankind but it also crushed the Bose's passion. After this in *August 1945* Bose, fleeing Southern Asia, reportedly died in a Japanese hospital in Taiwan as a result of burn injuries from a plane crash. Kulke and Rothmund commented on Bose and wrote that his life and his appearance on this earth were like a meteor which enters the earth's atmosphere, but burnt brightly on the horizon for a brief moment only.

At times it looked as if the above two great leader's movements did not contribute much, at that moment, but had great influence on forthcoming nationalist activities especially after 1942 or towards the end of the World War Two.

World War Two and India's Independence

(1) There were many reasons which forced the British Government to grant independence to India and the most important was the strength of the nationalist movement. The movement under the leadership of Mahatma Gandhi had become so strong that the grant of independence could not be postponed for longer, The "Quit India" Movement had shown that the people of India could go to any length to bring to an end the British Raj in the country. They made tremendous sacrifices to paralyse the administrative machinery. The British Government was fully aware of the slogans "Do or Die" and "Now or Never". The organisation of the Indian national Army under Subhash Chandra Bose and the cry of "Dilli Chalo" made the British Government realise the folly of resisting the demand of the people of India for independence.

(2) Another cause was that the British Government lost faith in the loyalty of the armed forces in India, particularly the Navy. Throughout, Great Britain had relied upon force and military superiority for maintaining its hold over India. Force was always available to crush any revolt on the part of the Indians. However, circumstances changed to such an extent during the Second World War that the loyalty of the

Indian forces could not be depended upon. Thousands of Indians from all over India joined the armed forces during the Second World War. They not only fought for the victory of the Allied Power but also hoped that India would get independence after the war. No wonder when the war was over, these persons began to clamour for the freedom of India.

(4) There had been a feeling in India that the British power was invincible. However, the impression was removed during the Second World War as a result of the reverses suffered by the British troops at the hands of the Japanese. British troops were forced to evacuate Hong Kong, Singapore, Malaysia and Burma. Their best ships "The Repulse" and "Prince of Wales," were sunk. Great Britain was not in a position to demonstrate in Asia the background of strength and influence which had for some time enabled her to rule a million people with one man on the spot.

(5) Great Britain had to spend so much during the Second World War that she was completely exhausted. She was forced to borrow on an enormous scale. She had depended upon other countries not only for foodstuffs but also for raw materials to run factories. She depended upon American help in every field. The Englishmen had many problems to tackle at home. It was felt that it was not wise to keep her involved in India when all her energy was required at home. The American Government also put pressure on the British Government to grant India independence as the Allied Party had been fighting for freedom and democracy. Even die hard like Churchill began to feel that it was not of any advantage to keep India under bondage.

(6) Mr Attlee, Prime Minister of England at that time, had a lot to do with the granting of independence to India. He had always taken keen interest in the Indian affairs. When he became Prime Minister of England in 1945, he came to the conclusion that even if Great Britain was able to keep India in bondage with the help of force, that would not be

profitable to her as by doing so, she was bound to lose the goodwill of the people of India and in that case the Indo-British relations were bound to suffer in the long run. His view was that Great Britain was bound to gain if she was able to win the goodwill of the people of India by giving them independence. To begin with, he sent the Cabinet Mission to India, but when that failed, he sent Lord Mountbatten to complete the process of transfer of power in India.

(7) Another reason why Great Britain decided to leave India was that she got involved in the cold war after the Second World War. Both the United Stated and the Soviet Union accused each other. The Russians had an advantage over the Americans in the cold war. They could always point out the fact that Great Britain was keeping India in chains. Great Britain could be in a better position if she granted India Independence.

(8) A large number of persons advocated the cause of India's freedom abroad. Among them were Louis Fischer (Jewish-American journalist), Pearl Buck (Civil Activist and Nobel prize winner for Literature wrote a novel on India- Ancient culture), Lin Yu-tang (Chinese writer wrote on China and India wisdom), Norman Thomas (follower of socialist party in America) and J.J. Singh (Indian in America played important role towards India's independence, from there). The Indian viewpoint was put forward before the Conference at San Francisco which met to finalise the Charter of the League of Nations. Great Britain was not only a signatory to the Charter but her delegates played an important part in framing it. This fact was bound to affect the entire attitude of the British Government towards India. She could not talk of freedom while keeping India in bondage.

(9) Another factor which influenced the British decision to leave India was a change in the concept of British Commonwealth. In July 1917, the Commonwealth Relations Office was set up. If the British could treat Other Dominions in that manner, there was no reason why the same could not

be done with regard to India. It was felt that even after India was given independence, she would be persuaded to be part and parcel of the Commonwealth of Nations and hence no loss to Great Britain.

(10) The view of Maulana Azad was that the British Government decided to leave India only after making sure that she could continue to have a foot-hold on the Indian sub-continent. The British decision to partition India and then to transfer power was the culmination of the policy of "divide and rule." The partition of India in which the Muslim majority provinces formed a separate and independent state would give Britain a foot-hold in India. A state dominated by the Muslim League would offer a permanent sphere of influence to Great Britain.

(11) Indian masses were reliably informed by some respectable Indians who returned to India from England the year immediately following the end of the Second World War that British soldiers who had first-hand knowledge of the poverty of the Indian masses spoke about it feelingly to their friends and relatives. That knowledge filtered down to the people. A feeling was created in England that perhaps with the independence, the Indians might be able to improve their economic condition. That explains the unanimous support given by the members of Parliament to the Indian Independence Bill in *July 1947.*

(12) The view of Prime Minister Attlee was that the independence of India was fulfillment of Britain's mission in India. The British were leaving India after fulfilling their mission in the country. They had taught the Indians to govern themselves and they were now leaving the reins of Government in their hands.

As such one can argue that the World War Two, indirectly, did contribute to the independence of India.

8

The Drive to Independence, Partition and Transfer of Power 1939-47

Introduction

The contradictory nature of the reality of *15th August 1947* continues to intrigue historians and torment people on both sides of the border to this day. A hard-earned, prized freedom was won after long, glorious years of struggle but a bloody, tragic partition as under the fabric of the emerging free nation. India's independence on 15th August 1947 was received with mixed feelings. Many Indians called it a 'Sad Morning'. The massive land of India was partition into two countries and *14th August* was the day when Pakistan came to be in existence with its two wings namely West and East Pakistan. Two questions arise. Why did the British finally quit? Why was the Partition accepted by the Congress?

The chapter looks into the causes behind the partition of India and investigates whether it could have been possible to prevint India's partition.

The Drive to Independence

The imperialist answer is that independence was simply the fulfillment of Britain's self-appointed mission to assist the Indian people to self-government. Partition was the unfortunate consequence of the age of old Hindustan by the mass actions of 1946-47 in which many Communists participated, often as leaders. But the bourgeois leaders of the congress, frightened by the revolutionary upsurge struck a deal with the imperialist power by which power was transferred to them and the nation paid the price of partition.

Once it was recognised that British rule could not survive on the old basis for long, a graceful withdrawal from India, to be effected after a settlement had been reached on the modalities of transfer of power and the nature of the post-imperial relation between British and India, became the overarching aim of British policy-makers. The British Government was clear that a settlement was a must both for good future relations and to bury the ghosts of a mass movement. Since failure could not be afforded, the concessions had to be such as would largely meet Congress demands. With the Congress demand being that the British quit India; the Cabinet Mission went out to India in *March 1946* to negotiate the setting up of a national government and to set into motion machinery for transfer of power. It was not an empty gesture like the Cripps Missions in 1942 the Cabinet Mission was prepared for a long stay.

Congress Demand for One Nation

The Congress demand was for transfer of power to one centre, with minorities' demand being worked out in framework ranging from autonomy to Muslim provinces to self-determination on secession from the Indian Union but after the British left. The British bid was for a united India, friendly with British and an active partner in Commonwealth defense. It was believed that a divided India would lack depth in defence, frustrate joint defense plans and be a blot on British's diplomacy. Pakistan was not seen by Britain as her natural future ally, as the Government's policy of fostering the League ever since its inception in 1906 and the alignment today between Pakistan and the Western imperialist bloc may suggest.

British policy in 1946 reflected this preference for a united India, in sharp contrast to earlier declarations. Attlee's *15 March 1945* statement that a 'minority will not be allowed to place a veto on the progress of the majority' was a far cry Iron Wavell's allowing Jinnah to wreck the Simla Conference in *June-July 1945* by his insistence on nominating all Muslims. The Cabinet Mission was convinced that Pakistan was not viable and that the minorities' autonomy must somehow be safeguarded within the framework of a united India. The Mission Plan conceived three sections, A-comprising Madras, Bombay, Uttar Pradesh, Bihar, C.P. and Orissa; B-consisting of Punjab, NWFP and Sind; and C-of Bengal and Assam-which would meet separately to decide on group constitutions. There would be a common centre controlling defence, foreign affairs and communications.

The Congress and League interpreted the Mission Plan in their own way, both seeing it as a confirmation of their stand. This, Patel maintained that the Mission's plan was against Pakistan, that the League's veto was gone and that one Constituent Assembly was envisaged. The League announced its acceptance of the Plan on *6th June* in so far as the basis of Pakistan was implied in the Mission's plan virtue of the compulsory grouping. Nehru asserted the Congress Working Committee's particular interpretation of the plan in his speech to the AICC on the *7 July 1946*: 'We are not bound by a single thing except that we have decided to go into the Constituent Assembly. The implication was that the Assembly was sovereign and would decide rules of procedure. Jinnah seized the opportunity provided by Nehru's speech to withdraw the League's acceptance of the Mission Plan on *29th July, 1946.*

This was the situation in which Lord Mountbatten came to India as Viceroy. He was the last Viceroy and charged with the task of winding up the Raj by *30th June 1948*. Mountbatten has claimed to have introduced the time limit into the *20 February* settlement, 'I made the great point about it. I had thought of the time limit, and I had great difficulty in bringing him (Attlee) up to it...I think the time limit was fundamental. I believe if I'd gone out without a time limit, I'd still be there.

Mountbatten had a clear cut directive from His Majesty's Government, he did not write his own ticket, as he has claimed. He was directed to explore the options of unity and division till

October, 1947 after which he was to advise His Majesty's Government on the form transfer of power should take. Here again he soon discovered that he had little real choice. The broad contours of the scenario that was to emerge were discernible even before he came out. Mountbatten found out within two months of his arrival that more flogging would not push the Cabinet Mission plan forward, it was a dead horse. Jinnah was obdurate that the Muslim would settle from nothing less than a sovereign state. Mountbatten found that he was unable to move Jinnah from this stand: 'He gave the impression that he was not listening. He was impossible to argue with…He was, whatever was said, intending on his Pakistan.'

The British could keep India united only if they gave up their role as mediators trying to affect a solution Indians had agreed upon. Unity needed positive intervention in its favours, including putting down communal elements with a firm hand. This they chose not to do. Attlee wrote late, "We would have preferred a United Indian. We couldn't get it, though we tried hard."

Transfer of Power

The rationale for the early date for transfer of power, *15 August 1947*, was securing Congress agreement to Dominion Status. The additional benefit was that the British could escape responsibility for the rapidly deteriorating communal situation. As it is, some officials were more than happy to pack their bags and leave the Indians to stew in their own juice. As Patel said to the viceroy, the situation was where 'you won't govern yourself and you won't let us govern'. Mountbatten was to defend his advancing the date to *15th August, 1947* on the ground that things would have blown up under their feet had they not got out when they did. Ismay, the viceroy's Chief of Staff in British India Army and diplomat, felt that August, 1947 was too late, rather than too early. From the British point of view, a hasty retreat was perhaps the most suitable action.

Formation of Pakistan

The Punjab massacres that accompanied Partition were the final indictment of Mountbatten. His loyal aid, B. Ismay, wrote to his wife on *16 September, 1947*, 'our mission was so very nearly a success: it is sad that it has ended up such a grim and total failure'. The early date, *15th August 1947*, and the delay in announcing the Boundary Commission Award, both Mountbatten's decisions, compounded the tragedy that took place. A senior army official, Brigadier Bristow, posted in Punjab in 1947, was of the view that the Punjab tragedy would not have occurred had partition been deferred for a year or so. Lockhart, Commander-in-Chief of the Indian Army from *15 August* to *31 December 1947*, endorsed this view. Had officials in every grade in the civil services, and all the personnel of the armed services, been in position in their respective new countries before independence Day, it seems there would have been a better chance of preventing widespread disorder. The Boundary Commission Award was ready by *12th August, 1947* but Mountbatten decided to make it public after Independence Day in the Punjab and Bengal saw strange scenes. Flags of both Indian and Pakistan were flown in villages between Lahore and Amristar as people of both communities believed that they were on the right side of the border.

It is forgotten that Nehru, Patel and Gandhi in 1947 were only accepting what had become inevitable because of the long-term failure of the Congress to draw in the Muslim masses into the national movement and stem the surging waves of Muslim communalism, which, especially since 1937, had been beating with increasing fury. This failure was revealed with stark clarity by the 1946 elections in which the league won 90 cent Muslim seats. Though the war against Jinnah was lost by early 1946, defeat was conceded only after the final battle was mercilessly waged in the streets of Calcutta and Rawalpindi and the village lanes of Noakhali and Bihar. The Congress leaders felt by June 1947 that only an immediate of power could forestall the spread of Direct Action and communal disturbances. The virtual collapse of the Interim Government also made Pakistan appear to be an unavoidable reality. Patel argued in the AICC meeting on *14th June, 1947* that we have to face up to the fact that Pakistan was functioning in Punjab, Bengal and in the Interim Government.

15th August, dawned revealing the dual reality of Independence and Partition. As always, between the two of them, Gandhi and Nehru mirrored the feeling of the Indian people. Gandhi prayed in Calcutta for an end to the carnage taking place. His close follower, Mridula Sarabhai, sat consoling a homeless, abducted 15 year-old girl in a room somewhere in Bombay. Gandhi's prayers were reflected of the goings on in the partition of India. The partition of India in 1947 was the outcome of many forces although the main cause was the isolationist policy of the Muslim in India. Under the influence of Sir Syed Ahmed Khan, Muslims started feeling that their interests were different from those of the Hindus and they had nothing in common with them. They went to the extent of contending that their interests were opposed to those of the Hindus. If India was given a responsible government, the Hindu majority was bound to dominate the Muslim of India who was in a minority in the whole country. The Muslim also felt that they were educationally backward and consequently could not compete with the Hindus, with the passage of time; they drifted more and more away from the Hindus.

However, it cannot be denied that the Muslims were helped immensely by the British Government in India. After the Mutiny of 1857, the Government of India wanted allies in the country and they found the Indian princes, *Zamindars* and the Indian Muslims ready to cooperate with them. The Government of India followed a policy of "Divide and Rule" and kept partitioned to please the Muslims. The Muslims were given separate representation in 1909. They were given weightage in the legislatures. Seats were reserved for them on the Indian Council and the Governor-General Executive Council. Whatever the Congress offered to win over the Muslims, the Government of Indian and the British Government offered more. Under the circumstances, the Muslims of India began to look to the British Government for everything and were not in a mood to come to any compromise with the Congress or the Hindus. It was this attitude that was responsible for the partition of India at the time of her liberation from the foreign yoke. It is a well-known fact that the British bureaucracy in India helped the Muslim League agitation in 1946 and 1947. As a matter of fact, it was their encouragement that the Muslim Leagues had the guts to stage demonstrations without any interference or beating by the Government.

Critics point out that the Indian National Congress as also partly responsible for the Partition of India. Congress adopted an attitude of appeasement towards the Muslims and thus encouraged them, without wishing it, to go on adding to their unreasonable claims. In its passion to woo the Muslims, it frequently made sacrifices of principle. The communal malady was into proportioned height and ultimately led to the division of India. The Congress unfortunately never tried to understand the Muslim character of isolation and aggression and, to the end, continued to dally with the false hopes that, somehow or other, some turn of event would remove communal problem. The initial mistake was made by the India National Congress in 1916 when it entered into the Lucknow Pact. It ought not to have conceded separated electorates to the Muslims. It ought not to have agreed to give the Muslims a fixed percentage of representatives in the legislatures. That was the initial blunder. The Congress attitude towards the Communal Award of 1932 also helped the isolationist policy of the Muslims. Congressmen ought to have understood the Muslim character correctly and talked the problem with a firm hand from the very beginning.

The announcement of the British Government in *February 1947* that it was determined to put power into the hand of the Indians at a very early date worsened the communal situation in the country and helped the cause of Pakistan. While making the declaration, His Majesty Government had hoped that it would be possible for the major parties to co-operate in the working out of the Cabinet Mission's plan of May 1946, and evolve for India a Constitution acceptable to all concerned. However, that hope was not fulfilled as no pressure was put on the Muslim League to take part in the deliberation of the Constituent Assembly. The British Government also accepted the Muslim League's point of view that the grouping of the provinces under the Cabinet Mission scheme was a compulsory one.

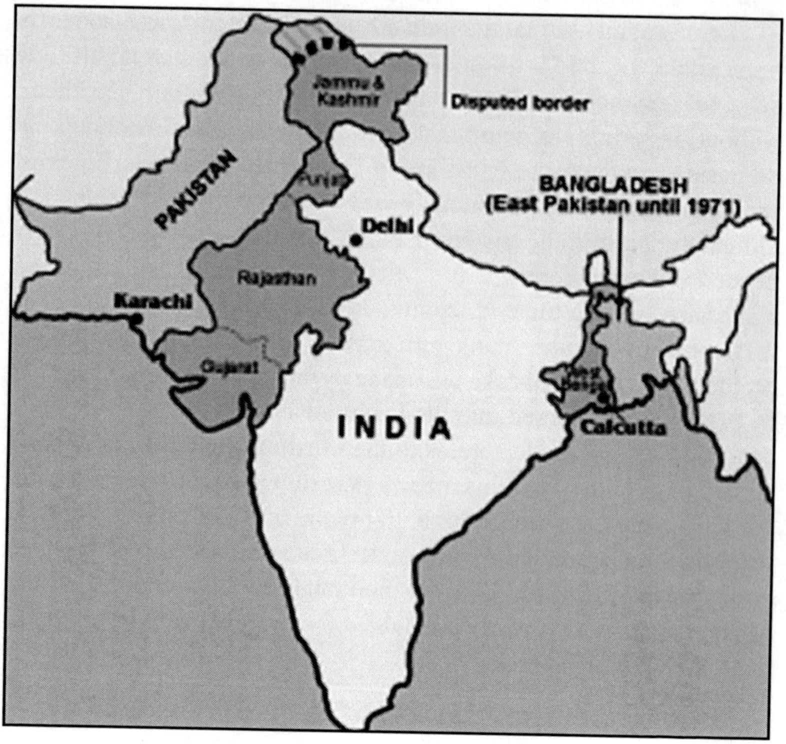

Map 3: Divided India 1947

9

Fate of Princely States and Consolidation of India as a Nation

Introduction

This chapter presents the methods that were used by the Indian government to absolve or merge the princely states with India. The Independence Act, 1947, terminated the Crown's sovereignty and Paramountncy over British India and Princely states; all treaties and agreements etc. Between the Crown and the Princely States lapsed with effect from *15th August, 1947*. Thus, the Princely States became legally independent. In fact they were given a choice, just before *August 1947*, to merge their states with Free India or Free Pakistan, depending on geographical proximity or remain independent. As many as 554 from approximately 562 states preferred to integrate with India but for the rest, Indian government persuaded to sign instrument of Accession and Standstill Agreement. In return, they were offered compensation in various ways.

The uncertain constitutional position of the princely states posed a grave problem. These states were constitutionally linked directly to England, a relationship embodied in the doctrine of paramount. In essence, the British government was responsible for their defense, foreign relations, and communication, while they remained autonomous in their internal relations.

Newly formed Indian Government through the instrument of accession and standstill agreement, as methods, used to merge the princely states of India that involved enormous task and various actions that were taken by Sardar V. Patel, the minister of states in integrating not only the numerous minute princely states but also large ones such as Junagadh, Hyderabad, Trivendrum and Jammu Kashmir. Sometimes it is a topic of debate and needs to be evaluated the necessity behind the use of force for this purpose.

Regional Cases

The uncertain constitutional position of the princely states posed a grave problem. These states, were constitutionally linked directly to England, a relationship embodied in the doctrine of paramountcy. In essence, the British government was responsible for their defense, foreign relations, and communications, while they remained autonomous in their internal relations. Lord Louis Mountbatten, the last viceroy of India, announced on June 3, 1947 that "paramountcy" would lapse on *August 15, 1947*, but the Indian Independence Act, passed in *July 1947*, had been silent about the status of the princes after the transfer of power. By default the Act appeared to grant them freedom of action to accede to India, to Pakistan, or to assert their independence.

Vallabhbhai Patel headed the Ministry of States from its creation on *July 5, 1947*. Accession, democratisation, and integration were the principles of the new policy. The Instrument of Accession was a device designed to fill the void left by the lapse of imperial paramountcy. Through it the rulers transferred to the Indian government control over the three subjects, which had formerly been in the care of the "paramount power", namely defense, foreign affair, and communications. In all other respects the princes retained control over their affairs. Thus, out of some 570 princes all but three acceded to the new India before the formal transfer of power on *August 15, 1947*. The three were Kashmir, Junagadh, and Hyderabad.

Sardar Vallabhbhai Patel: Tough Negotiator

Patel was Indian Barrister and statesman, one of the leaders of the Indian National Congress during the struggle for India's independence. He was even called ***Loh Purush*** (iron man) of India. He was born on *15 December 1875* in Nadiad, Gujarat. From 1917 to 1928 he served as the First Indian Municipal Commissioner of Ahmadabad. In 1928, Patel successfully led the landowners of Kheda *satyagraha* in 1919 when the British government agreed to suspend collection of revenue and rolled back the rates. In 1928, Bardoli Taluka in Gujarat suffered from flood and famine. In this hour of distress the British government raised the tax by thirty per cent. Patel instructed the farmer not to pay the tax and the government had to bow before him. It was during the struggle and after the victory in Bardoli that caused intense excitement across India, that Patel was increasingly addressed by his colleagues and followers as *Sardar* (leader). He was elected Congress President in 1931. He however, was a revolutionary. He supported Gandhi's Non-Cooperation Movement and as President of Gujarat Congress, helped in organising bonfires of British goods in Ahmadabad. He gave up his English cloths and started wearing *Khadi*. He emphasised the need to foster Indian self-reliance and self-confidence, but, unlike Gandhi, he did not regard Hindu-Muslim unity as a prerequisite for independence.

In August 1942, the Congress launched the Quit India movement. The government jailed all the important leaders of the congress, including Vallabhbhai Patel. No doubt, that the National Government of India and Home Minister Sardar Patel used various methods-persuasion, diplomatic pressure an even arm-twisting to get the Princely rulers' agreement to join the Indian Union by the end of 1947, though Junagarh and Hyderabad signed the Instrument of Accession in 1948. During the first three years of Indian independence after 1947, he served as Deputy Prime Minister, Minister of Home Affairs, Minister of Information, and Minister of States.

On 15th August, Lord Mountbatten paid the following tribute to Sardar Patel: "Thanks to that far-sighted statesman, Sardar Vallabhbhai Patel, Minister in charge of the States Department, a scheme was produced which appeared to me to be equally in the interests of the States as of the Dominion of India. It is a great triumph for the realism and sense of responsibility of the rulers and the

Plate 5

Sardar Vallabhbhai Patel

governments of the States as well as for the Government of India that it was possible to produce an Instrument of Accession, which was equally acceptable to both sides, and one moreover so simple and straightforward that within less than 3 weeks, practically all the States concerned had signed the Instrument of Accession."

Junagadh: Junagadh was an important State in the group of the Kathiawar-States. It was bounded by other Indian States except the South and South-west where the Arabian Sea lies. This State had no geographical continuity with Pakistan. The distance between Port Veraval of Junagadh and Karachi is about 300 miles. More than 80 per cent of the people were Hindus. There were many islands of the Junagadh State in the States of Gondal, Bhavnagar and Navanagar. Parts of the states which had acceded to India were interspersed with Junagadh territory and access to them was possible only through

Junagadh. The railways and posts and telegraphs of the state were an integral part of the Indian system. The railway police, telegraphs and telephones were administered by the Government of India. The *Nawab* of the State lived a life of luxury and his chief pre-occupation in life was dogs of which he had hundreds.

There was speculation that Junagadh was going to join Pakistan and the *Nawab* took pains to contradict it. Sir Shah Nawaz Bhutto, a Muslim League politician of Karachi, was appointed a member of the State Council of Ministers of Junagadh. In May 1947, he was appointed the *Dewan* (Prime Minister) of the state. The *Nawab* of Junagadh came under the influence of the Muslim League.The Government of India sent an Instrument of Accession to the *Nawab* of Junagadh for his signatures. On August 13, 1947, Sir Nawaz sent the reply that the matter was under consideration. In spite of it, the Government of Junagadh issued the following communiqué on *August 15, 1947*, announcing her accession to Pakistan.

The Government of Junagadh did not communicate to the Government of India that fact of its accession to Pakistan. There was a lot of correspondence between the Governments of India and Pakistan about Junagadh and ultimately on *September 13, 1947*, the Government of Pakistan informed the Government of India that she had accepted the accession of Junagadh to Pakistan and also signed a Standstill Agreement. There is no doubt about the fact that there were prolonged secret negotiations between the *Nawab* and the *Dewan* on the one hand and the Government of Pakistan and Mr M.A. Jinnah on the other.

The situation in Junagadh was deteriorating day by day. More than a lakh of Hindus ran away from the state of Junagadh. Law and order in the whole of Kathiawar practically collapsed. It was at this stage that the Congress leaders of Kathiawar announced in Bombay on *25 September, 1947*, the establishment of a provisional Government (*Arzi Hakumat*) of Junagadh. The provisional Government consisted of 6 members with Samaldas Gandhi as President "with all power, authority and jurisdiction heretofore vested in and exercised by the Nawab of Junagadh prior to *15th September, 1947.*" When Samaldas

Gandhi (an Indian Freedom Fighter who headed the *Aarzi Hukumat* or temporary Government of the eastwile princely state of Junagarh) and his colleagues journeyed from Bombay to Rajkot, they were greeted by large crowds at the wayside railway stations. They set up their headquarters at Rajkot and enrolled a large number of volunteers. Junagadh troops entered the State of Mangrol which had acceded to the Dominion of India. It was then decided to send Indian troops to occupy the State of Mangrol. It was found that the Khan of Manavadar was arresting local leaders and harassing the people. In order to prevent a flare up in the State, that State was also taken over on 22nd October, 1947.

When the *Nawab* of Junagadh found that help from Pakistan was not enough to keep him on the throne, he ran away from the state towards the end of October 1947. He took with him to Karachi not only the members of his family but also all his jewellery and all the available cash in the State treasury.

Finding his position precarious, Sir Shah Nawaz opened negotiations with Samaldas Gandhi on *7th November, 1947* through Captain Harvey Jones, Senior Member of the Junagadh State Council, requesting Samaldas Gandhi to take over the reins of Government and restore law and order in the State. However, the Muslims of Junagadh prevailed upon Shah Nawaz to handover the Government not to Samaldas Gandhi but to Mr Buch who at that time was the Regional Commissioner, Western India and Gujarat States. It was under these circumstances that Mr D. Buch (the Regional Commissioner of Saurashtra in the Government of India) took over the administration of Junagadh on *9th November, 1947*. Sir Shah Nawaz had already left for Karachi a day earlier.

As soon as normal conditions were restored, the Government of India arranged a referendum of the people of Junagadh with regard to the question of accession. C.B. Nagarkar, I.C.S., supervised the referendum which took place on *20th February, 1948*. Out of a total of 201,456 registered voters, 190,870 exercised their right of vote. Only 91 voters voted for accession to Pakistan. A referendum was also held in the States of Mangrol, Manavadar, Babariawad, Bantwa, and Sardargarh. Out of 31,434 votes cast for all these States, only 39 voted for accession to Pakistan. It was in this way that the problem of Junagadh was solved.

Hyderabad: Geographically, Hyderabad occupied a pivotal position in the heart of India. This State was surrounded by the Central Provinces in the North, Bombay in the West and Madras on the East and South. Its population was nearly 60 million and the annual revenue was Rs 26 crores. Its area was more than 82,000 square miles. It had its own coinage, paper currency and stamps. Although the Hindus formed more than 85 per cent of the total population of Hyderabad, their representation in the Civil Services and the army was practically nil and the Government machinery was a monopoly of the Muslims. Although it was a very important State, it was not given any privileged position by the British Government. The latter asserted its right to intervene in its affairs whenever it considered being necessary. After the announcement of *3rd June 1947* plan by the British Government, the *Nizam* (the Ruler) of Hyderabad issued a firmaan (notice) declaring his intention not to send his representatives to the Constituent Assembly of either India or Pakistan. He made it clear that after *15th August*, 1947, he would be a completely independent sovereign ruler. The intention of the *Nizam* was to make Hyderabad a Dominion of the Commonwealth of Nations.

On July 11, 1947, the *Nizam* sent a delegation to Delhi to meet Lord Mountbatten. One of the members of the delegation was Sir Walter Monckton. The discussions centred round three points: the retrocession of Berar to *Nizam*, the grant of Dominion Status to Hyderabad and the accession of the State of Hyderabad to the Indian Union. The delegation was told that it was not possible to hand over Berar to the *Nizam*. The delegation was also told that it was not possible to grant Dominion Status to Hyderabad. The members of the delegation went to the extent of saying that if the *Nizam* was pressed hard, he might join Pakistan. The delegation was told that the Government would not enter into a Stand-still Agreement without the State of Hyderabad acceding to India. The *Nizam* asked for two months to consider his position and that time was allowed to him.

Lord Mountbatten was hopeful that ultimately Hyderabad would accede to India.

In spite of the difficulties in the way, a Standstill Agreement was signed between the Government of India and the *Nizam* on November 29, 1947. It was provided that until new arrangements were made all the agreements and administrative arrangements on matters of common concern, including defense, external affairs and communications which had existed between the Crown Representative and the *Nizam* before the transfer of power, would be continued as between the Government of India and the Nizam. The Government of India and the *Nizam* also agreed to appoint their agents in Hyderabad and Delhi respectively and give them every facility for the discharge of their functions. The Government of India was not to exercise any paramountcy function in their relations with Hyderabad.

The Standstill Agreement was taken in different lights. Lord Mountbatten hoped that the Agreement would provide a basis for a satisfactory long-term solution. He hoped that before the Standstill Agreement expired, it would be possible for Hyderabad to accede to India. The view of Jawaharlal Nehru was that the Agreement would purchase communal peace in the south for a least one year. Sardar Patel was doubtful about the *bona fides* of the Government of Hyderabad. The Nizam and his advisers took the Agreement as something which gave them breathing space in which they were to secure the withdrawal of the Indian troops from Hyderabad and ultimately become independent.

K.M. Munshi was appointed as India's Agent-General in Hyderabad. Unfortunately, the attitude of the *Nizam* Government towards him was positively hostile from the very beginning. He was not given even a building for his residence or office. Ultimately, two of the buildings belonging to the Indian army were put at his disposal.

The *Nizam* began to press for the speedy withdrawal of the Indian troops and the supply of arms and ammunition for the Hyderabad army and police. The *Nizam* also issued two Ordinances by which he put restrictions on the export of all precious metals from Hyderabad to India and also made Indian currency as not legal tender in the Hyderabad State. The Government of Hyderabad also advanced a loan of Rs 20 crores to Pakistan in the form of Government of India's securities. The Government of India protested against these developments but nothing was done to remove the objection. At this time, the activities of the *Razakars* (private militia organised by Quasim Rizwi to support the rule of *Nizam*) increased tremendously. Kasim Rizvi and his followers made all passions inside and outside of Hyderabad. Rizvi declared that the *Razakars* were the liberators of the Muslims and of India. The *Razakars* began to attack the neighbouring provinces like Madras, Bombay and the Central Provinces. The situation became so serious that the common saying was that the *Razakars* ruled by day and the Communists ruled by night. The Government of Madras asked for military help to save its people from the raids of *Razakars*. This state of affairs continued for many months. Shri K.M. Munshi was practically a prisoner in his house in Hyderabad. El Edroos, the Commander-in-Chief for the Hyderabad forces, called upon the people in a radio talk to be ready for any emergency. In his speech delivered on *March 31, 1948*, on the occasion of the inauguration of the Hyderabad Weapons Week, Kasim Rizvi urged the Muslims of Hyderabad not to sheathe their sword until their objective for Islamic supremacy was achieved.

After the departure of Lord Mountbatten, the relations between India and Hyderabad began to worsen. Charges of border raids and breaches of the Standstill Agreement were made on both sides. Sidney Cotton, an Australian, was employed by the Hyderabad Government to smuggle arms and ammunition into Hyderabad. The Government of Pakistan began to cash a portion of the Rs 20 crores of the Government of India Securities which the Government of Hyderabad had offered to the Government of Pakistan as a loan. There was a reign of terror. People were being killed and their eyes were being taken out. Women were being raped and houses were being burnt down in large numbers. The situation was becoming intolerable. Both the press and the public opinion in India caused the Government of India of inaction in the face of repeated violations of Indian territory. The stories brought by the evacuees from Hyderabad madc the people indignant. Attacks on the trains created panic. It was under these circumstances that the Government of India decided to take action.

In the early hours of *13th September, 1948*, Indian forces commanded by Major-General J.N. Chaudhuri under the direction of Lieut. General Maharaj Shri Rajendrasinhj who was then the General Officer Commanding-in-Chief, Southern Command, entered the Hyderabad State. There was still some resistance on the first and second day and after that the same collapsed. On the evening of *17th September, 1948* the Hyderabad Army surrendered. On *18th September, 1948*, the Indian troops entered Hyderabad city. The police action lasted for 108 hours. It was learnt that if action had not been taken on *13th September, 1948*, Lt. T.T. More who was captured with his jeep full of explosives, would have destroyed all the important bridges in the State and it would have been very difficult for the Indian army to move forward.

On *18th September, 1948*, Major-General Chaudhuri took charge as Military Governor. On 19th September, Kasim Rizvi was arrested. The *Razakars* were disbanded and many of them were detained under the Public Safety Regulations. Strong action was taken against the Communists and their resistance was crushed.

The administration under Major-General Chaudhuri lasted up to December 1949 when Shri M.K. Vellodi, I.C.S., took over as Chief Minister. In 1950, four representatives of the Hyderabad State Congress were appointed as Ministers. In March 1952, general elections were held and a Congress Ministry was installed with the *Nizam* as a constitutional head. In 1956 was passed the States Reorganisation Act by which the State of Hyderabad was split up and it ceased to exist. Most of its territories went to the State of Andhra Pradesh.

Jammu and Kashmir: The State of Jammu and Kashmir had strategic importance on account of its international boundaries. To the East was Tibet, to the North-East was the Sinkiang province of China and to the North-West was Afghanistan. The majority of the population of the State of Jammu and Kashmir consisted of Muslims although the Buddhists were in majority in Ladakh. At the beginning of 1947, Maharaja Hari Singh was the ruler of the State and Pt. Ram Chandra Kak was its Prime Minister.

After the announcement of June 3 Plan, Lord Mountbatten visited Kashmir and for four days discussed the question of accession of the State of Jammu and Kashmir with Maharaja Hari Singh. He told him that independence was not practicable and the State would not be recognised as a Dominion by the British Government. He gave an assurance to the Maharaja that up to *15th August, 1947*, he could join any Dominion and there would be no difficulty. Even if he accepted to Pakistan, India would not raise any objection. However, it was desirable to ascertain the wishes of the people before acceding to any Dominion as the majority of its people were Muslims. Lord Mountbatten failed in his mission as the Maharaja refused to commit himself. After *15 August, 1947*, Lord Ismay went to Srinagar and tried to persuade the Maharaja to join one Dominion or the other but his mission also failed.

It cannot be denied that it was easy for the Maharaja to make a decision. He was himself a Hindu and he would not like to join Pakistan at once. Moreover, he was not sure of the fate of his Hindu subjects in the event of his joining Pakistan. There was also the possibility of the opposition from the National Conference which was the most powerful and vocal organisation in the State. If he acceded to India, there was also the possibility of adverse reactions in Gilgit and certain other areas which were contiguous to Pakistan. Moreover, the road communications were with Pakistan. Till the declaration of the Radcliffe Award there was no land communication between India and the State of Jammu and Kashmir. Moreover, Maharaja Hari Singh was thinking in terms of becoming an independent ruler.

Shortly before *15th August, 1947*, Pt. Ram Chandra Kak was replaced by Major-General Janak Singh as Prime Minister. The Government of Jammu and Kashmir announced its intention of entering into Standstill Agreements both with India and Pakistan. India was not enthusiastic about it even after the announcement of the Radcliffe Award which connected India with the State by Road. Pakistan signed a Standstill Agreement but with an ulterior motive. In spite of the Agreement, the Pakistan authorities cut off the supply of food, petrol and other essential commodities. Restrictions were put on the transit of travel between Kashmir and Pakistan. Goods belonging to the State lying in the towns of Pakistan were not allowed to be transported to the State of Jammu and Kashmir. The State had practically no petrol for its transport organisation. Military pressure was put on Jammu and Kashmir to accede to Pakistan. Mr M.A. Jinnah sent his British Military Secretary three times, to Srinagar to bring about Kashmir's accession to Pakistan. Mr Jinnah also wrote to Maharaja to allow him to spend the summer in Kashmir on account of his bad health and offered to make his own arrangements. Major Shah was sent to Kashmir to arouse the people in favour of Pakistan and also to intimidate the Maharaja to accede to Pakistan. There were hit and run border raids on the State. It was under these circumstances that Mr Justice Mehr Chand Mahajan took over as the Prime Minister of the State.

On *15th October, 1947*, the new Prime Minister complained to the British Prime Minister that the Government of Pakistan had broken the Standstill Agreement by discounting the supply of essential articles and by stopping, without any reason, the railway service from Sialkot to Jammu. He also pointed out that the whole of the State border from Gurdaspur to Gilgit was threatened with invasion and the same had already started in Poonch. He requested the British Prime Minister to advise the Government of Pakistan to deal fairly with the State of Jammu and Kashmir. However, he got no reply. On 18th October, 1947, a protest was sent to the Governor-General and the Prime Minister of Pakistan against the breaches of the Standstill Agreement and the raids on the State. Mr M.A. Jinnah, Governor-General of Pakistan, sent a reply on 20th October, 1947 in which he protested against the tone and language of the communication.

The all-out invasion of Kashmir started on 22nd October, 1947. The raiders included Afridis, Wazirs, Mahsuds, Swathis and the soldiers of the Pakistan Army on leave. They were led by regular officers who knew Kashmir well. They advanced from Abbottabad in North-Western Frontier Province along the Jhelum Valley Road. They captured Garhi and Domel and arrived at the gates of Muzaffarabad. All the Muslims in the State Battalion at Muzaffarabad deserted and acted as advance guard to the raiders' column. They marched towards Baramula, along the road leading to Srinagar. All the Muslims in the State Forces deserted and joined the raiders. Brigadier Rajinder Singh, Chief of Staff of the State Forces, gathered together about 150 men and proceeded towards Uri. He engaged the raiders for two days and in the rearguard action destroyed the Uri Bridge. Not only the Brigadier himself but all his men were cut to pieces in the battle. On *24th October, 1947*, the raiders captured the Mahura Power House which supplied electricity to Srinagar, and that plunged Srinagar in darkness. The raiders declared that they would reach Srinagar on *26th October, 1947* and celebrate the *Id* celebrations in the Srinagar mosque.

Such was the critical situation when the Government of India received an appeal for help from the Maharaja of Jammu and Kashmir on *24th October, 1947*. Even earlier than that, Field-Marshal Auchinleck, the Supreme Commander, had received a message from Pakistan Army Headquarters giving information about the advance of the raiders and their probable destination. Although the information was passed on to the Government of India, no action was taken on it. Even when the appeal came from the Maharaja on *24th October*, no immediate action was taken. On the morning of *25th October, 1947*, a meeting of the Defence Committee was held under the presidentship of Lord Mountbatten. It was decided that no immediate action be taken by the Government of India and Shri V.P. Menon be sent to Srinagar immediately to study the situation on the spot and report to the Government of India. Shri V.P. Menon immediately left by plane and reached Srinagar. The result of the negotiations on the morning of 26th October, 1947 was that at the persistent request of Prime Minister Mahajan, the Indian Cabinet agreed to accept the accession of the State and send its army to Srinagar on the morning of *27th October, 1947* to defend the State. Shri V.P. Menon again went to Jammu accompanied by the Prime Minister Mahajan and after getting the Instrument of Accession from the Maharaja, he flew back to Delhi. Sardar Patel was waiting at the aerodrome and both of them went straight to a meeting of the Defence Committee which was arranged for that evening. There was a long discussion and ultimately it was decided that the Accession of Jammu and Kashmir should be accepted subject to the provison that a plebiscite would be held in the State when the law and order situation allowed. It was also decided that an infantry battalion should be flown to Srinagar the next day. This decision had the fullest support of Sheikh Abdullah. It must be pointed out that Lord Mountbatten and the 3 British Chiefs of Staff of the Indian Army, Navy and Air Force pointed out the risks involved in the operation for which there was hardly any preparation.

In the early hours of the morning of *27th October, 1947,* more than 100 civilian aircraft and Royal Indian Air Force planes were mobilised to fly troops, equipment and supplies to Srinagar. It must be admitted that it was the heroism and enthusiasm shown by the civilian and Royal Indian Air Force pilots and the ground crews that made the air-lift a success. Some of the pilots did several sorties in the course of the day. It was in this way that the timely arrival of the Indian forces in the morning of *27th October, 1947* saved Srinagar.

Mr M.A. Jinnah was impatient with what was happening in Kashmir. His Private Secretary, Khurshid Ahmed, was already in Srinagar but after the arrival of the Indian troops, he was arrested and sent back to Pakistan. When M.A. Jinnah heard about the acceptance of the accession of Jammu and Kashmir by India and the arrival of the Indian troops in Srinagar, he gave orders to General Gracey, the Acting Commanding-in-Chief of the Pakistan Army, to send Pak troops to Kashmir but the General refused to do so without the approval of Field Marshal Auchinleck. The Field Marshal also flew to Lahore on the morning of *28th October, 1947* and explained to Mr Jinnah that the State of Jammu and Kashmir had acceded to India and if Pak troops entered Kashmir, there was every likelihood of a war between the two countries and if that happened, all British Officers serving in the Pakistan Army would be automatically and immediately withdrawn. It was under these circumstances that Mr Jinnah cancelled his previous orders for Pakistan troops to march into Kashmir.

On *30th October, 1947*, a statement was issued by the Government of Pakistan in which it was stated that accession of Kashmir to India was "based on fraud and violence and as such cannot be recognized." It was also stated therein that the State troops were the first to attack the Muslims in the State and the Muslim villages on the Pakistan border and that provoked the raiders to attack the State. It was also at this time that Pakistan established her control over Gilgit which was a part of the State of Jammu and Kashmir.

On *1st November, 1947*, Lord Mountbatten and Lord Ismay flew to Lahore and had a long conference with Mr M.A. Jinnah. The latter contended that the accession of Kashmir to India was brought about by violence and the reply of Lord Mountbatten was that the violence had come from the tribal raiders. Lord Mountbatten suggested a plebiscite under the auspices of the United Nations but Mr Jinnah pressed for a plebiscite under the joint control and supervision of the Governors-General of India and Pakistan. Many other things were discussed at the meeting but nothing came out of it and Lord Mountbatten came back to Delhi. On 4th November, 1947, Prime Minister Liaquat Ali Khan broadcast from Lahore in which he said that the accession of Kashmir to India was a fraud perpetrated on its people by its cowardly ruler with the aggressive help of the Government of India.

It was on the persuasion of Lord Mountbatten that the Government of India took their complaint to the United Nations against the Pak invasion of Jammu and Kashmir. A cease-fire was ordered with effect from *1st January 1949*. Many efforts were made by the United Nations to resolve the dispute between India and Pakistan but they did not succeed.

In 1965, Pakistan sent her infiltrators into the Kashmir Valley and then attacked the Chhamb area. That resulted in a war between India and Pakistan not only in the State of Jammu and Kashmir but also in East Punjab. As a result of the good offices of the Soviet Union, the war was brought to an end and the famous Tashkent Declaration was issued in January 1966, but in spite of this the relations between the two countries remained bitter on account of the question of Kashmir.

The accession of the State of Jammu and Kashmir has been criticised by Pakistan on many grounds. It is pointed out that the State of Jammu and Kashmir had an overwhelming population of Muslims and hence the State ought to have acceded to Pakistan. However, the fact must not be ignored that the partition of the country had not taken place on the two-nation theory. If that had been so, there was no necessity of holding a plebiscite in the North-West Frontier Province with its 90 per cent Muslim areas from the rest of India was in the nature of a political division. Moreover, it must not be forgotten that Muslims are even today the citizens of India and occupy the highest positions in the country and that also proves that the partition of the country did not take place on the basis of the two-nation theory.

It is well known that Mr M.A. Jinnah did his level best to secure the accession of the predominantly Hindu State of Jodhpur and Jaisalmer to Pakistan and offered tempting terms for that purpose. It is a different matter that he failed but it could not be denied that Mr Jinnah did his best to secure their accession to Pakistan. Moreover, the Muslim ruler of the State of Junagadh actually acceded to Pakistan and the Government of Pakistan accepted it. That also contradicts the two-nation theory as the population of Junagadh was over 85 per cent Hindu.

It must be observed that the Government of India was not enthusiastic about the accession of the State of Jammu and Kashmir to India. Nothing was done by the Government of India to force the hands of the Maharaja. As a matter of fact her attitude was one of indifference. It is possible that if the raiders had not attacked the State of Jammu and Kashmir, the Government of India which had her hands otherwise full would not have bothered about the State of Jammu and Kashmir. It was only when the raiders attacked the State of Jammu and Kashmir and there was the immediate danger of the fall of Srinagar into their hands that the Maharaja of Jammu and Kashmir had requested the Government of India to come to his help and as that help could be given only if that State acceded to India, the Government of India was forced to send her troops into the State of

Jammu and Kashmir. If the attitude of India was one of indifference, it is well known that Pakistan adopted all kinds of tactics to put pressure on the Maharaja to accede to Pakistan. It is also known that the leader of the raiders was one General Tariq who was later on identified as Major-General Akbar Khan of the Pakistan Army. It is this Akbar Khan who later on became the Commander-in-Chief of Pakistan.

Compensation to the Princely States

In return, the Government of India guaranteed through the Constitution, payment of Privy Purse (Private Purse) totaling around 3.2 million Pounds to the rulers. Their compensation differed from one region to another depending upon their wealth and size of the states. This had been reduced to half (1.6 million pounds) by September 1970 because with the death of an ex-ruler, his successor would get only half of it. Even to the ex-ruler other privileges were maintained, for example; immunity from prosecution, exemption from income tax, wealth tax, estate duty, local taxes and requisition of property refund of excise duty, public holidays on birthdays, recognition of titles and their private wealth, military hounors, free driving licenses and personal number plates, free medical attention, own flags, gun salutes, armed guards and escorts and postal and telegraph concessions. They were given privilege to contest for MP (Member of Parliament) and MLA (Member of Legislative Assembly) from the area they belonged.

Even in those days, some political parties criticised the generous terms given to the ex-rulers and as time passed, they were increasingly attacked. During the China war (1962) Nehru appealed to 100 ex-rulers to volunteer a 10 per cent cut in their purses but none of them agreed. Some rulers donated 10 per cent in total. Therefore, they evoked very little sympathy in the average man's heart. By *September 1970,* the Privy Purse system was terminated totally.

Consolidation of the Nation

A major problem, perhaps the most serious one that India has faced since 1947 has been of national unity or consolidation of the nation. The problem is also sometimes referred to as national integration or the integration of Indian people as a political community. The chapter discusses the ways in which India was consolidated as a nation. This was a difficult task for the government as it consists of a large number of linguistic, culture and geographic economic zones. India's diversity was a weakness and needed to be handled carefully without hurting any group's sentiment? People from deprived society needed to be uplifted and no doubt Government did frame policies accordingly. Indian Constitution, under democratic policy, gave right to all citizen of eligible age the right to vote, for education, religion etc.

There were already conflicts between religious groups at the time of independence and each group of people was to be given equal status to maintain India's unity. Along with above challenges government also looked into the development of science and modernisation of Indian to match with other countries. Newly formed Government was able to identify the challenges that the independent India faced which threatened her unity but could achieve their goal for consolidation of India as a nation by taking special measures. The Indian Government were convinced different group of people for better life and better education for all.

Unity in Diversity

The Indian nation is the product of a historical process and has been therefore in the making for very long, at least some five centuries. The roots of India's nationhood lie deep in its history and also in its experience of the struggle for independence. Pre-colonial India had already acquired some elements of common existence and common consciousness. Despite its immense cultural diversity, certain strands of a common cultural heritage had developed over the centuries, knitting its people together and giving them a sense of oneness, even while inculcating tolerance of diversity and dissent. As the poet Rabindranath Tagore put it, the unity of India is the 'unity of spirit'. Elements of political, administrative and economic unity had developed especially under the Mughals. The politics of the rulers and their territorial ambitions often cut across regions and were, at their most ambitious, sub-continental in their reach. Also, despite backward means of transport and communication, a great deal of Indiawide trade, specialisation of production and credit networks developed, especially during the late medieval period. A feeling of Indianness, however vague, had come into being, as testified by the currency of the concepts of *Bharat Varsha* and Hindustan.

The leaders of the national movement realised that the making of the nation was a prolonged and continuous process, and which was open to such disruption had already occurred in 1947. As founders of the Republic, these leaders were therefore fully aware that after independence too the process of unifying India and national integration was to be carefully sustained, promoted and nurtured through ideological and political endeavours. In fact, the leaders of India after 1947 saw the preservation and consolidation of India's unity as their biggest challenge.

India's complex diversity is legendry. It consists of a large number of linguistic, cultural and geographic-economic zones. It has followers of different religions, Hindus, Muslims, Christians, Sikhs, Parsis, Buddhists and Jews, apart from the tribals with a myriad belief systems. In 1950, the Indian Constitution recognised fourteen major languages, besides hundreds others, many of which were spoken by just a million persons.

Given this diversity, the leaders of the national movement realised that the Indian nation had to be built on a very broad foundation. India could be unified and its segmentation overcome only by accepting this immense diversity and not counter posing it to the process of nation-in-the-making. The emergence of a strong national identity and the preservation of India's rich diversity were seen as simultaneous processes. Regional cultural identities would develop not in conflict with but as part of the all-India identity.

It was, however, recognised that the diversity of India could also be a source of weakness. Diversity could be used for divisive purposes and transformed into disruptive tendencies, such as communalism, casteism, linguist, and regional exclusiveness. The problem of integrating diverse loyalties was therefore quite real, especially as rapid social changes led to increase in the scale and number of social conflicts. The issues of jobs, educational opportunities, access to political power and share in the larger economic cake could and did fuel rivalries and conflicts based on religion, region, caste, and language. Special efforts were necessary, different from those in other parts of the world, to carefully promote national unity. The broad strategy for national consolidation after 1947 involved territorial integration, mobilisation of political and institutional resources, economic development, adoption of policies which would promote social justice, remove glaring inequalities and provide equal opportunities.

The constitutional structure established in 1950 encompassed the demands of diversity as well as the requirements of unity. It provided for a federal structure with a strong Centre but also a great deal of autonomy for the states. The makers of the Constitution kept in view the difference between decentralisation and disintegration and between unity and integration and centralisation. The constitutional structure was not only conducive to national integration but provided the basic framework within which the struggle against divisive forces could be carried on. The political leadership was to use elections both to promote national consolidation and to legitimise its policies of integration. The parliament was the institution where basic and ultimate power resided and which acted as the open arena where different political trends could express themselves as also contend for power.

Also, political parties acted as a great integrating force. All the major post 1947 political parties – Socialist party, Communist Party of India, the *Jan Sangh* and later the *Swatantra* party – were all-India in character and in their organisation and ideology; they stood for the unity of the country. They strove for national goals and mobilised people on an all-India basis and on all-India issues even when their capacity to do so was limited to particular regions. All this was perhaps even more true of Congress in the post-independence years. It had a strong and large organisation covering almost all parts of the country.

The Indian army and administrative services were also a force for forging national unity. India developed after 1947 a national administrative service with recruitment to its top echelons, the IAS, the IPS, and other central services, taking place on the basis of individual merit, irrespective of caste or religion, from all regions and linguistic areas. These services were all-India in character and sentiment and all officers selected were given common training and owed allegiance to the central government, which also had the ultimate power to promote or discipline them. The central services, as also the state services, were basically non-political and accepted the authority of the party which was voted to power by the people. Likewise, the army was a national force whose officers and ranks were recruited from all parts of the country.

The Indian economy, national market, and transport and communication networks were further unified after 1947. Industrial development was promoted on a national scale and dams, steel mills, fertilizer plants, cement factories, and heavy machinery and electric plants soon became symbols of national endeavour as well as national unity.

Jawaharlal Nehru and other leaders saw economic development as essential for national consolidation. Soon after independence, the government set up a Planning Commission and took active measures for planned economic development.

National integration also required policies which would promote social justice and greater social and economic equality. The national movement had also linked the process of nation-in-the-making with socio-economic changes in the interests of the oppressed and the deprived. Consolidation of the nation after independence had to be judged in terms of how it affected their lives. The entire Indian people and not merely the middle and upper classes had to benefit from the coming of independence and processes of economic development and political democracy.

The Constitution laid the basis for reduction of social disparity by putting an end to any discrimination on grounds of religion, caste or sex. Redeeming the national movement's major pledge to the depressed sections of society, it provided reservations for Scheduled Castes and Scheduled Tribes in educational institutions, employment and in the legislatures. Soon after 1947, a number of social reforms and welfare laws were passed. Landlordism was abolished and there was some redistribution of land. A law was passed making untouchability an offence.

Independent India's foreign policy served as another unifying force. The policy of non-alignment and anti-colonialism and Nehru's growing stature as a world figure contributed to a sense of national pride in India among all sections of people all over the country and irrespective of their political alignment.

At the moment of freedom, the need for unity was urgent but also present was the problem of integrating diverse loyalties. The strategies and approached promoting integration required time but the people were in a hurry and there was plenty of scope for conflicts. Many observers, infact, predicted growing disunity and even break-up of the country.

The Language Problem

The language problem was the most divisive issue in the first twenty years of independent India, and it created the apprehension among many that the political and cultural unity of the country was in danger. People love their language; it is an integral part of culture.

The Indian Constitution recognises sixteen major languages, including English and Sanskrit. In addition, there are a myriad language spoken by the tribals and others, with or without their own scripts. The model that independent India has adopted is not that of assimilation into, or suppression of the many languages by one of them. This is in any case impossible in a democratic polity. The feasible option is to accept and live with this 'multiplicity' in a manner that conflict situations do not emerge or persist for long.

Economic Imbalances and Regionalism

Economic inequality among different states and regions could be a potential source of trouble. However, despite breeding discontent and putting pressure on the political system, this problem has not so far given rise to regionalism or feeling of a region being discriminated against.

At independence, the leadership recognised that some regions were more backward than others. Only a few enclaves or areas around Calcutta, Bombay and Madras had undergone modern industrial development. For example, in 1948, Bombay and West Bengal accounted for more than 59 per cent of the total industrial capital of the country and more than 64 per cent of the national industrial output. Under colonialism, agriculture had also stagnated, but more in eastern India than in northern or southern India. Regional economic disparity was also reflected in per capita income. In 1949, while West Bengal, Punjab and Bombay had per capita incomes of Rs 353, 331 and 272 respectively, the per capita incomes of Bihar, Orissa and Rajasthan were Rs 200, 188 and 173 respectively.

From the beginning, the central government adopted a whole range of policies to influence the rates of growth in poorer states and regions so as to reduce their economic distance from the richer states and regions. A major government instrument in bringing this about was the transfer of financial resources to the poorer states. Important in this respect was the role of the Finance Commission, provided for in the Constitution and appointed periodically by the President. The Commission decides the principles on which disbursement of central taxes and other financial resources from the central government to the states occurs. Various Financial Commissions have tried not only to do justice among the states but also to reduce inter-state disparity by giving preferential treatment to the poorer states, by allocating larger grants to them than their population would warrant and by transferring resources from the better-off states to them.

The Rooting of the Electoral Process

First of all came the entrenchment of democracy – an achievement which has endured so that it is now taken for granted. The process had begun with the framing of the Constitution after 1947 and its promulgation on 26th January 1950. Democracy took a giant step forward with the first general election held in 1951-52 over a four month period. These elections were the biggest experiment in democracy anywhere in the world. The elections were held on the basis of universal adult franchise, with all those twenty-one years of age or older having the right to vote. There were over 173 million voters, most of them poor, illiterate, and rural, and having had no experience of elections. The big question at the time was how the people would respond to this opportunity.

Many were skeptical about such an electorate being able to exercise its right to vote in a politically mature and responsible manner. Some said that democratic elections were not suited to a caste-ridden, multi-religious, illiterate and backward society like India's and that only a benevolent dictatorship could be effective politically in such a society. The coming elections were described by some as 'a leap in the dark' and by others as 'fantastic' and as 'an act of faith'.

India's electoral system was developed according to the directives of the Constitution. The Constitution created an Election Commission, headed by a Chief Election Commissioner, to conduct elections. It was to be independent of the executive or the parliament or the party in power.

After 1952, during the Nehru years, two other general elections were held for the Lok Sabha and state assemblies in 1957 and 1962. In both, the voter turnout improved – while in 1951-52 it was 46 per cent, in 1957 it was 47 per cent and in 1962 nearly 54 per cent. In both elections, the Congress again gained an overwhelming majority of seats in the Lok Sabha with a minority of votes; and neither the right nor the left could pose a serious challenge to it. Both, however, made inroads into the Congress hegemony in a few states. In 1957, the Communists were able to form a government in Kerala, which was the first democratically elected Communist government anywhere in the world.

Establishment of Democratic Institutions

Building on the traditions of the national movement, the Indian leaders, and above all Nehru, further strengthened the foundations of democracy in the country by the manner of their political functioning.

They gave due importance to the institutional aspects of the democratic system so that gradually attachment of people to parliamentary institutions grew. They adhered not only to the spirit but also to the forms of democratic institutions and procedures. Nehru, in particular, despite holding complete sway saw to it that political power was widely dispersed and diffused.

Civil liberties were put on a firm footing with the Press having a free play, even when it criticised the government severely. The independence of the courts was carefully nurtured, even when they turned down an important piece of popular legislation, namely agrarian reform.

Nehru treated the parliament with respect and made every effort to sustain its dignity, prestige and power, even though his party enjoyed an overwhelming majority in it. He tried to make it a major forum for expression of public opinion, and made it a point to sit through the Question Hour and to attend parliamentary debates. The Opposition too played its part by respecting the parliament and its procedures, functioning without fear in its portals, and keeping the standard of parliamentary debates at a high level. Moreover, parliamentary committees such as the Estimates Committee began to play an important role as critics of, and watchdogs over, the government administration.

Despite the dominance of the Congress party the role of the Opposition was strengthened during the period. Nehru gave full play and respect to the opposition parties and was quite responsive to their criticism.

Federalism, provided for in the Constitution, also was established as a firm feature of Indian polity during the Nehru years, with a genuine devolution of power to the states. Respecting the states' autonomy, Nehru would not impose decisions on the state governments or interfere with their policies, though he took care to inform them of his own thinking and occasionally advise or even insist on their acceptance of a particular policy. He also permitted the state Congress parties to choose their party. The Nehru years occurred when the Communist government in Kerala was dismissed in 1959 and President's Rule was imposed in the state.

The Administrative Structure

Immediately after independence, it was to be decided whether the government of independent India should carry on with the administrative structure and machinery inherited from the colonial regime and 'designed to serve the relatively simple interests of an occupying power'.

The kingpin of this structure was the Indian Civil Service (ICS). If the structure was to be replaced or overhauled, the beginning had to be made with the ICS. Initially, there were differences in approach to the question between Nehru and Patel, who, as Home Minister, dealt directly with the administrative services. Nehru was a staunch critic of the ICS and bureaucracy as a whole not only because of their colonial ancestry but also because of their basic conservatism.

Nehru accepted Patel's position, though grudgingly, for he too realised that there was no alternative to reliance on the existing all-India services if a breakdown of administration was to be avoided. Over time he too began to rely heavily on these services, admiring their administrative efficiency, especially as he realised that the other available human resources were rather poor.

Development of Science and Technology

A major achievement of the Nehru era was in the fields of scientific research and technological education. Nehru was convinced that science and technology were crucial to the solution of India's problems. As early as January 1938, he had said in a message to the Indian Science Congress: 'It was science alone that could solve these problems of hunger and poverty, of insanitation and illiteracy, of superstition and deadening custom and tradition, of vast resources running to waste, of a rich country inhabited by starving people.' This view was reiterated in the Scientific Policy Resolution passed by the Lok Sabha in March 1958 acknowledging the role of science and technology in the economic, social and cultural advancement of the country. After 1947, Nehru also became aware of the critical role that scientific research and technology would play in India's defence.

As part of the effort to promote self-sustaining scientific and technological growth, the foundation stone of India's first national laboratory, the National Physical Laboratory, was laid on *4th January 1947*. This was followed by the setting up during the Nehru years of a network of seventeen national laboratories, specialising in different areas of research.

Urgent steps were also taken to recognise the training of technical personnel sorely needed by the country. In 1952, the first of the five institutes of technology, patterned after the Massachusettes Indian Institute of Technology (IIT), was set up at Kharagpur – the other four being set up subsequently at Madras, Bombay, Kanpur and Delhi. The extent of the effort put in developing science and its success is revealed by the expenditure on scientific research and science-based activities which increased from Rs 1.10 crores in 1948-49 to Rs 85.06 crores crores in 1965-66, and the number of scientific and technical personnel which rose from 188,000 in 1950 to 731,500 in 1965.

India was one of the first nations to recognise the importance of nuclear energy. Nehru was convinced that nuclear energy would bring about a global revolution in the social, economic and political spheres, besides affecting nations' defense capabilities.

In August 1948, the Government of India set up the Atomic Energy Commission with Homi Bhabha, India's leading nuclear scientist, as chairman, in the Department of Scientific Research, which was under Nehru's direct charge, to develop nuclear energy for peaceful purposes. In 1954, the government created a separate Department of Atomic Energy under the prime minister with Homi Bhabha as Secretary. India's first nuclear reactor in Trombay, Bombay, also the first in Asia, became critical in August 1956. Though India was committed to the peaceful uses of nuclear power, its nuclear capacity could easily have been used to produce the atomic bomb and other atomic weapons.

India also took up space research. It set up the Indian National Committee for Space Research (INCOSPAR) in 1962 and established a Rocket Launching Facility at Thumba (TERLS). Krishna Menon, as Defence Minister, took steps to initiate defence research and development. Steps were also taken to increase India's capacity in production of defence equipment so that India gradually became self-sufficient in its defence needs.

Social Change

The vision of the founding fathers of the Republic went beyond national integration and political stability. Indian society had to move towards social change. Article 36 of the Constitution in the section on the Directive Principles of State Policy stated: 'The state shall strive to promote the welfare of the people by securing and protecting as effectively as may be a social order in which justice, economic and political, shall inform all institutions of the national life.' This conception of the new social order was encompassed in 1955 by the phrase 'socialistic pattern of society officially accepted by the Congress at its Avadi Session and later incorporated as its objective in the Second and Third Five Year Plans. Consequently, several important measures of social reforms, which some described as the beginning of a welfare state, were taken during the Nehru years. Very important measures in this respect were those of land reforms, the initiation of planned economic development and rapid expansion of the public sector which shall examine in separate chapters of this volume. In addition far-reaching labour legislation was undertaken, including recognition of collective bargaining, the right to form trade unions and to go on strike, security of employment and provision of health and accident insurance. There were also moves towards a more equitable distribution of wealth through progressive and steep income-tax and excise tax policies. Expansion of education and health and other social services, was also sought.

The Constitution had already incorporated a provision abolishing untouchability. The government supplemented this proviso by passing the Anti-Untouchability Law in 1955 making the practice of untouchability punishable and a cognisable offence. The government also tried to implement the clauses of the Constitution regarding reservations in educational institutions and government employment in favour of Scheduled Castes (SCs) and Scheduled Tribes (STs) and other weaker sections of society. Other necessary measures were taken to raise their social status, such as the provision of special facilities in the form of scholarships, hostels accommodation, grants, loans, housing, health care and legal-aid services.

Participating actively in the national movement for years, women's groups and organisations were demanding revision of laws regarding women's rights in the family and in Nehru they had a firm supporter. Already, before independence, Nehru had made his position on this issue clear and quoted Charles Fourier, the French philosopher, "One could judge the degree of civilisation of a country by the social and political position of its women."

A major step forward in this direction was taken when the Hindu Code Bill was moved in the parliament in 1951. The bill faced sharp opposition from conservative sectors of society, especially from *Jan Sangh* and other Hindu communal organisations. Even though actively supported by the vocal members of Congress party and women MPs and other women activists, Nehru decided to postpone enactment of the bill in order to mobilise greater support for it. He was, however, firm in his determination to pass the bill and made it an issue in the elections of 1951-52.

After coming back to power, the government passed the bill in the form of four separate acts which introduced monogamy and the right of divorce to both men and women, raised the age of consent and marriage, and gave women the right to maintenance and to inherit family property.

Education

The founding fathers were fully aware of the need for better and wider education as an instrument of social and economic progress, equalisation of opportunity and the building up of a democratic society. This was all the more urgent because in 1951 only 16.6 per cent of the total population was literate and the percentage was much lower, being only 6 per cent, in the case of rural families. To remedy this situation, the Constitution directed that by 1961 the state should provide free and compulsory education to every child up to the age of fourteen. Later, this target was shifted to 1966.

The government provided large sums for developing primary, secondary, higher and technical education. While the expenditure on education was Rs 198 million in 1952-53, by 1964-65 it had increased to Rs 1462.7 million i.e. by more than seven times. Since education was primarily a state subject, Nehru urged the state governments not to reduce expenditure on primary education, whatever the nature of financial stringency. If necessary, he suggested, even expenditure on industrial development could be reduced. He told the National Development Council in May 1961. "I have come to feel that it (education) is the bases of all and, on no account unless actually our heads are cut off and we cannot function, must we allow education to suffer."

The Nehru years witnessed rapid expansion of education, especially in the case of girls. Between 1951 and 1961 school enrolment doubled for boys and tripled for girls. From 1950-51 to 1965-66 the number of boys enrolled in classes I to V increased from 13.77 million to 32.18 million. The relevant figures for girls were 5.38 million and 18.29 million. The progress was equally rapid in case of secondary education. Between 1950-51 and 1965-66 enrolment increased from 1.02 million to 4.08 million (by nearly 4 times) in case of boys and from 0.19 million to 1.2 million (by nearly 6½ times) in case of girls. The number of secondary schools increased from 7,288 to 24,477 during these years.

At the time of independence there were eighteen universities with a total student enrolment of nearly 300,000. By 1964, the number of universities had increased to fifty-four, the number of colleges to about 2,500 and the number of undergraduate and post-graduate students, excluding intermediate students, to 613,000. The number of girl students increased six-fold and constituted 22 per cent of the total. However, the progress in primary education, though recognisable, did not match the needs or the intentions especially as the number of eligible students was growing fast because of the high rate of population growth. The constitutional target of free and compulsory education to all children was first shifted from 1961 to 1966 and then to a distant future. By the end of the Third Plan in 1965-66 only 61 per cent of the children between six and fourteen were in school, the figure for girls being only 43 per cent.

Community Development Programme

Two major programmes for rural uplift, namely, the Community Development programme and *Panchayati Raj* (village administration), were introduced in 1952 and 1959. They were to lay the foundations of the welfare state in the villages. Though designed for the sake of agricultural development, they had more of a welfare content; their basic purpose was to change the face of rural India, to improve the quality of life of the people.

The Community Development programme was instituted on a limited scale in 1952 covering 55 development blocs, each bloc consisting of about 100 villages with a population of sixty to seventy thousand. By the mid-sixties most of the country was covered by a network of community blocks, employing more than 6,000 Block Development Officers (BDOs) and over 600,000 Village Level Workers (VLWs or *Gram Sewaks*) to help implement the programme. The programme covered all aspects of rural life from improvement in agricultural methods to improvement in communications, health and education.

The emphasis of the programme was on self-reliance and self-help by the people, popular participation and responsibility. It was to be basically a people's movement for their own welfare. As Nehru stated at the very outset of the programme in 1952, the basic objective was "to unleash forces from below among our people." While it was "necessary to plan, to direct, to organise and to coordinate; but it [was] even more necessary to create conditions in which a spontaneous growth from below [was] possible." While material achievements were expected, the programme was much more geared "to build up the community and the individual and to make the latter a builder of his own village centre and of India in the larger sense." "The primary matter is the human being involved," he added. Another major objective was to uplift the backward sections, "We must aim at progressively producing a measure of equality in opportunity and other things. In 1952 and in the later years, Nehru repeatedly referred to the Community Development programme and the accompanying National Extension Service as representing 'new dynamism' and a 'great revolution' and as 'symbols of the resurgent spirit of India.'

The programme achieved considerable results in extension work: better seeds, fertilizers, and so on, resulting in agricultural development in general and greater food production, in particular, construction of roads, tanks and walls, school and primary health centre buildings, and extension of educational and health facilities. Initially, there was also a great deal of popular enthusiasm, which, however, petered out with time. It soon became apparent that the programme had failed in one of its basic objectives – that of involving the people as full participants in developmental activity. Not only did it not stimulate self-help, it increased expectations from and reliance on the government.

10

Debates on Economic and Social Alternatives

Introduction

Here the chapter highlights the independent India's plans to handle the rapidly growing population, availability of food, illegallity and unemployment in the Indian society. Under such condition it sought simultaneously of its laws and institutions, to raise the living standard of the common people by a rapid industrialisation of the country.

It must be a difficult task to identify the major economic sectors for enhancement and then to handle the situation effectively. They introduced and encouraged the farmers to new methods of agriculture using modern plough system and to plant seeds differently? Next challenge for the government was towards modern science and technology and development of manufacturing industries. The Government also handled the language problem successfully in a diverse society of India. Chapter here exposes the ways the newly formed Indian government managed to achieve these things by implementing different policies.

Agriculture System

Farming was the chief occupation in India. About 80 per cent of the population is engaged in farming but most farmers grow only enough to stay alive. Custom, tradition, and ancient farming methods kept food production down; farmers use handmade ploughs drawn by oxen, farm tools were expensive, scarce, and those which were used were often inefficient. Poor seed quality uneven distribution of rain, and the lack of fertiliser to restore the soil, were also responsible for poor crop yields.

Additional agricultural problems rose from the fact that most Indian farmland was cut up into tiny plots. Although the average size of farms was about 7.5 acres, many of the farmers have 2.5 acres of land or less. (The average size farm in the United States is 305 acres.) In India, the farmer and his family consume almost everything grown on the farm. There is almost no agricultural surplus for the cities. Farmers could grow enough to feed the 20 per cent of the population living in the cities. In the United States, the six per cent who are farmers grow enough to feed the rest of the nation and still provide a surplus.

Although India's agricultural production was one of the lowest in the world, the country instituted a bold new programme designed to increase farm production. The plan included educating farmers in modern methods of caring for their land, expansion of India's fertiliser industry, and the development of better seeds.

India's Economic Sectors

Although India is currently the world's second largest producer of rice, she must annually import large amounts of rice from Burma and the United States. India also produces a number of other important crops: oilseeds, cotton, sugar, tea, coffee, spices, and jute. There are two well-defined crop seasons – *Kharif* (or summer) and *Rabi* (or winter). Rice and cotton are among the most important *Kharif* crops, while wheat is an important *Rabi* crop. Sugar cane is a year-round crop.

India's cattle population is a huge drain on the country's food supply. The Hindu's refusal to kill cattle or to eat meat for religious reasons as well as to ban cattle slaughter results in an unusually long life span for animals. The animal population is estimated at 160 million cattle and 50 million buffalo. India has more cattle than any other country in the world. It is not unusual to see cattle roaming through fields of rice, corn, or millet, eating as much as they want. Cows are sacred in the Hindu religion; therefore few people disturb them.

Structure of Indian Industry

Indian industry may be divided into large-scale, small-scale, and cottage industries. India has several large-scale industries. The country has the world's largest jute manufacturing industry and is among the world's leading producers of cotton textiles, sugar, and motion pictures. India's iron and steel industries were founded not long after the start of the twentieth century. Other large-scale industries include cement, leather, glass, rubber, and paper. In recent years, a number of new industries have appeared-heavy chemicals, electric motors, machine tools, automotives, bicycles, and sewing machines.

A small industry in India is generally defined as one which employs fewer than 50 workers. Although there is no clear-cut difference between small-scale and cottage industries, the use of electric power is common in small-scale industries and infrequent in cottage industries. Usually, cottage industries are carried on wholly with the help of members of the family as full or part-time workers.

The Indian government believes that small industries – weaving on handlooms, handicrafts, the making of silk and *khadi* (homespun)– and cottage industries offer the most potential and best source of labour.

Five-Year Plans have reflected this belief, and the government has encouraged small industries, such as plants which manufacture aluminum utensils, umbrellas, electrical furnaces, cardboard boxes, bread and biscuits, preserved foods, soap, matches, shoe polish, and carpets.

Irrigation

Two crops a year can be raised in most parts of India if water is available during the dry season. For this reason, irrigation is vital. When India gained its independence in 1947, there were 15 million irrigated acres of land – more irrigated land than in any other country of the world. Since that time, the Indian government has built many new irrigation projects, and each Five-Year Plan has included the building of projects. Today, roughly 22 per cent of the land is under irrigation.

The Bhakra Nangal Project, in the Punjab in northwestern India, is the largest irrigation project in the nation and cost more than $327 million. It consists of one of the highest dams in the world (740 feet), with about 652 miles of canals. The project irrigates five to six million acres of land. The Rajasthan Canal, part of the Bhakra Nangal Project, irrigates about 500,000 acres. The Hirakund Dam Project in Orissa, 15,748 feet long, is the world's longest dam. This project irrigates almost 400,000 acres of land. The Damodar Valley Project and the Tungabhadra Project, along with others, have made a significant contribution to the Indian economy. The late Prime Minister of India, Jawaharlal Nehru, called India's dams "the temples of tomorrow".

The indifference and sometimes the opposition of village farmers to new irrigation projects has stopped India from making the fullest use of her water resources. Many Indian farmers believe it is best to continue with the methods of agriculture that have been used for generations. They also believe that they may not be doing their dharma if they change from old to new methods of agriculture. When land is irrigated, it is sometimes necessary for farmers to plough and plant seeds differently from their accustomed way. They must often build small canals of their own to secure the water. Many of them refuse to take these measures to ensure a good crop. It has been a slow struggle for the government to teach irrigation methods to the farmers and to have them accept these new ways of farming.

Power

India's power production is increasing, but the demand is still far ahead of present capacities. All of India's principal cities and villages with populations of over 50,000 are served to some extent by electricity. However, most of India's population lives in small villages (with populations of less than 2,000). The largest cities are served mainly by hydroelectric power, but in some areas thermal power, or coal-burning, steam driven generators are used.

In recent years the Indian government has become interested in the development of atomic power. India has an Atomic Energy Commission which is responsible for the development of atomic energy for peaceful purposes. India's first atomic power plant is at Tarapur, 60 miles from Bombay. A second nuclear power station is under construction at Rana Partapshear in Rajasthan. A site for a third nuclear power station has been selected in Madras State. These plants will greatly increase India's power production.

India's Money System

The basic unit of currency in India is the *rupee*, which is divided into 100 *naye paise*. The value of the rupee is 7.5018 rupees (Rs) to the United States dollar, a value that varies on the international money market. India devalued its currency when the British devalued the British pound. Thus, India maintains the value of the rupee unchanged in terms of sterling silver. The rate of exchange of the rupee has been maintained at 13.33 cents.

Communications

Most of India's communication services, including the postal, telephone and telegraph service, are owned by the government. Radio broadcasting is conducted by the government-owned enterprise known as All-India Radio. It operates through 28 radio stations and broadcasts in all the important languages of the country; news bulletins in English are broadcast four times daily. Musical programmes take up about half of the broadcasting time. All-India Radio accepts no commercially sponsored programmes. Television is still in the experimental state. Almost 500 daily newspapers are published in India; about 85 of these are printed in English.

Foreign Economic Relations

Great Britain is India's principal market supplier. Many Indian export items are traded through the British. Although Great Britain's commercial interests in India have decreased in recent years, it still has considerable influence in the jute and tea industries. India also continues to have financial relations with Britain because of the public debt India contracted under British rule.

During World War II, India and the United States strengthened their economic ties. The United States loaned a variety of products to India, including silver. In 1951, the United States gave India a loan of $190 million for the purchase of food. This loan, along with other loans and grants received from the United States since India became independent in 1947, totals over half of all the foreign aid received by India. In 1966, the United States sent one-fourth of its wheat crop to India. The United States has also given India aid in the form of technical assistance programmes. Many American farmers, teachers, miners, Peace Corps workers, and other trained people, have gone to India.

West Germany and Japan are among the free-world countries which have aided India in its economic development. West Germany provided assistance to India in building one of her large steel mills and has granted loans to India for a number of industrial projects. Japan has given money to India for purchases of Japanese goods, and has also provided a wide range of technical assistance. Japan and the United States government are now helping in the development of iron ore deposits in India. A number of Japanese companies are also establishing industrial plants there.

In the early years of India's independence, she had few ties with Communist China and the Soviet Union. Beginning in 1955, however, India became a prime target for economic aid from the USSR. Almost all of this aid came to India in the form of loans. Only a small portion of it was in direct grants-in-aid. The USSR helped to establish Indian plants for the manufacture of drugs, medicines, and surgical instruments. They have given aid to India's steel industry, helped her to get heavy machinery and mining machinery, and have aided India in oil exploration, refining, and production.

Economic and Social Problems

The Population Explosion. Today in India, a baby is born every 1.5 seconds – less time than it takes to read this sentence. With

554 million people already, India adds 13.5 million (or 2.5 per cent) yearly, more people than live in the state of Pennsylvania. This rate of increase is more than double that of the United States (one per cent yearly). At its present rate of increase, India's population will double in 28 years. It will take *seven centuries* for the slowest growing countries – Luxembourg, Belgium, and East Germany – to double their present populations. Population experts predict that by the year 2000 there will be one billion people living in India. What is *one billion*? A billion is 1,000 football stadiums each holding 100,000 football fans. Meeting some of the minimum needs of this population increase requires an additional 1.2 million tons of grain and 126,000 new schools yearly. So long as the population explosion increases the country's basic needs this rapidly, there is little hope of improving the life of the Indian people.

One of the reasons for this enormous increase in population is the great effort Indians are making to wipe out disease. This effort has caused the death rate to drop and population figures to soar. Today, the life expectancy of an Indian at birth is 50 years. In 1945, it was 28 years. The Indian government has fought a hard campaign against disease and has decreased the number of deaths from smallpox, dysentery, malaria, and yellow fever.

The Indian government was among the first national governments to sponsor family planning programmes. These programmes are part of a nationwide movement to provide a better life for the individual, family, and for the community. The main goal of India's large, well-publicised programme is to hold families to two or three children, and to reduce the birth rate in India from the present 43 per 1,000 to 25 per 1,000 by 1973. The States of Maharashtra and Kerala are now down to 27 births per 1,000 people. Another aim of the program is to provide married people with an education that will bring about an acceptance of a small family, knowledge about family planning methods, and readily available supplies available. More than 13,000 doctors and some 120,000 medical workers have been trained in family planning techniques. Yet, making the programs available in a country where there are some 565,000 far-flung villages, is difficult. The population picture is not bright for a country that already has

410 people per square mile and crowds 14 per cent of the world's population into 2.4 per cent of the earth's land area.

Food, Housing, Literacy, and Jobs. The increase in population and improved health measures mean that Indians need more of everything to maintain even their present standard of living, let alone raise it. India has to run harder if it wants to stand still, otherwise it will slip backward. Providing a food supply adequate for the population is a serious problem. Although India's yearly population increase of 2.5 per cent requires an additional 1.2 million tons of grain, the food production increase is only 2 per cent yearly.

The income per person throughout India is presently close to $90 per year – less than $2 per week. In the United States, the average yearly income per person is close to $3,500 a year – nearly $70 weekly. In addition to their poverty, about 70 to 75 per cent of the Indian people can neither read or write. In the United States, about 3 per cent of the population is illiterate. Most young Indians do not have a primary education when they begin work, and few village children are enrolled in primary schools. Of those enrolled, some never attend school and many drop out.

The minor gains which have been made in easing the housing shortage in India have been wiped out by the rise in population. Today, there is a critical need for 2.5 million new housing units each year. Employment shortages present another serious problem. Nearly four million new jobs are required each year to employ the young people entering the labor market.

Because most Indians have little income, they must spend what they earn filling their minimum needs: food, clothing, and shelter. The average person in India earns one rupee (13.33 cents) a day for hard manual labor. There is nothing left over to save for "a rainy day". Since there is little capital for investment, industrial development is slow, and jobs are hard to find. Poor economic growth and few jobs mean little income; and the cycle begins again. It is a cycle which must be broken if India is to provide her people with a decent standard of living.

The Moslem-Hindu Problem. There are 55 million Moslems living in India. Some of them have their tiny shops on a narrow lane in Old Delhi, not far from the beautiful palaces erected by the Moslem rulers of the Mogul Empire. From these Moslem shops, it is only a 20-minute ride to the streets of New Delhi. Yet, there are practically no Moslems in New Delhi, for most of them feel out of place there. Moslems often say "New Delhi is for Hindus".

The majority of these 55 million Indians who make up the world's third largest Moslem community (after Pakistan and Indonesia) face the problem of being a minority group in India. Some Indians look on Moslems as "Pakistani spies". The mistrust between the two countries is still basically mistrust between Moslem and Hindu.

The Pakistan press and radio often magnify incidents in which Moslems in India suffer some misfortune. Some Moslems take this as proof that Hindus want to destroy them. Indian Moslems are insecure and cling to each other and their traditions. Their withdrawal into their own communities and their lack of involvement in Indian political life only deepend Hindu suspicion of them.

Although Moslem loyalty to India is often questioned, a number of Indian Moslems fought bravely against Pakistan in the Indo-Pakistani conflict of 1965. The highest Indian decoration was given to a Moslem sergeant who destroyed two Pakistani tanks and damaged a third. In 1967, a Moslem nationalist, Dr Zakir Husain, was elected India's Third President; another Moslem became Chief Justice of the Indian Supreme Court.

Most Moslems believe they are discriminated against in colleges, private industry, and government service. Although a brilliant Moslem will be favoured over an average Hindu, it is probably true to say that an average Hindu will always be favoured over an average Moslem. Moslems account for less than one-half of one per cent of the workers holding government jobs.

Prejudice. Color is not a basis for prejudice among Indians. But Indians do discriminate on the basis of class. Any person of any color with money, manners, decent education, and friends who will introduce him to people of a higher class, will have few problems socially. He will have an even easier time in life if he is involved in some way with government life, such as being a member of Parliament. His colour will not bar him from even the highest political posts.

How can lower-class Indians obtain a higher class status when most of them are poor and illiterate? How can they become well read, widely travelled, and socially sophisticated when they are starving and earning $90 a year or less? How can they send their children to private schools to be taught by Roman Catholic priests when they cannot afford the tuition? All of these advantages are necessary, but next to impossible, in order to obtain a higher class status.

Prejudice in India is not based on color or race but rather on caste, class, language, and religion. This prejudice runs deep and is difficult to stamp out even through laws forbidding it. Yet, the government continues to seek ways of eliminating prejudice because of respect for the dignity and worth of the individual.

Medical Care. The ancient Moslem and Hindu medical sciences were the most advanced in the world until the middle of the eighteenth century when they began to decline. A doctor was so honored that he was permitted to have a servant hold an umbrella over him at all times.

The introduction of Western practices with their emphasis on preventive medicine, cleanliness, surgery, hospitalisation, and various special fields of study caused a great deal of trouble in India. Many Indians thought that Western medical practices were irreligious and degrading. Gandhi wrote that "doctors are injurious to mankind, but European doctors are the worst of all. They violate the religious instincts, for many of their medical preparations contain either animal fat or liquor, which are taboo to Hindus and Moslems". Western medicine ran into further trouble when the English tried to stop the Indians from disposing of dead bodies in the Ganges River. Indians drank the waters of the Ganges, which they regarded as sacred. The English tried to reason with the Indians that the water became polluted by dead bodies, but some Indians believed this was an attack on the Hindu religion. Many Indians also refused disease-preventing vaccines because the serums came from animals. Some Indians were willing to bring their sick to hospitals.

Today, the growth of medical science in India may be judged by the improvement in the health of the people. The government has made tremendous efforts to conquer such diseases as malaria, cholera, and the plague. There have been extraordinary results – a decrease in the death rate of 52.9 per cent since World War II. On the other hand, the average Indian has no understanding of disease. He believes that evil spirits cause illness and depends on prayers and charms for a cure.

Directives Taken by Ruling Party for Economic Revival

The constant flow of wealth from India to England for which India did not get an adequate economic, commercial or material return has been described by the Indian nationalist leaders and economists as 'economic drain' from India. Sometimes this drain of wealth was interpreted as an indirect tribute extracted by imperial Britain from India year after year.

Now, after the independence, leaders of India had to combat the legacy of British rule. They advocated for a democratic century as they must have thought that 'Democracy gives an individual opportunity to develop'. According to Nehru 'from political democracy we advance to the concept of economic democracy', to call it a welfare state.

Among the directives of the Constitution were, to provide an adequate means of livelihood to all citizens, equitable distribution of material resources, and avoidance of concentration of wealth and means of production in a particular class. Thus, the principle as defined in parliament in 1954, was the adoption of 'a socialist pattern of society,' pragmatic socialism, as Nehru said. The aim of Indian planning was largely on these basic lines. A general all round improvement in the condition of the people was aimed at in regard to education, employment, prosperity, standard of living and so forth, on the one hand; and on the other a substantial progress of the country in industry, agriculture and other resources. Emphasis was placed on assisting the weaker section of society and on doing away with inequalities in wealth.

Have you ever thought the situation in India, after acquiring independence from her colonizers (the British) who ruled India for about 190 years? Do you think how it must be challenging for the newly formed Indian Government to come with a policy which could suite a country which had large population with people having different languages, religion and culture?

This chapter even assesses the success and failure of the economic policies that were undertaken by the Indian Government under the premiership of Nehru from the period 1947 to 1964.They should further give an outline of the Five Year Economic plans that were put in place by Government by highlighting major areas of concentration in an effort to combat colonial economic legacy that was characterised by underdevelopment.

The First Plan (1951-52 to 1955-56)

The first five-year plan had a twofold objective, viz., 'to correct the disequilibrium in the economy caused by the second world war and the partition of the country and to initiate simultaneously a process of all-round balanced development which would ensure a rising national income and a steady improvement in the living standards over a period of time.'

The outlay of the first plan was initially for 2,069 crore (1 crore is equivalent 10 million) of rupees(Indian currency- Rupees [Rs] and Paise [p]) which was later raised to 2,378 crore. The actual expenditure, allowing for the price change during the period, was about 1,960 crore of rupees, i.e. a shortfall of about 418 crore. As the country had to import foodgrains on a large scale in 1951, the plan gave first priority to agriculture, community development, irrigation and power which took about 44.6 per cent of the outlay. Thereafter in descending order, were transport and communication, industry and mining and social services.

In the original plan, borrowing and budgetary resources of the centre and state government were expected to provide about 1,258 crore of rupees. This included revenues, income from railways, loans from the public, small savings and deposits and other miscellaneous sources. The gap of 811 crore (Rs 2,069-1,258 crore) was to be filled in the following manner-521 crore by external assistance, additional borrowings and if necessary by deficit financing; and 290 crore by deficit financing alone. The size of the plan being raised to Rs 2,378 crore, the original gap was increased to Rs 830 crores. External aid was available for a limited amount and ultimately most of the gap (Rs 532 crore) had to be met by deficit financing. On the whole the first plan made satisfactory progress. The chief danger in supplementing the plan expenditure through foreign aid and deficit financing, was inflation. This was avoided and at the end of the first plan prices were lower by 13 per cent than what they had been at the start. The all-India cost of living index in 1955 averaged 96 compared to 100 in 1949. Money supply in public hands increased by about 208 crore of rupees, and national income by about 18 per cent. The Reserve Bank's holding of foreign securities, together with its balances abroad rose from 723.07 crore of rupees to 746.1 crore. The Indian per capita income recorded an increase of 10.5 per cent. The 1955-56 output of foodgrains, which was 64.8 million tons, was more than 10 per cent, since the beginning of the plan. Industrial production showed an overall increase of 40 per cent, the main gains being in cotton textiles, jute manufactuing, sugar and so forth. Over 16 million acres of land were brought under irrigation by major and minor works. The generation of electric power was up by 4,425 kwh. Commerce, transport, cement manufacture, fertilisers, cables, telephone, locomotives, machine tools, newsprint and drugs like penicillin – all showed a rise. Manufacture of Indian made steel was greatly pushed up in order to meet industrial requirement. A new trend noticeable was state ownership and trading. Preliminary work on the installation of three steel plants and a heavy electrical plant was completed in the first plan period.

Much of the agricultural prosperity achieved was due to good monsoons, even though, as said above, there was increase in power production and irrigation.

The first plan assumed a population growth rate of 1.25 per cent per annum for twenty years from 1952. Thus the unanticipated part of growth rate set all calculation awry. Little or no impact was made, for example, on the unemployment problem, and the plan left a backlog of 5.3 million.

The plan did not achieve a balanced economy. It ignored machine manufacturing industries, which was to prove a great drawback in necessitating import of machinery in the future.

It could not integrate physical achievements to money spending. Physical targets were reported to be overachieved despite shortfalls in outlays. The integrated plan did not have annual break ups of physical targets. Hence, reviews and correctives could not be timely made and applied. There was absence of crop planning, crop allocations and crop insurance, which were essential aspects of agricultural planning. The first plan was really an experiment in planning. It spelled out, for example, the conceptual significance of 'deficit financing' as follows:

'to denote the direct addition to gross national expenditure through budget deficits, whether the deficits are on the revenue or on the capital account. The essence of such a policy lies therefore in government spending in excess of revenue it receives in the shape of taxes, earnings of state enterprises, loans from the public, deposits and funds, and other miscellaneous sources.

The government may cover the deficit either by running down its accumulated balances or by borrowing from the banking system'.

A large part of the first plan was, in fact, 'a collation and systematisation' of schemes already existing. As Jawaharlal Nehru said of it 'We just took what there was and called it a plan.' The plan was nevertheless a successful experiment and achieved much of what it envisaged target-wise, though not in terms of the socialistic pattern principle.

The Second Plan (1956-57 to 1960-61)

The first plan had succeeded beyond expectations and the flush of achievement hardly left scope for lessons to be learnt. This was unfortunate for future plans. A Taoist proverb says: 'Failure is the foundation of success, and the means by which it is attained.' The mistakes of the first plan were not only repeated in the second, they were augmented as well.

The second five-year plan sought to rebuild rural India, to lay the foundations of industrial progress and to secure to the greatest extent feasible, opportunities for the weaker and under-privileged sections of people and the balanced development of all parts of the country.

The main aims of the plan were:

1. An increase of 25 per cent in the national income.
2. Rapid industrialisation with particular emphasis on the development of basic and heavy industries.
3. Large expansion of employment opportunities.
4. Reduction of inequalities in income and wealth and a more even distribution of economic power.

The plan aimed at increasing the national income from 7 to 11 per cent by 1960-61. Its stress was on industry-increased production of iron and steel, heavy chemicals and nitrogenous fertilisers. It was in favour of developing heavy engineering and machine building industry.

The development (public sector) outlay was 4,800 crores of rupees (£3,600 million), shared between the states and the centre, the former contributing Rs 2,241 crore and the central government Rs 2, 241 crore. This meant an average annual expenditure of Rs 850 crore, a colossal figure. Industries and mining took away about 19 per cent in the first plan, transport and communications 29 per cent, out of which railways accounted for 19 per cent (as against 11 in the previous plan). The financing of the plan was a ticklish affair. Rs 1,200 crore were to be obtained by deficit financing, Rs 800 crore surpluses from current revenues, Rs 1,200 crore by borrowings from the public, Rs 400 crore by other budgetary resources, and Rs 800 crore by resources to be raised externally. This still left a gap of Rs 400 crore, which was proposed to be covered 'by additional measures to raise domestic resources'. A serious snag was 'the running down of foreign reserves at a much quicker rate than had been planned'. The second plan envisaged a number of large scale industries which required equipment from abroad. The plan anticipated a foreign exchange deficit of Rs 1,100 crore (£ 560 million approximately).

Foreign loans and grants, apart from the strings attached, took time for negotiation. A frantic effort was, therefore, made to curb the out-flow of foreign exchange by severe cuts on imports, minimising travel abroad, and rigorous scrutiny of foreign expenditure. But the amount was far too high to be covered by such devices, helpful though they were, and ultimately a heavy leaning on foreign aid was inevitable. This was mainly obtained through the World Bank which formed what came to be known as the 'Aid India Consortium'.

Despite the financial bottlenecks, the achievements of the second plan were much better than could be imagined. The national income was up by 20 per cent against the target of 25 per cent. The index of agricultural production (with the three years ending 1961-62 as base) rose from 84.4 at the end of the first plan to 102.7 at the end of the second. There was an eight per cent increase in the per capital income. Production of foodgrains increased from 65.8 million tons to 76 million tons and the net irrigated area from 51.5 million acres to 70 million. Particular progress was made in community development, co-operatives and extension services.

In industries there was a cumulative rate of growth in industrial output of seven per cent per annum. Three new steel plants were opened in the public sector and two in the private sector. Machine building industries registered a growth. The value of graded machine tools increased from Rs 34 lakh in 1950-51 to Rs 550 lakh in 1960-61. A coal mining machinery plant was set up at Durgapur and a foundry at Ranchi. Many new industrial items began to be produced indigenously, as for example locomotives, tractors, electrical goods, sewing machines, drugs and so forth. Village and small industries were expanded. Cloth production – *khadi,* handlooms, and other textile – was increased.

The result of the big-sized plan and its unrealistic mode of financing was bound to be felt in the long run, and some of it, as for example the price rise, was immediately discernible. Prices rose by 30 per cent in the five years of the second plan, i.e. six per cent each year. More money, accompanied by shortfall in production, particularly of foodgrains, and investments with no quick returns brought about increased pressure of money demand against limited availability of goods. The ensuing inflation led to concentration of wealth in the hands of the few, and produced conditions just the reverse of the equalisation and the socialistic pattern of society which the plan aimed at. What was worse, the disturbed economy led to undesirable activities such as hoarding, black-marketing and black money. There was the swelling population to add to the confusion.

11

The Government of India

Introduction

After the independence Indian leaders had a major task to lay the structure of the Government of India.There was another challenging task was the framing a constitution. And this stupendous task was given to one of such distinguished statesman and intellectual Dr B.R.Ambedakar. He not only accepted the responsibility of the Chairmanship of the drafting Committee but also raised the expectation of the Constituent assembly and the people of Inda. Ambedkar was eminently qualified to occupy this position by virtue of his academic distinction as a constitutional expert. A new constitution came into existence, under which India became republic (that is, British sovereign ceased to be the sovereign of India). India is a Federal country that is, it was at that time divided up into 20 (now 29 states and 7 union territories) states, and each of it had its own capital and its own parliament and government to deal with the local affairs of the states. The capital of the whole country is New Delhi and the national parliament meets there to make laws for the whole country.

The Prime Minister of India, as addressed in the Constitution of India, is the chief of government, chief of adviser to the President of India, head of the Council of ministers and the leader of the majority party in the parliament. The Prime Minister leads the executive branch of the Government of India. He is elected by the people but appointed by the President by convention, based on appointee's ability to command confidence in the Lok Sabha. The first Prime Minister of India was Pandit Jawaharlal Nehru. Who was elected in 1951 under congress pary and served the nation until his death in office in 1964.

The President of India is the formal head of executive, legislature and judiciary of India and is the commander-in-chief of the Indian force. The President is indirectly elected by the people through elected members of the Parliament of India (Lok Sabha and Rajya Sabha) as well as of the Legislative Assemblies (Vidhan Sabha) and each of the Union Territories in States of India. Although Article 53 of the Constitution of india states that the President can exercise his power directly or by subordinate authority, with few exceptions, all of the executive power is exercised by the Government of India. The executive power is exercised by the Prime Minister with the help of the Council of Ministers. The President opens the Parliament with an address. In addition to that, the President summons and prorogues the two Houses of Parliament from time to time. The first President of India was Rajendra Prasad.

Plate 6

(a) Pandit Jawaharlal Nehru
First Prime Minister

(b) Rajendra Prasad
First President

The Structure of Government

The organisation and principles of the Indian government reflect the best features of British, French, American, and other democratic governments. The idea of democracy is not new in India. Government by the people can be found in India's past. Historians claim that in one place or another there has been a republican form of government in India from the sixth century B.C.

The Constitution of India was adopted by the Constituent Assembly on *November 26, 1949*, and came into force on *January 26, 1950*. The preamble to the Constitution states that it was written to secure for all citizens "justice, social, economic, and political; liberty of thought, expression, belief, faith and worship; equality of status and opportunity; and to promote among them all fraternity, assuring the dignity of the individual and the unity of the Nation." Article 236 of the Constitution gives the right to vote to every person who is a citizen of India, 21 (now 18) years of age, and "not otherwise disqualified under the Constitution or any other law on the ground of non-resident, unsoundness of mind, crime, or corrupt or illegal practice."

The Indian Constitution lists individually the responsibilities of the various branches of government. Although in this sense it differs from the American Constitution and from British practice, the general principles of the Indian Constitution are similar to those of both American and British law. India, according to her Constitution, is a democratic republic with a division of power between the central and the state governments. The Indian system differs from the American, however, in that the central government can make laws in many more areas than can our national government.

The Executive Branch. The Union Executive consists of the President of India, the Vice-President, and the Council of Ministers with the Prime Minister as its head. The President is elected for a term of five years by an electoral college consisting of the elected members of both houses of parliament and of the Legislative Assemblies of the states. The President's duties are largely ceremonial, but the may proclaim (without the consent of parliament) a state of emergency and suspend the normal operation of constitutional law. This may be done only for a maximum period of two months unless the time is further extended by approval of both houses of parliament. The vice-President of India is elected by an electoral college consisting of the elected members of both houses of Parliament.

The Legislature. The Indian Parliament consists of the President, the Lok Sabha (House of the People), and the Rajya Sabha (Council of State). Although the Indian legislature is bicameral (that is, it has two houses), the government must have a majority in the Lok Sabha only. The members of the Lok Sabha are elected by the people and hold office for five years.

The Rajya Sabha is a permanent body, who are elected by the elected members of the Legislative Assemblies of the States. Twelve members are named to serve by the President. These are persons with special knowledge or practical experience in literature, the sciences, the arts, and social services. One-third of the members of the Rajya Sabha retire every two years. Although the Rajya Sabha cannot originate laws concerning money, it can introduce other measures. In the event of a disagreement between the two houses, a vote may be taken at a joint session.

The Judiciary. An important feature of the Constitution of India is the inclusion of a list of Fundamental Rights and Directives of State Policy. The Fundamental Rights guaranteed by the Constitution include freedom of religion, freedom of speech and association, a guarantee against arbitrary arrest and imprisonment, the outlawing of untouchability, and the forbidding of discrimination of any kind because of race, caste, religion, sex, or place of birth. The Supreme Court of India and its independent judiciary is the guardian of these rights. The judiciary guarantees the people rights and freedoms by interpreting the Constitution. All Supreme Court and High Court officials throughout India are appointed by the President; district court officials are appointed by state governors. The independence of the judiciary is safeguarded by a number of provisions. Judges cannot be removed except on grounds of failing to fulfill properly the function of their office and only with the approval of two-thirds of the members of both Houses and Legislature.

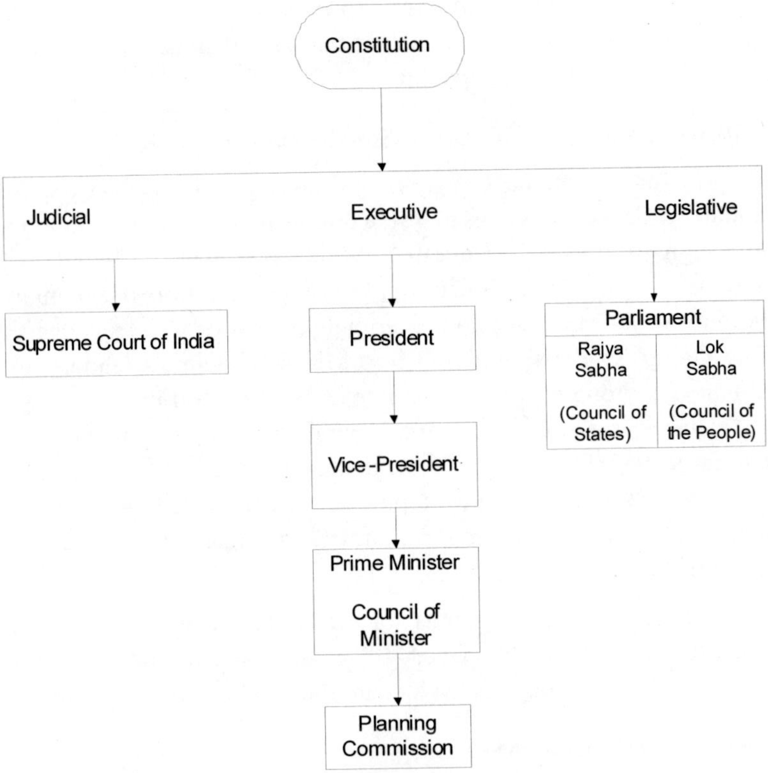

All persons, including non-citizens, are guaranteed equality before the Law. No person can be deprived of life, property, or personal liberty except by due process of the law, and no person can be prosecuted for the same offense more than once or be forced to testify against himself. All persons have a right to be brought before a judge within 24 hours of arrest except enemy aliens or persons arrested under preventive detention laws. It is interesting to note that the government has enacted laws under which persons who have not committed a crime may be jailed for one they are expected to commit. These persons however, have the right to know the grounds on which they are held and must be given an immediate opportunity to question the order. The Indian Constitution also includes a set of directives which makes the state undertake, within its means, a number of welfarc mcasures. These are intended to insure the citizen an adequate job, to raise the standard of living, to improve public health, and to provide education for children. It is the task of India's judiciary to protect these rights of the people.

Political Conditions in India after Formation of Self- Rule

The Indian National Congress, or Congress Party, which led India to independence, continues to be the dominant political party in India although its power has declined. The Party has the benefit of association with Gandhi's name and has kept the confidence of many because of its leadership in the struggle for national independence. The Congress Party, under Prime Minister Nehru's leadership, obtained a strong majority in parliament and control in all the state legislatures as a result of the first general elections held in late 1951 and early 1952. In the second general elections, 1957, the party gained slightly in the percentage of popular votes polled (48 percent compared with 45 percent in 1952). In 1967, Congress Party majorities slipped badly.

The Congress Party stands for moderate social and economic changes, that, a "socialist pattern of society," and for the separation of religion and politics. Its leaders are the wealthy and well born.

Ruling Party: Congress

India is virtually the only post-colonial nation to sustain a system of parliamentary government for over 65 years after independence. It is, of course, true that throughout the Nehru years Congress was dominant politically and retained power at the Centre and in almost all the states. But simultaneously, a multi-party system based on free competition among parties and strong parliamentary institutions also developed from the beginning. The nature and working of the party system in place at the time of independence with several political parties – the Congress, the Socialist Party, the Communist Party, the *Kisan Mazdoor Praja Party* and the *Bharatiya Jan Sangh* – functioning actively and successfully in 1951-52 was crucial to the development of parliamentary democracy in India.

Though the opposition parties remained individually quite weak compared to Congress in terms of mass support as also seats in the parliament and the state legislatures, they were quite active and politically did not play just a peripheral role. They vigorously campaigned for alternative sets of economic and political policies. More significantly, non-Congress candidates polled more votes than the Congress in the general elections of 1951-52, 1957, and 1962; and, despite the first-past-the-poll electoral system, they captured 26 per cent of the Lok Sabha seats in 1952, 25 per cent in 1957 and 28 per cent in 1962. They fared even better in the state assemblies where their strength was 32 per cent of the seats in 1952, 35 per cent in 1957, and 40 per cent in 1962. What is even more important, they put considerable pressure on the government and the ruling party and subjected them to consistent criticism. In practice, they also wielded a great deal of influence on public policies, in fact, quite out of proportion to their size.

One reason why the opposition parties remained weak in this period was because of their inability to unite. They found they had more in common with one or the other wing of Congress than with each other. This was not accidental because except for the communal and casteist parties all the other opposition parties had before 1947 been part of the national movement and the Congress. It was only when the left and right parties could unite, formally or informally, that they could defeat the Congress in 1977 and 1989.

The Indian National Congress was then the most important political organisation in India at independence and, in fact, throughout the Nehru era. There was no alternative to it on the horizon. It enjoyed immense prestige and legitimacy as the leader and heir of the national movement. Its reach was national; it covered the entire sub-continent. Its social base extended from the metropolitan cities to the remotest of villages and from the big capitalists to the rural poor. Congress gave the country a stable government; it was a major instrument of the political stability India enjoyed for several decades.

Jawaharlal Nehru, on the other hand, was convinced that it was both possible and necessary to retain the all-embracing consensual character of Congress and that without its leadership the country would neither be politically stable, nor capable of economic and social development. He was therefore unwilling to divide the partly along left-right lines and stayed with Congress as did a large number of the Congress Socialists who saw Congress and Nehru as more effective instruments of socialism and social change. However, realising that the departure of the Socialists would adversely affect the socialist aspirations of Congress, he made, as we shall see, several attempts to bring them back into the party or at least to get their cooperation in his nation-building efforts. He also constantly strove to reform Congress and give it a left-turn, however arduous the task. He also adopted a reconciliatory approach towards political opponents other than the communalists.

Congress did, of course, become after 1947 a distinct political party, competing with other parties for political power but it did not become a monolithic party. It retained its amorphous and national consensual character with a great deal of ideological flexibility and vagueness. Though the party observed a certain degree of discipline, its functioning and decision-making remained democratic and open. There was still a great deal of debate within it as also tolerance of different viewpoints, tendencies and open dissent. The views of the party members got reflected in the All India Congress Committee and the annual sessions of the party. The district and provincial party organisational structures also functioned effectively and conveyed to the leadership the different points of view prevailing in the party. Important in this respect was the role of Nehru who functioned as a democrat inside the party as also in relation to the opposition parties.

During the Nehru era, Congress remained basically a party of the Centre or middle with a left orientation – in other words, a left-of-the-centre party – though it had right and left minorities at its flanks. Broadly, it stood for nationalism, economic development, social justice, redistribution of wealth and equalisation of opportunities encompassed by the broad idea of democratic socialism. As a centrist party it had three important features. First, the opposition parties, other than the communal parties, were able to influence it through their mass agitations or through like-minded groups within it, for there always existed inside Congress groups which reflected the positions of the opposition parties. Second, this conciliatory attitude led to the opposition parties being open to absorption. Congress was able to absorb the social base, cadres, programmes and addition there was to be a ceiling on land-holdings and state trading in foodgrains. The Nagpur decisions faced opposition both within and outside the party and were quietly jettisoned. Land ceilings were circumvented by the state governments under the pressure of capitalist farmers and rich peasants supported by the middle peasants. The small experiments in cooperative farming were a failure, and state trading in foodgrains was soon found to be unworkable. Nehru was quite willing to learn and discard unworkable policies, and except for the land ceilings, other aspects of the Nagpur Resolution were soon abandoned. However, the commitment to socialism was once again vigorously asserted at the Bhubaneshwar session of the Congress in January 1964.

While refusing to let the Congress be divided sharply on a left-right basis, Nehru kept the Congress on a left-of-the-centre course. He consistently attacked the right-wing parties and individuals and treated the left parties with respect even while criticising them and making clear his differences with them.

Decline of Congress

The stronger assertion of its commitment to socialism did not stop the rot in the Congress party. There was growing criticism of the party in the country as also disillusionment with it. Also internal divisions in the party were growing more serious. The old leaders had grown jaded while new suitable leaders were not coming forth. The party organisation continued to weaken; the party had been in power too long. A large number of Congressmen were no longer satisfied with party work – they hungered for official positions, influence and patronage. Administrative corruption was beginning to go beyond tolerable limits. The Congress was drifting away from the people and losing ground to the opposition in the states. The growing weakness of the party was revealed by the loss in 1963 of three prestigious Lok Sabha by-elections in the party strongholds. People had begun to ask the questions: After Nehru, who? And after Nehru, what?

Nehru, aided by the Madras Chief Minister, K. Kamaraj, now made a last effort to infuse new life into the party and restore the balance between the party and the government. This was sought to be achieved through what came to be known as the Kamaraj Plan, produced in August 1963 at a meeting of the Congress Working Committee. The essence of the Plan was that a number of leading Congressmen who were in the government as Union cabinet ministers or as chief ministers in the states should voluntarily resign from their posts and take up party organisational work in order to revitalise the party. Nehru was to decide whose resignations were to be finally accepted. This would also enable Nehru to cleanse the party at the top.

Opposition Parties

The Communist Party of India is the chief opposition party in Parliament and today is represented in almost every state legislature. It received 10 per cent of the popular vote in 1957, more than doubling its vote of 1952. In the third general election, 1962, it made even greater gains. Various socialist parties in India include the Praja Socialist Party and the Samyukta Socialist Party. Many splinter groups also exist which differ among themselves, largely in matters of tactics and personalities. The *Hindu Mahasabha*, the *Jan Sangh*, and the *Ram Rajya Parishad* all uphold, in varying degrees, the ideals of Hindu orthodoxy and the concept of a Hindu-dominated state. The *Swatantra* Party was formed in opposition to the socialist economic policies of the Congress Party.

The Socialist Party

Of all the political parties that emerged immediately after independence the Socialist Party held the greatest promise. In Jayaprakash Narayan it had a leader next only to Jawaharlal Nehru in mass popularity. It has also several other brilliant leaders, for example Acharya Narendra Dev, Achyut Patwardhan, Asoka Mehta, Dr Rammanohar Lohia and S.M. Joshi. However, the first problem the Socialists faced – and this was a problem they continued to face to the end – was that of their relationship with Congress. The Socialist

Party had been born in 1934 and had remained since then a part of Congress, though it had its own separate constitution, membership, discipline and ideology.

The Communist Party

Communist Party of India (CPI) was a part of Congress since 1936 but, unwilling to accept the Congress discipline, it left the party in 1945. From 1942 to 1945 it had a remarkable growth, even though it got isolated from the mainstream of the national movement and consequently suffered in terms of its hegemonic influence over the people. In 1947, CPI started out with certain advantages; it had several able leaders and thousands of devoted, disciplined and hardworking cadres who were active among the peasants, workers, students and the intelligentsia.

The CPI had gone through a great deal of inner turmoil and division during 1947. Initially, it recognised that India had become free and advised all progressive forces to rally round Nehru against the reactionary communal and pro-imperialist forces. Later, under Soviet guidance, it declared in *December 1947* that India's independence was fake (*yeh azadi jhooti hai*), *15 August* was a day of national betrayal, Congress had gone over to imperialism and feudalism, Nehru had become a stooge of imperialism, the government was ruling in a fascist manner, and the Constitution that was being framed was a charter of slavery. The Communists had, therefore, to take up the anti-imperialist and anti-feudal tasks, fight for freedom and democracy and initiate an armed struggle.

CPI finally split in 1964, with one party, representing the earlier 'right' and 'centrist' trends, being known as CPI and the other party, representing the earlier 'left' trend, being known after sometime as the Communist Party (Marxist) or CPM. Apart from personal and factional differences, the split took mainly a doctrinal form.

Bharatiya Jan Sangh

The *Bharatiya Jan Sangh*, founded in October 1951, was basically a communal party and has to be studied as such. A communal party is one which is structured around communal ideology. A communal party cannot be defined by specific policies, for it can discard any of its programmatic and policy elements and sometimes adopt the very opposite ones. Its economic, political and social policies are generally a husk or a mask which can be changed at appropriate moments to suit its electoral or other political needs, which it perceives as essential for the capture of political power, which in turn the party needs to implement its communal agenda. A communal party is not a conservative party for it is not committed to the conservation of large elements of the existing social, economic and political structure. It is, however, a right-wing party for it cannot communalise the state and society without strengthening the reactionary and exploitative elements of the economy.

The *Jan Sangh* could not, however, openly profess its communal ideology as it had to function within two major constraints. Being an electoral party, operating in a secular democratic polity, it had to try to cobble together an electoral majority and therefore appeal to non-communal voters, as also obey electoral laws forbidding political appeals to religion. Further, because of the firm ideological commitment of the national movement and the anti-communal sentiment in India, especially after the assassination of Gandhiji, communalism had a bad odour about it.

The Swatantra Party

The Swatantra Party, the first authentic all-India secular conservative party, came into being in early *August 1959*. It had a number of distinguished leaders, most of them old Congressmen, for example, C. Rajagopalachari, Minoo Masani, N.G. Ranga and K.M. Munshi. Right-wing groups and parties had, of course, earlier existed at the local and regional levels, but *Swatantra's* formation was the first attempt to bring these highly fragmented right-wing forces together under the umbrella of a single party. The provocation was the left turn which the Congress took at Avadi and the Nagpur Resolution.

Favouring the nineteenth century conception of the 'night watchman' or *laissez-faire* state, *Swatantra* stood for free, private enterprise and opposed the active role of the state in economic development. It wanted to radically restrict centralised planning and the role of public sector, as also state-regulation of the economy. It opposed any nationalisation of private enterprise and any extension of land reforms, especially fixation of ceilings on land holdings. *Swatantra* was fully committed to secularism and that was one reason it found it difficult to merge or form a general alliance with Jan Sangh, though it entered into seat-sharing arrangements with it. In fact, many conservative intellectuals, businessmen and political leaders welcomed the formation of *Swatantra* because it provided a non-socialist, constitutionalist and secular conservative alternative to the Congress. *Swatantra* leaders accused Congress of accepting communist principles and trying to abolish private property. Totally misrepresenting Nehru's position, they accused him of trying to introduce collective farming and Chinese-type communes. Nehru, Rajagopalachari said, was treading 'the royal road to Communism'. *Swatantra*, on the other hand, was 'dedicated to saving India from the dangers of totalitarialism'.

Communal and Regional Parties

A large number of communal and regional parties existed between 1947 and 1964. Among the communal parties, *Hindu Mahasabha* was an old party, but it soon faded from the political scene after 1952, when it had won four seats in the Lok Sabha, as it gradually lost its support base to *Jan Sangh*. Same was the case with *Ram Rajya Parishad*. Because of its association with the demand for Pakistan, Muslim League lay dormant, with many of its demoralised leaders and activists joining Congress and other parties. However, it revived in parts of Tamil Nadu and in Kerala where first Congress and then CPI and CPM gave it respectability by making it an alliance partner. *Akali Dal* was another major communal party, though limited to Punjab.

12

India under Jawaharlal Nehru Democracy and Development

Introduction

Jawaharlal Nehru can be justifiably considered an architect of modern India. One of the great Indians of the twentieth century, he has been variously described as a democrat, socialist, humanist and visionary, but he was all these and more. Any assessment of his role in the making of independent India would need to take cognizance of his immense stature and extraordinary personality and would, therefore, inevitably be complex and somewhat controversial.

What was it about Nehru which makes so many Indians today look back on the Nehru era with such nostalgia? That period was even more full of misery and poverty than the present. Then why did his presence make so much of a difference? What are the abiding elements of Nehru's contribution to the making of independent India; what is his legacy? What did he, and under his leadership the Indian people, achieve? What abiding values did he try to inculcate among Indians that are today treated as a guide and measure of their own and their leaders' actions, pronouncements, and ideas? And was he 'equal to his opportunities'? It is the answers to these questions which will determine his place in history and not what he failed to achieve and what remains to be done.

This Chapter also briefly describe the early life of Jawaharlal Nehru and also identify the role he played in India's social, political and economic dimensions. Finally, this chapter critically analyses the strengths and weaknesses of Nehru's leadership.

No doubt, Nehru played an important role in framing Indian constitution and was a great supporter of both political and economic democracy. He had a vision to make India an industrialised country and called industries as Temple of new India. He was very close to Mahatma Gandhi and took a lot of interest in liberating neighbouring countries including Africa.

Early Life

Nehru came from a family of Kashmiri Brahmins, who had migrated to the plains early in the eighteenth century. He was the son of Motilal Nehru, a renowned lawyer and one of Mahatma Gandhi's prominent lieutenants. Jawaharlal was the eldest of three children, two of whom were daughters. His sister, Vijayalakshmi Pandit, later became the first woman president of the UN General Assembly.

Until the age of 16, Nehru was educated at home by a series of English governesses and tutors. Jawaharlal also had an Indian tutor who taught him Hindi and Sanskrit. In 1905 he went to Harrow, a leading English School, where he stayed for two years. Nehru's academic career was in no way outstanding. From Harrow he went to Trinity College, Cambridge, where he spent three years earning an honours degree in natural science. On leaving Cambridge, Nehru joined the InnerTemple in 1910 to read law, where in his own words he passed his examinations "with neither glory nor ignominy". In London he was drawn to the Fabian socialists, also known as the Bloomsbury group. He returned home in 1912 after seven years of education in England.

Four years after his return to India, in March 1916, Nehru married Kamala Kaul, who came from a Kashmiri family settled in Delhi. Their only child, Indira Priyadarshini, was born in 1917; she would later (under her married name of Indira Gandhi) also serve as Prime minister of India.

For Nehru independence had to go beyond mere political independence. He was also strongly committed to change and development, the building of an equitable and egalitarian, just and democratic society – a socialist society -, laying down the foundations of a democratic and civil libertarian polity and the consolidation of India as a nation. And he tried all his life – both before and after the attainment of independence – to link his dual commitment to nationalism and socialism.

This was an unchartered path. Neither Marx nor Gandhiji, two long-term influences on him, provided guidelines on how to go about building a nation. But he set upon this hard task with a degree of excitement and optimism. He had always believed that India's greatest need was 'for a sense of certainty concerning her own success.' This sense of excitement and faith in the coming success he did not abandon even after the defeat and betrayal of the Indo-China war of 1962. And, what is more important, he succeeded in imparting this sense to millions of Indians.

Democracy, rule of law, respect for the freedom and dignity of the individual, social equity and equality, non-violence, rationality in the guidance of human affairs and morality-based politics were the pillars of his basic approach to nation building. Personal integrity, love and confidence in the Indian masses were his major assets in this task.

Consolidation of Indian Independence

Maintenance, strengthening and consolidation of India's independence were among Nehru's most pressing tasks. In a world that was sharply divided between the two superpowers – the United States and the Soviet Union – which were determined to extend their hegemony over the rest of the world, Nehru resisted all pressures and refused to become their pawn. India's internal policies – right or wrong – developed outside the direct influence of the superpowers, and India remained in full control of her internal as well as her external policies. Nehru also successfully resisted penetration of India's political and economic structure and institutions by outside agencies.

Clearly, independence depended on the economic strength of a country. Given this, Nehru set out, with a great deal of success, to build an independent and self-reliant economy and made an all-out effort to break out of colonial underdevelopment and to ensure self-sustaining and self-generating growth, both in agriculture and industry. He put a great deal of emphasis on self-reliance and cautioned against dependence on other nations. Rapid industrialisation, particularly growth of heavy industries, planning, development of the public sector, atomic energy and science and technology, technical modernisation and the training of a large technical and scientific cadre were regarded by Nehru as necessary parts of the effort at independent economic development and self-reliance.

Forging National Unity

Nehru succeeded in maintaining and strengthening the national unity forged during the freedom struggle and rendered fragile by the manner of the transfer of power in 1947. He also succeeded in checking the disruptive forces, consolidating the nation and the independent state, promoting the psychological integration of the Indian people. This was no mean task. Casteism, provincialism, tribalism, linguistic chauvinism – largely transcended during the freedom struggle – were surfacing again; the princely states were there, and, of course, there was the ever present danger of communalism.

Nehru recognised that India was not yet a structured nation but a nation-in-the-making. He also kept in view and made allowance for India's immense variety and diversity. He constantly urged the people to develop 'an outlook which embraces all this variety and considers it our very own.' A specific expression of this strategy of unity in diversity was his policy towards the tribal people. Overall, despite the persistence of many disruptive forces, at times dormant, at time active, there is no doubt that Nehru succeeded in keeping them under check, and provided the much needed political stability and push forward to the process of national integration, of nation-building. In fact, he subordinated all other questions and issues to this task. Behind the Five Year Plans lay the concept of national unity.

Nurturing Democracy and Parliamentary Government

Carrying on the traditions of the national movement, Nehru carefully nurtured and entrenched democracy and parliamentary government in independent India. He fought three general elections on the basis of universal adult franchise and secret ballot and made elections the norm, not an exception.

Nehru's commitment to democracy and civil liberties was total. To him they represented absolute values and not means to an end. He would not subordinate them to any other goals, whether of social change or socio-economic development. He was aware that the parliamentary system had its weaknesses, and made efforts to remove some of them. But he would not, he declared, 'give up the democratic system for anything.' He also helped create an institutional structure which was democratic and in which power was diffused: a Constitution with basic civil liberties enshrined in it, a sovereign parliament elected on the basis of universal suffrage and regular elections, a free Press, a cabinet government and an independent judiciary.

This commitment to democracy was rooted in Nehru's deep and unqualified faith in and respect for the common man. 'That is enough religion for me.' He once declared. He was willing to back fully 'the free market of ideas' because he believed that in the long run people could discriminate between different ideas. At the same time, he was aware of the authoritarian tendencies in the country and even in his own party. 'Our democracy', he said in 1951, 'is a tender plant which has to be nourished with wisdom and care.' And so he tried his best to instil in the commonfolk, a taste for democratic concepts. He regularly toured the land sharing his ideas with the people, trying to educate them in the ways of rational and democratic thinking. When asked what his legacy to India would be, he repeated 'Hopefully, it is four hundred million people capable of governing themselves.'

Democracy was intrinsic to Nehru's idea of social and political development. Democracy would enable the people to mobilise themselves and to exert pressure from below to achieve social justice and equality, as well as reduction of economic inequality, which over time would lead to socialism. The political party in power would either implement the popular mandate or would get swept away. He was aware that this process might take time, for parliamentary system and universal suffrage gave the right to govern but not necessarily the power to do so. But sooner or later, he believed, the power would follow the right, and he did his best to bring this about. This is one reason why he placed so much emphasis on elections, besides community development projects, Panchayati Raj, cooperatives and decentralisation of all kinds of power.

Particularly, to ensure the unity of a diverse society like India's, Nehru argued democracy was essential. No amount of force or coercion could hold India together. 'In India today,' he said in 1960, 'any reversal of democratic methods might lead to disruption and violence.'

Nehru was aware of the formidable, novel and unprecedented character of his effort to develop the country economically on the basis of a democratic and civil libertarian political structure. No other country had attempted this so far. Most other nations and societies had used authoritarian and administrative measures and institutions during the period of their economic take-off. Nehru was aware that his path of development might slow down the rate of economic development. But Indian people, he felt, were willing to pay this price for the sake of a democratic political order.

Throughout his life Nehru opposed dogma and a dogmatic mentality. This was his major objection to religion and became a major ground for his favouring a scientific temper and outlook on life and its problems.

Building Socialism

Nehru rejected the capitalist developmental and civilisational perspective and, instead, worked for fundmental transformation of Indian society in a socialist direction. Clearly, he did not succeed in building a socialist society and there was a large gap between his precepts and practice. But he did, over the years, grapple with the problem of initiating socialism in an underdeveloped country with a democratic polity. It was Nehru, above all, who carried the socialist vision to millions and made socialism a part of their consciousness.

What did socialism mean to Nehru? In fact, Nehru never defined socialism in terms of a definite scheme or rigid general principles. To him, generally, socialism meant greater equality of opportunity, social justice, more equitable distribution of higher incomes generated through the application of modern science and technology to the processes of production, the ending of the acute social and economic disparities generated by feudalism and capitalism, and the application of the scientific approach to the problems of society. Socialism also meant the eventual ending of the acquisitive mentality, the supremacy of the profit motive, and capitalist competitiveness and the promotion instead of the cooperative spirit. It also meant the gradual ending of class distinctions and class domination. Socialism also laid down the large-scale social ownership or control over the principal means of production. But Nehru insisted that, first of all, socialism concerned greater production, for there could be no equal distribution of poverty. In fact, to him socialism was equal to greater production plus equitable distribution.

In Indian conditions, Nehru regarded socialist transformation as a process and not as an event. Socialism was then not a clearly pre-defined, pre-laid-out scheme towards which the process of transformation moved. Instead, socialism was expected to go on being defined, stage by stage, as the process advanced. There was to be no sudden break but gradual change. Socialist transformation was to be viewed in terms of a series of reforms which would occur within the orbit of the existing socio-economic structure, but which would, over time and in their totality, amount to a revolution or a structural social transformation. Nehru described these reforms as 'surgical operations'. Socialist revolution would, thus, consist of a series of 'surgical operations' performed through the due process of law by a democratic legislature. Nehru believed that democracy and civil liberties had to be basic constituents of socialism, and were inseparable from it.

India of the Nehru era was quite often criticised for being a soft state and Nehru was accused of being a weak ruler. But Nehru did not agree, for he was aware of the danger of authoritarianism posed by too strong a state and too strong a ruler. Just before his death, he said in 1964, "One should not mistake gentleness and civility of character for weakness. They should criticise me for my weakness, but this is too large a country with too many legitimate diversities to permit any so-called "strong man" to trample over people and their ideas."

One reason Nehru adopted an open-ended approach towards socialism was because of his belief that it was not possible to mobilise a large majority around a clear-cut, structured, ideological definition of socialism. A large majority could be mobilised only by uniting diverse interests and multiple views and ideological strands around a common socialist vision of broad framework.

Over time Nehru came to believe that a socialist society could be achieved through peaceful and non-violent means. While recognising the existence and significance of the class struggle he believed that it could be resolved through non-violent means and the rule of law.

Planning for Economic Development

Nehru looked upon rapid economic development as basics for India's independence and unity and for the removal of poverty and implementation of his social welfarist policies. The three pillars of Nehru's development strategy, representing 'a fairly widespread intellectual consensus of the time,' were planning for rapid industrial and agricultural growth, a public sector to develop strategic industries and a mixed economy. Nehru popularised the concept of planning and made it a part of Indian consciousness. India was to have a mixed economy as a transitional stage, with the private sector functioning for a long time to come though within the framework of planning. In the long run, the state was to occupy the commanding heights of the economy, owning or controlling all basic industries and strategic sectors of the economy. The public sector was not to be based only on state-run enterprises. Nehru was very clear that the cooperative principle should be encouraged and cooperatives in trade, industry and agriculture should play an increasingly larger role.

Above all Nehru wanted to build an independent self-reliant economy, for independence depended on economic strength and the capacity to resist economic and political domination. Emphasis on rapid industrialisation and agricultural self-sufficiency, planning, public sector and heavy, capital goods industry, minimal use of foreign capital and aid, science, technology and technical modernisation, the training of a large technical and scientific cadre, and atomic energy was seen by Nehru as necessary parts of the effort at independent economic development. In achieving this, there is hardly any doubt that he was eminently successful. India did make the transition from a colonial to an independent economy, though a capitalist economy. Whatever the weaknesses that emerged later, Nehru's economic policy did prove to be the right one for India and as a result her economic achievement was quite substantial.

Opposing Communalism

Nehru's commitment to secularism was unsurpassed and all-pervasive. Communalism went against his grain, and he fought it vigorously throughout his life. He helped secularism acquire deep roots among the Indian people; and prevented the burgeoning forth of communalism when conditions were favourable for it. Though on almost all issues he believed in consensus and compromise, communalism was the exception, for as he said in 1950, any compromise on communalism 'can only mean a surrender of our principles and a betrayal of the cause of India's freedom.'

Keeping in view India's specific situation, Nehru defined secularism in the dual sense of keeping the state, politics and education separate from religion, making religion a private matter for the individual, and of showing equal respect for all faiths and providing equal opportunities for their followers. He defined communalism as the ideology which treated Hindus, Muslims, Sikhs or Christians as homogeneous groups in regard to political and economic matters, as 'politics under some religious garb, one religious group being incited to hate another religious group.'

Nehru was one of the first to try to understand the socio-economic roots of communalism, and the first to try to understand that it was primarily a weapon of reaction, even though its social base was formed by the middle classes. He also most perceptibly described communalism as the Indian form of fascism. In contrast, he regarded secularism as an essential condition for democracy.

He also did not distinguish between Hindu, Muslim, Sikh or Christian communalisms. They were, he said, different forms of the same ideology and had, therefore, to be opposed simultaneously. While he was very clear that secularism meant giving full protection to the minorities and removing their fears, at the same time, he was as opposed to minority communalisms as to the communalism of the religious majority. He also argued most convincingly that secularism had to be the sole basis for national unity in a multi-religious society and that communalism was, therefore, clearly a danger to national unity and was anti-national.

Opposing Conservation

Nehru did not devote much time and effort to social reform in the narrow sense of the term. But he was opposed to social conservatism; and, realising that men and women do not live by bread alone, he regularly emphasised the necessity of bringing about changes in the social sphere along with economic and political changes. One of his greatest achievements as prime minister was the passage of the Hindu Code Bills. Another was the care with which he promoted education among girls and public employment of middle-class women.

Pursuing Foreign Policy

Nehru's foreign policy was a many splendoured phenomenon. Nehru used foreign policy as an instrument to defend and strengthen India's newly won independence and to safeguard India's national interests and to develop the self-reliance, self-confidence and the pride of the Indian people, even while serving the cause of world peace and anti-colonialism. It is significant that successive prime ministers after Nehru, till today, have continued to follow the broad framework of his foreign policy.

Assessing Nehru as the First Prime Minister of India

Nehru's place in history should rightly take into account his political weaknesses. This in no way diminishes him for he still emerges as a person towered over his contemporaries.

A critical weakness of Nehru's strategy of consolidation of the Indian nation, economic development and social transformation flowed from his non-adherence to the Gandhian strategy of non-violent struggle in one crucial aspect – its emphasis on the mobilisation of the people. Nehru did see the necessity of involving a large number of people in nation building. But he had an overpowering belief in spontaneity, in the poor mobilising on their own; he believed in the reductionist notion that the exercise of franchise would gradually educate the masses to vote in their own interest. He also harboured the nineteenth-century liberal notion that his speeches or those of other right type leaders would by themselves arouse and activise the masses.

There is no doubt that Nehru felt deeply and passionately for the people; his sway over the masses was immense as was his capacity to communicate with them, to sense their feelings and to win their love, affection and trust. But an active involvement of the people in politics and their own social liberation required organisation and mobilisation, a party, however loosely structured, cadres, however democratically organised, and a minimum of ideology, however broad, non-dogmatic and open-ended. In fact, Nehru's own model of development and social transformation depended on active pressure from below by the deprived, the exploited and the dominated. Such active popular participation in politics alone would enable parliamentary democracy to serve as an instrument of nation building, social change and equity.

But Nehru failed to help create any institutions or structures or agents through which the people or even the lower-level cadres of his own party could be mobilised and activised and politically educated. The only form of mobilisation was his extensive tours through which he communicated with the people, educated them and created popular support for his policies. Before 1947, the political harvest of his tours had been gathered by the local Congress committees and the nationalist cadres. But after 1947, in the absence of any popular level organisation to follow-up the outcome of his tours, the political and organisational benefits were more often than not reaped by the party bosses from the local to the state level.

The Nehruvian period, it is noteworthy, did not witness greater participation by the people in the political processes except in the form of elections. Actually, there was gradual demobilisation of the people and the weakening over time of the link between politics from below and the national leadership in power as also between politics and social and constructive work; at least in the medium run-to be calculated in decades, electoral politics strengthened the hold of the local economic and political elite.

Nehru also failed to build institutions and organisational structures to implement his vision or policies or to mobilise the people behind them; he created no social instruments and this led to a general weakness in execution of his policies and ideas, and was a major reason for the shortcomings in the implementation of the land reforms, the execution of the Community Development project and the management of the public sector.

The Congress party could have played the role of organising secular and nationalist forces to back Nehru's policies and to popularise and to mobilse the people behind them. But Nehru also neglected party-building, even after he acquired complete control over it in 1951. He had never been a builder or organiser of the party before independence. But this weakness became a serious flaw after Gandhiji and Sardar Patel, stalwart organisers of the party before 1947, left the scene and Nehru became its sole leader. One result of this was that Congress was increasingly weakened as an organisation and began to lose its role as an instrument for social change or the implementation of government policies or even education in the party ideology. Instead, it gradually veered towards machine politics.

The consequence was that Nehru increasingly started relying on government administration and bureaucracy for implementing his policies. Even the Community Development programme and the Panchayati Raj, the two great efforts to involve the people in their own development, ended up under bureaucratic control; and the village level social worker, the kingpin in rural reconstruction, became a cog in the bureaucratic machine and spent as little time as possible in the village. Furthermore, the administrative structure and the bureaucracy remained unreformed and unreconstructed and as distant from the people as before.

To conclude, as the first prime minister of independent India, Nehru was faced with daunting tasks. In spite of this, measured by any historical standards his achievements were of gigantic proportions. He rooted certain values, approaches, objectives, goals and an outlook and made them an integral part of the ethos of the Indian people. As one of his biographers, Geoffrey Tyson has said, 'If Nehru had been a different kind of man, India would have become a different kind of country.'

Nehru and the Nehru era have receded into historical memory. Most Indians – even those who during his life-time were his harsh critics – hark back to the Nehru era, identify with him, and draw inspiration from his life and work, his social vision, and the values he sustained in the endeavour to build a happier and healthier society in which class, caste and gender oppression would cease to exist. The legacy he left behind is in many respects a sheet-anchor for the Indian people who are today buffeted about in a sea of despair. What more could a people ask from a leader? Has any society, any people the right to ask a leader, however great, to solve all its problems once and for all?

Indian Democracy and Development

Here the book discusses the Indian Democracy and Development after its independence. India alone among the post-colonial countries has sustained a democratic and civil libertarian policy since its inception. India has impressive achievements to its credit in the political and economic arena. Further it has been noticed that a prominent and positive feature of Indian political development in the post-independence period has been the steadily growing political awareness among the people and their greater direct and indirect participation in the political process.

India since independence is able to maintain her democracy and is called as the largest democracy in the world. After ups and down in economic sector, India is an industrial hub in region and due to such development she is considered as one of the largest growing economy in Asia. Food production has been increased and she is now self-sustained country.

Democratic Political Systems

The great success story of independent India has been its secular, federal and multi-party political system. The nation has had to face tasks of immense magnitude and confront numerous problems, e.g., having to function in a backward economy with an impoverished citizenry, being torn by violent social conflicts, having to wage three major wars and face high costs of national defence since 1947, gradual weakening of many of its institutions and being constantly under international pressure. Despite all this, the political system has, however, shown remarkable resilience and flexibility and has stood the test of time and exhibited an ability to overcome several crises.

Political stability has been an important characteristic of independent India's political system. There have been since 1967, rapid changes of governments in the states and since 1989, at the Centre, but political stability has persisted. Different political forces and formations have, waged their political battles in the political arena prescribed by the Constitution. Changes in governments have taken place according to constitutional and democratic rules and have invariably been quietly and often gracefully accepted by those voted out of power by the parliament or the electorate.

The political system has also acquired more or less unquestioned legitimacy, the few who have questioned its basic tenets having fallen in line in the end. Thus, the Communists for several decades challenged, though only in theory, the basic constitutional structure as being geared to domination by the ruling, exploiting classes. But today they are among the more vocal defenders of the Constitution. The communalists have been trying from the outset to undermine the secular character of Indian society and polity but even they pay verbal obeisance to secularism though they try to distort its character redefinition.

Entrenchment of Democracy

Perhaps the most significant of India's achievements since 1947 is the firm entrenchment of political democracy and civil liberties which have become a basic feature of Indian life. Indians enjoy today a free Press, the freedom to speak, travel and form associations, the right to freely criticise the government; they have competitive elections, unrestricted working of political parties, an independent judiciary, the right to participate in political life and to change the government through the ballot-box, and freedom from fear of arbitrary arrest.

India alone among the post-colonial countries has sustained a democratic and civil libertarian polity since its inception. Commitment to democratic values has deepened over the years among most Indians. Paradoxically, even the experience of the Emergency underlined this attachment. The belief has also taken root that social transformation through a democratic political framework is possible. Nationalisation of banks and several industries, land reforms – even quite radical as in Kerala and West Bengal – and effective functioning of *Panchayati Raj*, with its provision for 30 per cent reservation of seats for women, and successful and unopposed working of the system of reservations for the Scheduled Castes and Tribes in several states, has shown that political democracy as such is not an obstacle to social transformation and socio-economic reforms in the direction of equity and equality.

A prominent and positive feature of Indian political development in the post-independence period has been the steadily growing political awareness among the people and their greater direct and indirect participation in the political process.

People have also become aware of the power and value of their right to vote at various levels from the panchayats to the parliament and of the benefits to be derived from its exercise. The politics of booth-capturing, sale and purchase of votes, vote-banks and patronage have been gradually receding and the voter's choice becoming more autonomous. People now tend to vote according to issues, policies, ideologies or group interests so as to garner greater advantage from the government's development and welfare schemes.

It is true that the role of caste in electoral politics has increased in recent years, but quite often caste as a political factor has come in primarily when other social, economic and political issues have been absent in the electoral arena or when such issues have got grouped around caste as in the case of jobs and educational opportunities. However, caste as a factor in politics has invariably receded when broader national issues have come to occupy centre-stage as in the *garibi hatao* election of 1971, the JP Movement of 1974-75, the anti-Emergency election of 1977 and the 1984 election, after the assassination of Indira Gandhi, when the country was seen to be in danger.

The voters have not only become more sensitive to the larger social, economic and political issues but are also more assertive and demanding – the people they vote for have to respond more actively to their needs and demands.

Forms of Political Protest

Political protest, along with the right to vote, is one of the basic ingredients and a normal part of democratic politics. For the oppressed sections of society, it is a critical part of their effective participation in politics and essential for the expression of their demands and grievances. India is, therefore, going to have more, not less, protest as different sections of society awaken to political life and work for faster changes in their social condition. Protest movements are also very important means for the people to force those in authority, particularly those wielding political power, to respond to their demands.

Popular protest movements by political parties, students, workers, farmers, government employees and common citizens have most often taken the form of demonstrations, hunger strikes, *hartals*, strikes in the work place or educational institutions, dharnas, bandhs, gheraos, blockages of roads (*rasta roko)*, *satyagraha*, civil disobedience or disobedience of laws, leading to mass arrests, and rioting. The purpose of such protest movements is, however, not to convince the concerned authority of the justness of their demands, or to win it over by 'changing his heart', to use a Gandhian phrase, but to erode its authority and to coerce it to accept their demands.

Economic Performance

Independent India's economy has been quite vibrant and its performance on the whole satisfactory. It has made long strides in almost all different aspects though the extent of achievement is not what was possible and what was needed.

India has overcome economic stagnation and broken through the vicious circle of poverty-underdevelopment-poverty. It has also broken from the colonial economic structure and has been successful in laying the foundations of a self-reliant, independent economy. It has thus fulfilled the design of the founders of the Republic, to go from political independence to economic independence.

Immediately after independence, India successfully developed an economic pattern of its own, namely, a mixed economy, which placed equal emphasis on the active economic role of the state and the market and developed a complementary relationship between the public and the private sectors. In the last decade of the millennium, India has also been able to carry through economic reforms; dismantling bureaucratic controls and licence-quota *raj* and developing a closer integration with the world economy, through a gradual process, without hurting the economy or the people's living standards.

India has also been able to transform its landlord-ridden, semi-feudal agrarian structure, though with many weaknesses and not to the benefit of the landless.

Stagnation of the colonial period in agricultural production and productivity has come to an end with agriculture growing more than three and a half times since 1950. India has achieved self-sufficiency in food with foodgrains production having grown at three per cent per year. Famines have become a distant memory, despite periodic droughts. The effect of the monsoons on agricultural production lessens with the passage of time.

Industry has grown more than seventeen times since 1950. It has moreover, undergone structural transformation and considerable diversification. The weakness in the basic and capital goods sector has been overcome to a considerable, though not to the desirable extent. The share of this sector in total industrial production has gone up sharply, and India's dependence on the advanced countries for basic goods and capital equipment has been greatly reduced.

There has also been a massive expansion of power, transport and banking sectors. India has also become more or less self-sufficient in defence production with capacity to produce long-range missiles and atomic weapons, though it still has to purchase some items of highly sophisticated defence equipment from abroad. It has also acquired a large trained scientific and technical force.

India's national income has grown more than seven-fold since 1950 and its per capita income by two and a half time despite a very high rate of population growth.

India has during the last few years entered a period of high economic growth and is on the way to becoming an important global economic power. As such it is bound to play a major role in the world economy of the twenty-first century.

Economic Problems and Dangers

Under Nehru and Indira Gandhi it was attempted to bridge the gap between India and the advanced countries by concentration on heavy industry and electricity generation. This was a necessary task for India had to compress in a few decades what Europe had achieved in more than 150 years. But while we were running to catch up with the past, the present was moving into the future in the advanced parts of the world. While the vision and the objectives of the Nehru era – that of catching up with the western world while being self-reliant and retaining economic independence and on that basis building a more egalitarian and just society – have to continue to inspire the Indian people, the means and goals of technological transformation have to undergo a change. The world economy has entered a new, momentous phase. Application of science to industry, agriculture, trade and communication has taken another leap forward.

Planning and an active role of the state in economic development, including the role of the public sector in production, still retain their great significance for without them Indian cannot hope to compete in the new technology sector. However, the public sector has to be not only maintained but also made more productive through the more efficient use of resources and competition with the private sector. It also needs to be freed from the stranglehold of political patronage and the ill-fitting and incompetent bureaucracy.

The Areas of Darkness

Wide prevalence of poverty, inequality and social injustice and the poor quality of life of the vast majority of the people are the major areas of darkness in India's social and economic development. A change in the social and economic condition of the people has occurred since independence but at too slow a rate.

Putting forward the social objectives of planning before the parliament in 1954, Jawaharlal Nehru had said:

> "We are starting planning for the 360 million human beings in India...What do the 360 million people want?...it is obvious enough that they want food; it is obvious enough that they want clothing, that they want shelter, that they want health...I suggest that the only policy that we should have in mind is that we have to work for the 360 million people; not for a few, not for a group but the whole lot, and to bring them up on an equal basis."

Poverty

In the early sixties, the Planning Commission formulated the concept of the poverty line. Below this line were people whose consumption, especially of foodgrains, did not come up to a minimum level in terms of calories. While no figures were available for the colonial period or the early years after independence, it was calculated that in 1970-71 nearly 59 per cent of the population was living below the poverty line. Since then, this figure has been steadily going down. It had declined to 51.3 in 1977-78, 44.5 in 1983, and 36 in 1993-94. the obverse side of these figures is that over 300 million people, equal to the population of India at the moment of freedom, are still below the poverty line. Moreover, poverty varies across different states, being as high as 63 per cent in Bihar, and 20 per cent in Punjab and Haryana in 1993-94. The main brunt of poverty is borne by landless agricultural labourers, small and marginal farmers and the urban poor.

The reduction in poverty levels was largely the result of various anti-poverty, mostly employment generating programmes initiated in the mid-seventies by the Indira Gandhi government under the guidance of one of India's finest and socially committed economists, Sukhamoy Chakravarty. These programmes have been pursued more vigorously, though still inadequately financed, since 1984-85. As the figures show, they have had a significant impact despite corruption and the failure to always reach the targeted groups. Particularly effective has been the Employment Guarantee Scheme (EGS) in Maharashtra. In this context, it may be pertinent to point out that what made possible the taking-up and implementation of the anti-poverty programmes, was the radical restructuring of the Indian economy brought about by the Nehruvian planning strategy during the fifties and sixties.

Even apart from the proof of the poverty line statistics, it is observed that Indians no longer live in abysmal poverty as they did under colonialism. The mass starvation of that period has been conquered. India has not had a major famine since the Bengal famine of 1943. In the worst drought of the century in 1987-88 very few died of hunger or disease. The same was the experience of the serious droughts of 1965-67 and 1972-73.

Similarly, in the colonial period and the immediate post-independence years a vast number of Indians went without two meals a day, several months in a year, and sometimes without even one meal. A recent study has shown that the number of people who could not obtain two square meals a day had dropped to 19 per cent of the households in 1983 and to less than five per cent in 1994.

The reduction in the incidence of poverty is also indicated by the greater availability of foodgrains and other food items over the years. For example, while per capita foodgrains consumption fell by over 24 per cent between 1901 and 1941, it increased from 394.9 grams per day in 1951 to 468.8 grams per day in 1971 and 507.7 grams per day in 1995 – an overall increase of 28 per cent. This growth in availability is also evident in the case of several other items of consumption. The annual availability of cloth per head was 9 metres in 1950, 15 metres in 1960 and 29.3 metres in 1995.

We have already pointed out earlier, that per capita income, a crucial aspect of standard of living, has increased by 250 per cent from 1950 to 1995. From 1975 to 1995, it has grown at the rate of 2.8 per cent per year, which compares favourably with the rates of increase in per capita income in advanced countries at a comparative stage of development.

The Health Care and Education

An Indian's life expectancy at birth which was 32 years in 1950 rose to 45.6 years in 1970 and to 63 years in 1998 – very creditable indeed. But it was already 69.8 and 73.1 years in 1997 in China and Sri Lanka respectively. The rise in life expectancy in India was basically the result of the steep fall in death rate per thousand from 27.4 in 1940 to 14.9 in 1970 and 8.9 in 1997.

Infant mortality rate per 1,000 live births which was 227 in 1941 had fallen to 130 in 1970 and to 71 in 1997. However, it was much lower for China (38) and Sri Lanka (17) in 1997. Another sad fact observed is that too many women still die in India during childbirth. The current maternity mortality rate per hundred thousand live births in India is as high as 507 compared to 95 in China and 140 in Sri Lanka. One reason for this is that 60 per cent of all child births in rural India are still attended to only by untrained persons.

Promises to Keep

No doubt we still have 'promises to keep and miles to go...' We still face challenges of poverty, disease, illiteracy, inequality, social backwardness, and gender and caste discrimination and oppression. But there is no ground for pessimism or resignation, for frustration or lack of pride. Many of our current problems are the outcome of the tremendous changes we have undergone and not because of regression or stagnation. Despite many maladies and shortfalls, India has impressive achievements to its credit in the economic and political arena. It has made significant progress towards social justice. As a result to economic development and transformation of the agricultural and industrial production base of society during the last half century, India has now the resources to further its social agenda.

The major reason for our optimism lies in our belief that a vibrant democracy can find a solution for these problems. Women, the rural poor and the oppressed castes have increasingly come to believe that a better, more humane life is possible. They have woken up to the political power that is inherent in them. India's democratic political system, despite many weaknesses, provides them the framework in which to exercise that power. The power of the people in a democracy is the 'liberating deluge' that can, and we are sure will, sweep away the accumulated dirt of the ages. This is, of course, all the more reason for the preservation and deepening of democracy in India.

13

The Impact and Legacy of British Rule in India

Introduction

The polemical debate about the nature of British impact on India started in the second half of the nineteenth century and continues even to-day. Nationalist writers like Dababhai Naoroji, R.C. Dutt, D.E. Wacha, S.N. Banerjee began the task of assessing the merits and defects of British rule in India and developed the theme that Britain was exploiting India and draining away her wealth. Such writings and the challenge of Indian nationalism put the British historians on the defensive. To counter this nationalist viewpoint, administrator-historains like J.F. Stephen, John Strachey, Alfred Lyall, W.W. Hunter developed the theory of 'paternalism and trusteeship' and dwelt at length on the 'civilising mission' of Britain in India, ignoring altogether its impact on Indian society and the Indian response to British policies.

The shock of the First World War, the growing popularity of the nationalist movement and the wider appeal of the anti-imperialist slogans after the Russian Revolution of 1917 brought some change in the complexion of the 'balance sheet' debate. Though British writers like Ramsay Muir, P.E. Roberts, H.H. Doodwell et al still not tired of recounting, 'the immeasurable services to the peoples of India'. 'the priceless gifts of Britain to the Indian people', yet some of them, P.E. Roberts for example, admitted 'the inherent reasonableness of

India's claim to manage her own affairs'. Indian nationalist writers like Tilak, Lajpat Rai, Gandhi, Rajendra Prasad, Nehru et. al. became increasingly critical of Britain's 'negative role' in India and held her responsible for most of the ills of Indian society and economy.

In the post-independence period English writers like Percival Spear, Percival Griffiths, Philip Woodruff[1], Michael Edwards et. al. have endeavoured to strike a balance between the plundering and constructive role of Britain in India. Woodruff, for example, finds the ultimate justification of British rule in the reaction it provoked which in turn stung political life into India. Edwards dwells on Britain's scaffolding of Free India and Pakistan and points out that out of exploitation came a unity of purpose and out of tyranny a sense of nationhood. Philips Mason in a somewhat comic style likens to the Anglo-Indian association to a forced marriage between the masculine John Bull and the docile Indian girl which ended in divorce on *15th August 1947* now in a reminiscent mood both parties have some pleasant memories and some regrets and have decided to forgive and forget and be friends on equal terms.

Whatever developments – political, administrative, economic, social or intellectual – India witnessed during two centuries of British rule here were not planned by the colonial rulers out of any philanthropic mission for the good of India, but were merely offshoots of the imperial rulers larger aim of keeping firm their bold over India or for promoting the political, economic or material interests of their own country. It may be even more correct to say that political and social changes came in spite of the British or as an incidental or unexpected consequence of their activities. Jawaharlal Nehru has rightly commented that "changes came to India because of the impact of the West, but these came almost inspite of the British in India... They succeeded in slowing down the pace of those changes".

The impact of British rule may be summarised under the following heads:

Political

Political unification of India under one centralised government was perhaps the most significant development under British Rule.

The inexorable logic of imperialism worked a full circle till the whole of India from the Himalayas to Cape Comorin and from Chittagong to the Khyber Pass passed under British control. If the British Indian provinces were under 'direct' British rule, Indian States came under 'indirect' imperial rule. The British could rightly take pride that the British empire encompassed more extensive territories than the Mauryan or Mughal empires ever did.

Britain also gave to India – what British writers are never weary of emphasising – the Blessings of Peace. She maintained a strong army both for external defence and maintenance of internal security. Britain also organised a strong police for maintenance of law and order-all at a heavy expense to the Indian taxpayer.

Jawaharlal Nehru made a pertinent observation that the British undoubtedly rescued India from chaos and anarchy – that chaos and anarchy which was partly at least due to the aggressive and ambitious policy of the East India Company and their representatives in India. Further, the British used the strong military and police forces not for maintaining peace in the country but also for suppression of popular movements.

Another impact of British rule was the emergence of the spirit of Indian nationalism and the growth of the Indian nationalist movement. If political necessities compelled the imperial rulers to have a single administrative set-up for the whole of India, considerations of military defence and economic exploitation goaded them to develop the means of transport and communications through a network of roads and railways and efficient organisation of the post and telegraph systems. These developments gave India the appearance of unity and fostered the spirit of one-mindedness. The emergence of an English-education middle class intelligentsia and the development of the modern press fostered the modern concepts of nationalism, nationality, political rights etc. which in turn cleared the ground for the formation of an all India political organisation like the Indian National Congress.

Enlightened imperialists like A.O. Hume, William Wedderburn, George Yule, Alfred Webb, Henry Cotton et. al. tried to keep the Indian National Congress as a 'loyal and innocuous' organisation in the beginning and even used its official platform for pro-British and anti-Russian propaganda. The Indian National Congress came of age in the beginning of the twentieth century and started questioning the very moral right of Britain to rule India. The demand for *Swaraj* followed.

The development of Indian nationalism was never to the liking of British rulers of India. They used a thousand and one methods to weaken the movement. The Anglo-Indian bureaucracy which looked upon the Congress as a Hindu organisation worked hard to keep the Muslim community away from political agitation. The introduction of the system of reservation of seats for different communities in the Central Legislative Council, Provincial Legislative Councils and even Local Bodies; the principle of reservation of government jobs on communal basis in the junior civil services, in the police, in the army and other services – were all calculated to hinder the development of a healthy political and social outlook on national issues. The British also regimented the Indian Princes as a Third Force in Indian politics. The policy of 'counterpoises' roped in not only the Indian princes, but also the big *zamindars* and even the scheduled castes among the Hindus. Thus British policies struck at the very root of the solidarity of Indian nationalism. Before Britain quit India in 1947, it partitioned India into two independent states of India and Pakistan and left the Indian princely states a potential source for mischief. The fear of Balkanisation stared India in the face. Thus the Indian National Congress' goal of a strong undivided free India was shattered, mainly due to the machiavellian policies of imperial Britain. The British who had always claimed credit for creating a strong unified India left behind a divided and weak India. Truly, had Karl Marx prophesied that Britain's role in India was 'swinish' and it would 'Irelandise India'.

Britain also claimed to have introduced in India a parliamentary system of government with the larger ideal of a democratic setup for the country. British writers are never weary of reiterating the existence of oriental despotism from the earliest times down to the Mughal times, particularly emphasising that no other system of government has been known in the country. Britain, it is claimed, inherited the autocratic system of government, but decided to introduce a liberal scheme of administration. The origin of democratic political ideals is traced since the governor-generalship of William Bentick. A beginning towards the introduction of a representative system was made by the Indian Councils Acts of 1861, 1892 and 1909. It is also claimed that a conscious direction to British policy in India towards self-government was given by the Government of India Act, 1919 and extended by the Government of India Act, 1935 through the introduction of diarchy and provincial autonomy. Sir Verney Lovett, writing in 1919, reiterated, "Britain is pledged to establish a democratic system of government over two-thirds of India" and yet the British system of government in India remained despotic till its end in 1947.

True, British despotism succeeded oriental despotism. The colonial rulers cloaked British despotism in a constitutional garb and made it a 'constitutional autocracy'.

Law and Administration

Perhaps the most abiding impact of British rule has been in the field of law and administration. The British rulers introduced the Rule of Law in their territories. Even the meanest subject enjoyed personal liberty. For example, the principle of *habeas corpus* provided that no person could be arrested or kept in prison without a written order from the local executive-cum-judicial authority, even if the viceroy desired otherwise. Even Government servants, for acts done by them in their official capacity, could be sued in the law courts. A natural corollary to the principle of rule of law was the principle of Equality before the Law. This certainly was a novel feature in a caste-ridden society. Further, the British rulers carried out a Codification of Law, The Code of Civil Procedure (1859), the Penal Code (1860) and the Code of Criminal Procedure (1861) laid down in clear, precise and exact language the law applicable to all citizens, high and low irrespective of the caste, creed or religious professions of the parties involved. The British also set up a gradation of courts, civil and criminal, for the trial of petty to heinous crimes with the right to appeal to High Courts and even an appeal to a Committee of the Privy Council in civil suits.

The legal system introduced by the British was not without its shortcomings. It was complicated and beyond the comprehension of the common man. It was very expensive and the rich had the opportunity to wear out the poor and the uneducated. Falsehood, chicanery and deceit paid high dividend. The inordinate delay in the decision of cases was another negative feature of the system. The lawyer class had vested interest in prolonging cases and pleading for clients who could afford to engage them. Even the government of the Free India has not been able to remove these deficiencies from the legal system. Perhaps, the worst aspect of the legal system in British times was the special procedure laid down for trial of Europeans in criminal cases. The Ilbert Bill highlighted the injustice involved in racial discriminations in judicial matters but provided no remedial measures.

The organisation of an Indian Civil Service which worked according to set rules and with machine-like efficiency and impartiality was another striking feature of the administration in contrast to the personal rule of the monarch or his governors as the case might have been in pre-British times. The I.C.S. officers worked as Collectors, Magistrates and Judges and maintained a high standard of impartiality and integrity unmindful of the likes or dislikes of the Governor General or even the Prime Minister of England. Professor B.B. Misra writes, "Among the contributions of British rule in India the creation of the Indian Civil Service is one of the most remarkable. It constituted in fact the spine of the Indian body politic, and to it the people generally looked for the protection of person and property, of life and liberty".

The much-praised I.C.S. was not without its drawbacks. In spite of repeated resolutions of the British parliament and announcements by the British monarchs about recruitment to the I.C.S. on the basis of competitive examination irrespective of racial considerations, the I.C.S. remained a close preserve of Europeans. Various subterfuges like holding the examination in London alone, keeping low the maximum age limit for entrance, drawing the syllabus to suit English boys, interview evaluation, riding tests-were used to keep the Indians out of these services. Further, the much-praised virtue of efficiency became a vice because it was, as Rabindranath Tagore put it, 'untouched by hand' i.e. they became insensitive to the feelings of the people and to the new currents of thought and never bothered to gain the goodwill and co-operation of the people whom they despised. Worst still, the I.C.S. developed a cult of its indispensability for India and unconsciously developed the sense of identifying India with their own interests. As Jawaharlal Nehru has put it, "They ran India, they wore India and anything that was harmful to their interests must of necessity be injurious to India". Indian nationalists rightly resented the fabulous salary and liberal allowances and still lavish pensionary benefits paid to the I.C.S. and interpreted these as a big channel in the drain of wealth from India. Dadabhai Naoroji described the I.C.S. as 'leeches' which sucked Indian blood.

Today the I.A.S. officers are advised not to be guided by the old imperial tradition, but to accept new social responsibilities and work as useful limbs in the working of a democratic set-up.

Education, Oriental Studies and Indian Renaissance

Intellectually eighteenth century India presented the picture of a stagnant society. The traditional system of education had greatly suffered during the political instability of the period. The new Renaissance spirit of scientific enquiry, skepticism, humanism and aggressive materialism which was rapidly transforming the West had not reached India. The political confusion of the eighteenth century which European intervention further accentuated delayed the infiltration of progressive ideas into India.

The Christian missionaries of Serampore – Carey, Ward & Marshaman – with the Cross in their hands were the first to open schools for Indian children. Their educational endeavours were just a means for their higher aim of proselytisation. Compulsion of administrative organisation, commercial penetration and need for cheaper clerks to man the lower rungs of the administration goaded the British government to provide in the Charter Act of 1813 a clause requiring the East India Company to annually set apart a sum of one lakh of rupees on the improvement of education in India. Some progressive Indians like Ram Mohun Roy urged the government to spend this fund on instructing Indians in mathematics, natural philosophy, chemistry, anatomy and other useful sciences. The Company's authorities dilly-dallied for two decades before a final decision was taken by the Committee of Public Instruction in 1835 under Lord Macaulay's chairmanship and adopted by William Bentinck's government to spend the allocated amount for "English education alone". Macaulay's aim was, in his own words, "to create a class of persons who would be Indians in blood and colour but English in tastes, in opinions, in morals and in intellect", apart from banishing idolatry in India.

Some painstaking British scholars devoted themselves to the study of Sanskrit, Philology, Indian culture and Indian history. Sir William Jones identified Chandragupta Maurya with Sandrokottus of Greek historians and this proved a landmark in Indian chronology, James Prinsep and Henry Masser deciphered the *Brahmi* script translated the Asokan inscriptions and many texts of Buddhist literature. This opened a new chapter in the history of ancient India. Further, the efforts of William Jones, founder of the Bengal Asiatic Society, Jonathan Duncan and other orientalists rekindled interest in the study of ancient Indian literature.

English writers take credit for England having heralded the Indian Renaissance. Percival Griffiths writes, "Whatever else of good or evil Britain may have achieved in India, she may justly claim to have brought about the great Indian Renaissance". It is hard to believe that modern political thought and scientific advances of the eighteenth and nineteenth centuries would not have reached India but for the British imperial rule in India. From times immemorial India had followed an open-door policy and even during the age of primitive means of transport and communications had maintained effective trade and cultural links both with the East and the West. Thus, the wind of new ideas from the west would have reached India even without

British rule. Jawaharlal Nehru rightly puts it, "some beneficent changes came inspite of them or as an incidental and unexpected consequence of their activities". Rather, it would be more correct to say that British imperial rule diluted the beneficent impact of world progressive developments in India.

The British over-emphasis on education through the English medium and faith in the 'infiltration theory' limited the spread of education to an elite class and neglect of the education of the masses, thus creating a gulf between the English – educated and the masses. The government turned its face even against spread of higher education towards the last quarter of the nineteenth century when it found its spread working against imperial interests. Further, the overemphasis on liberal education and utter neglect of technical education produced the phenomenon of educated unemployed.

The British pattern of liberal education and educational policies contained some inner contradictions. The emergence of modern political consciousness, political organisations and political agitations were as much a result of British educational policies as a reaction to imperial policies. It was a section of the English educated intelligentsia which exposed the true nature of imperial rule and provided leadership to modern political movements. Taken in this light the Macaulayan scheme of education proved beneficent to it.

Social and Cultural Impact

Western impact has been all pervading in the fields of Indian social life, has greatly influenced art, architecture, painting, literature, poetry, drama, novels and even Indian religions and philosophy. The pace-setters in these fields have been English public servants and men of letters and the carriers were largely the English – educated class who dominated the few professions of journalists, teachers, lawyers, doctors etc. It was this Indian intelligentsia who spearheaded most of the social and political organisations in the country.

Western models, or better still modern world models in social etiquette, dress, eating habits, dwelling units, furniture designs, better awareness about private and public hygiene, new modes of entertainment have penetrated deep into Indian life though traditional Indianness is writ large in the countryside.

Change is a continuous process and India certainly would have witnessed social changes with or without British contact. Even after the British have quit India, world currents in social outlook, dress, food habits, movie styles and even fashions and hair styles are penetrating deep into Indian life just as Indian models in some spheres are influencing world models.

The British rulers built town-halls after the Renaissance. Railway stations in the Gothic cathedral style, government buildings and secretariat offices in the western style with an admixture of traditional Mugahal models. The Western-educated class copied these models in their private buildings and personal residences. In the field of painting Ravi Varma, Abanindranath, *gogonenedranath*, Jamini Ray and Amrita Sher-Gil were greatly influenced by the Western style. In the field of literature Rabindranath Tagore, Aurobindo Ghosh, Sarojini Naidu, Mulk Raj Anand, R.K. Narayan to mention only a few names were influenced by the English pattern. In 1913 Rabindranath Tagore's talent was recognised by the award of a Nobel Prize for Literature.

English words and idioms have penetrated into vernacular languages. Words like station, railway, cinema, hospital, vote, election, restaurant, hotel, union etc. are understood even by the illiterate living in remote villages of Inda. Similary, phrases like Government's responsibility, right to work, right to food, shelter and social security, right to organise the workers, right to equality before the law, right to freedom of speech, debate, movement etc. etc. have become common place idioms in Indian life.

Economic Impact

Since the main motivation behind British intrusion and subsequent domination of India was commercial and economic, the British impact in the economic sphere has been the most deleterious and devastating. Britain used the most sophisticated methods to exploit India's vast and rich economic potential. If even after two centuries of the most close contact and complete control of Indian economy by the British – technologically the most advanced nation in the world – India in 1947 presented the picture of an economically underdeveloped nation with hunger, poverty, low national income, the responsibility must lie squarely on the shoulders of the British imperial rulers.

Indian agriculture received the maximum care under the East India Company primarily because the main source of state income was land revenue. The company tried various experiments to maximise the land revenue by resorting to the method of 'open auction to the highest bidder'. The system of farming of land revenue did not work. Cornwallis introduced the Permanent Settlement of Land Revenue in Bengal, Bihar and Orissa in 1793. Subsequent administrators introduced the Ryotwari system in Bombay Presidency and most parts of the Madras Presiency, the *Mahlwari* system (a) variation of the *Zamindari* system) in U.P. and with some further variations in the Punjab. The *Zamindari* system encouraged absentee landlordism and created a host of intermediaries between the state and the cultivator – all working to the misery of the cultivator. Even in the *Ryotwari* (revenue collection) tracts, the excessive land revenue demand – periodically revised upwards – bought in the money-lender as an important factor in rural India. Rural indebtedness, backward methods of cultivation, inadequate irrigation facilities resulted in pauperisation of the rural masses. Famines visited frequently claiming a heavy toll of life. In the latter half of the nineteenth century 24 famines, modest and severe, scourged India and claimed an estimated toll of three crores of the population.

Indian industry suffered the maximum at the hands of the British intruder. The superiority and extensive sale of Indian handicrafts in Europe and even in the British markets was anathematic to the interests of the commercial East India Company. The Whig government of the early eighteenth century imposed heavy duties on Indian textile imports in Britain. However, after the Napoleonic wars, the Indian markets were increasingly thrown open to British industrial products. The same British government which had earlier excluded Indian cotton goods from English markets by high protective legislation, now permitted British machine-made goods to be poured into India duty free or at nominal duties. This policy of one way free trade which ruined Indian handicrafts was the price India had to pay for the loss of her freedom. Even a British writer, H.H. Wilson has conceded that Britain "employed the arm of Political injustice to keep down and ultimately strangle a competitor with whom he could not have contended on equal terms." Karl Marx, writing in 1853 commented, "It was the British intruder who broke up the Indian handloom and destroyed the spinning wheel. England began with depriving the Indian cottons from the European market; it then introduced twist into Hindustan and in the end inundated the very mother country of cotton with cottons". Even William Bentinck wrote in 1834, "The misery hardly finds a parallel in the history of commerce. The bones of the Indian weavers are bleaching the plains of India". Thus Indian handicrafts declined in the nineteenth century.

Could Indian handicraft industry stand the challenge posed by rising capitalism and industrial Revolution? The capitalist mode of production and bourgeoisie commerce had destroyed handicraft industries in European countries too. While in Europe the destructive process had been accompanied by a corresponding growth of new forces of industrial production, the peculiar unhappy situation in the Indian economic scene was that the loss of the old world was without the emergence of a new world. The process of industrial regeneration did not start in India because of British imperial policies in India.

Far from not planning the industrialisation of India, the imperial rulers deliberately followed policies to the de-industrialisation of this country. Britain's interest laid in converting and preserving India as an 'agricultural farm' of industrialised Britain. Thus, the British rulers deliberately carried out the policy of 'ruralisation' and 'peasantilisation' of Indian economy. Whatever few Indian industries developed under the situation created by World War I and the economic depression of 1930s suffered from another disability that these were mostly controlled by British finance and capital. True, textile, cement, jute, paper, sugar, pig iron industries started in India, but the country lagged behind in the development of iron and steel, heavy engineering and metallurgical industries.

The 'gestation theory' popularised by modern Anglo-American scholars does not hold good even after a casual scrutiny of facts and figures. England's role in India was imperial, the Englishman's mission in India was economic exploitation, the Whiteman's Burden' was the burden of wealth that the Whiteman carried out of India.

Undoubtedly, British rule has left behind indelible marks, for good or for bad, on almost every aspect of Indian life. European ways of thinking and European patterns have taken firm roots among urbanities who control the strings of India's destiny. The rich legacy of difficulties particularly in the economic field, are an ever present reminder of the exploitative character of European imperialism in India. If at all there were some traces of modernisation on the Western model, the British imperial rulers took care of deprive the people of India of a significant share in the benefits.

It was realised that free India cannot at one stroke write off the deep influences of two centuries of British imperial rule in India. The British rulers created a new structure of colonial institutions a colonial economy, a colonial society and even a colonial idealogy. The institutions of landlordism, politically loaded casteism, communalism, regionalism etc, which were encouraged by imperial rulers to perpetuate their rule are evils defying easy eradication. Further, 'distorted modernisation' has created new problems. Thus, Britain left behind in 1947 a bleeding polity, a ruined economy, a sick society and above all, the ever present danger of neo-colonialism lurking all around.

Bibliography and Notes

1

Bakshi, S.R. *British Diplomacy and Administration in India*. New York: Rastiya Printing Works, 1971

Beauchamp, J. *British Imperialism in India*, London: Martin Lawrence Ltd., 1934.

Brown, G.N. *Great Britain in the Indian Ocean,* London: Oxford University Press, 1967.

Carringtone, C.E. *The British Overseas*, London: Macmillan, 1950.

Fergusson, N., Empire: *How British made the Modern World,* London: Penguin, 2004.

Furnivall, J.S. *Colonial Policy and Practice*, New York: New York University Press, 1956.

Guuicharnaud, J. *History of the India*, London: Routledge and Kegan Paul, 1966.

Grover, B.L and Grover, *S. A New Look at Modern Indian History.* New Delhi: S. Chand & Company Limited, 2001.

Hughes, E.R. *The Invasion of China by the Western World*, London: Adam and Charles Black, 1968.

Langer, W.L. *European Alliances and Alignments* 1871-90, New York: Alfred A. Knopf, 1965.

Mukherjee, S.N. *A Study of Eighteenth Century British Attitudes to India*, Cambridge: Cambridge University Press, 1968.

Munro, T., *British Imperialism 1750-1950*, Cambridge: Siomn C. Smith, 1998.

Pearson, M.N.,*The Portuguese in India*,NCHI,pt 1, vol.1, Cambrigde, 1987.

Spear, T. *History of British India Under Company and Crownford*, Oxford University Press, 1952.

Stein, *B. A History of India,* (2nd Edition), West Sussex: Blackwell Publishers Ltd 2010.

2

Bhattacharya, A., *A History of Modern India*, 1757-1947, New Delhi: Ashish Publication house, 1983.

Chhabra, G.S., *Advance Study in the History of Modern India*, New Delhi, Sterling Publishers PVT.LTD, 1971.

Keay, J.,A. *History: India*, New Delhi: Herper Collins Publishers, 2004.

Kopf, D., *The Brahmo Samaj and the Shaping of the Modern Indian Mind*, Prinston, 1979.

Kulke, H. & Rothermund, D., *A History of India* (4th ed.) London: Routledge, 2004.

Lamb, B.P. India: *A World in Transition*, New York: Praeger Publisher, 1975.

Masani, R.R., *Britain in India*, London: Oxford University Press, 1960

Metcalf, D.B. & Metcalfe R.T., *A Concese History of Modern India* (2nd Ed.), Cambridge: Cambridge University Press, 2006.

Panikkar, K.N., *Culture Idiology Hagemony, Intellectual and Social Conciousness in Colonial India*, New Delhi: Sterling Publishers, 1995.

Spear,.P., *The Oxford History of Modern India, Modern India 1740-1947,* London: Oxford University Press, 1965.

Spear, P., *A History of India: from Sixteenth Century to the twentieth century,* Penguin Books India Pvt Ltd: Penguin Books, 1965.

Spear T., *History of British India under Company Rule and Crown,* London: Oxford University Press, 1952.

Stein, B., *A History of India* (2 nd ed.), West Sussex: Blackwell Publishers Ltd, 2010.

Thapar, R., *A History of India*, Delhi: Viking Press, 1991.

3

Ball,.Charles, *History of the Indian Mutiny*, 2 vol, London, 1858-59.

Bhattacharjee, A., *A History of Modern India, 1757- 1947*. New Delhi: Ashish Publishing House, 1983.

Chaudhuri, S.B., *Civil Rebellion in the Indian Mutiny1857-1969*, Calcutta: 1957.

Granger, David, *The Indian Mutiny of 1857: Causes and Consequences*. London: Oxford University Press, 2002.

Grover, B.L.and S.Grover, *A New Look at Modern Indian History*. New Delhi: S. Chad and Company Ltd., 2001.

Heehs, P., *India's Freedom Stuggle, 1857-1947: A Short History.* London: Oxford University Press, 1991.

Hibbert Christopher, *The Great Mutiny: India 1857*, Allen Lane, London, 1978.

Josh, P.C., (ed.), *Rebellion: 1857*. London: Oxford University Press, 1981.

Majumdar, R.C., *The Sepoy Mutiny and the Revolt of 1857*. Calcutta: 1963..

Mukheri, R. *The Rise and Fall of East India Company: A Sociological Appraisal,* London: Monthly Review Press, 1974.

Roberts, P.E., *History of India.* London: Oxford University press, 1965.

Smith, V.A. & Spear, P., *The Oxford History of India,,* Oxford University Press, 1981.

Spear, P., Modern India: 1740 – 1947. London: Oxford University Press, 1965.

Spear, T., *History of British India under Company Rule and Crown.* London: Oxford University Press, 1952.

Royle,T.*The Last Days of the Raj*, New Delhi: Raj Co., 2002.

4

Chabra, G.S., *Advance Study in the History of India,* New Delhi: Sterlin Publishers Pvt, Ltd, 1991.

Dalrymple,W.,*The Last Mughal : The Fall of a Dynasty*, Penguin Books India Pvt Ltd: Penguin, 2006.

Dodwell, H.H., *The Cambridge History of the British Empire,* Vol.vi, Reprinted in India, 1989.

Gopal, S. *British Policy in India*, 1858-1905, Cambridge, 1965.

Guicharnand, J., *History of the India,* London: Routledge and Kegan Paul, 1966.

Hughes, E.R. *The Invasion of China by the Western World*, London: Adam and Charles Black, 1968.

Lamb, B P., India: *A World in Transition,* Revised edition, New York: Praeger, 1968.

Mehrotra, S.R. *India and the Commonwealth 1885-1929*, London: George Allen and Unwin Ltd, 1965.

Mehrotra, S.R., *Emengence of Indian National Congress,* New Delhi:1971.

Sarkar, S. *Modern India 1885-1947,* New Delhi: Macmillan India Limited, 1983.

Spear, T., History of British India Under Company and Crown, London: Oxford University Press, 1952.

Royle, T.,*The Last Days of the Raj*, New Delhi: Raj Co., 2002.

Wood, J. R., Rajkot: *Indian Nationalism in the Princely Context; The Rajkot Satyagraha of 1938-39*, in Robin Jeffre, editor, People, Prince and Paramount Power, New Delhi; 1978

5

Bose,A.C..,Indian Revolutionaries Abroad 1905-22, Patna: 1971.

Das, S., The Indian Sepoy in the First World War, Cambridge, 2005.

Gollant, W., *The Long Afternoon: British India 1601-1947*, London: Hammilton, 1975.

Gordon,A.D.D., *Businesmen and Politics: Rising Nationalism and Modernising Economy in Bombay*, 1819-1933, Delhi: 1978.

Omissi, D. *Indian Voices of the Great War*, Basingstoke: MacMillan Press, 1999.

Panandikar, S.G., *Some Aspect of the Econmic Consequences of the War For India,* Bombay:1921.

Percival,*S. A History of India: From Sixteenth Century to Twentieth Century,* Penguin Books India Pvt Ltd, 1965.

Sarkar,S.,*Modern India: 1885-1947*, New Delhi: Macmillan India Limited, 1983.

Seal, A., *The Emergence of Indian Nationalism: Competition and Collaboration in the Later Nineteenth Century,* Cambridge: The University Press, 1968.

Verney Lovett, *A History of Indian Nationalist Movement,* New York, A. Stoke Company, 1920.

6

Andrew,C.F.*Mahatma Gandhi's Idea*, New York: The Macmillan Company, 1931.

Bose, N.K., *Studies in Gandhism,* Calcutta: Indian Associated Publishing Company, 1947.

Bose, S.C. *Indian Struggle, 1920-1934*, Calcutta: 1948.

Bolitho, H., *Jinnah,* London: John Murray, 1954.

Brown, J.M., *Gandhi's Rise to Power: Indian Politics, 1915-1922,* Cambridge, 1972.

Brown J.M., *Gandhi: Prisoner of Hope,* Delhi: 1989.

Coupland, R., *Indian Politics, 1936-42*, Bombay: 1944.

Diwakar, R.R.,*Glimpses of Gandhi, Bombay: Hind Kitab, 1949. Doke, J.J., M.K.Gandhi: An India Patriot in South Africa*, Benaras: Akhil Bharat Sarva 1959.

Elwin, *V., Mahatma Gandhi*, London: Golden Vista Press, 1932.

Fisher, L., *The Life of Mahatma Gandhi,* New York: MacMillan, 1962.

Huttenback, R.A., *Gandhi in South Africa,* New York: Ithaka, 1971.

Kamath, *M.K., Gandhi Coolie: Life and Time of Ramkrihna,* Bajaj, Allied Publishers, 1995.

Moore, R., *The Crisis of Indan Unity, 1917-1940*, Oxford, 1974.

Payene,R., *The Life and Death of Mahatma Gandhi*, New York: Smith mark publishers, 1969.

Sitaramayya, P., *A History of Indian National Congress*, 1885-1935, NP, 1935.

Vincent, N., *Mahatma Gandhi: A Great Life in Brief,* New Delhi: Ministry of Information and Broadcasting, 1968.

7

Bolitho, H., *Jinnah: Creator of Pakistan*, New York, The MacMillal Company, 1955.

Bomford, P.C., *History of Khilafat and Non-Cooperation Movement,* Delhi, 1925, reprinted 1985.

Bose, C.,*The Indian Struggle 1920-42,* Oxford: Oxford University Press, 1998.

Chandra, B., (et.al.), *India's Struggle for Independence*, New Delhi: Penguin Book Pvt. Ltd, 1987

Coupland, R., *Indian Politics 1936-1942*, Madras, 1944.

Fisher, D. & Read, A. *The Proudest Day: India's Long Road to Independence,* London & New York: W.W.Norton and Company, 1998.

Hrdy, P., *The Muslims of British India*, Cambridge, 1972

Jog, N.G., *In Freedom's Quest: A Bibliography of Netaji Subhash Chandra Bose*, New Delhi: Longman, 1969.

Lawrence,J.,*The Rise and Fall of the British Empire*, Great Britain: ABACUS, 1994.

Rolland, R., *Gandhism and Modern India,* London: Oxford University Press, 1978.

Sarkar, S., *Modern India, 1885-1947,* New Delhi: MacMillan India Limited, 1983.

Tomlinson, B.R., *The Indian National Congress and Raj, 1929-42, The Penultimate Phase*, London: 1976.

8

Campbel- Johnson, A., *Mission with Mountbatten,* London, 1953.

Collins, Larry and Lapiere, Dominique, *Freedom at Midnight,* London: Collins, 1975.

Granu, D. British *Withdrawal from India, 1945-47*, New Delhi: H.K.Publication, 1990.

Kulke, H. & Rothermund, D., *A History of India,* London: Routledge, 2004

Leonard, M., *The Last Days of the British Raj*, London: Weidenfeld and Nicolson, 1961.

Menon, V.P., *The Transfer of Power*, London: Longmans, 1953.

Moon, P., *Divide and Quit*, London: Chatto and Windus, 1961; (ed.), Wavell: *The Viceroy's Journal*, London: OUP, 1973.

Philips, C.H., & Wainwright, W. (eds), *The Partition of India; Policies and Perspectives,* 1935-1947, London:1970.

Sharma, A., *History of Modern India*, Delhi: H.K. Publication, 1992.

Stein, B., *A History of India* (2nd ed.), West Sussex: Blackwell Publishers Ltd, 2010.

Wolpert, S., *The Last Years of the British Empire in India,* New York: Oxford University Press, 2006.

Wolpert, S., Jinnah of Pakistan, New York: Oxford, 1984.

9

Datta, N., Indian History, *Encyclopaedia Britannica,* New Delhi: Encyclopaedia Britannica (India) Pvt Ltd, 2003.

Desai, M., *The Story of Bardoli*, Ahmadabad: 1957.

Moorhouse G., *India Britannica*, London: Harvill, 1983.

Parikh, N.D., *Sardar Vallabhai Patel,* Vol I, Ahmadabad, Navjivan Publishins, 1953.

Phadnis, U., *Towards the Integration of Princely States,* 1919-1947, Bombay: 1968.

Sankar, S., *Modern India 1885-1947*, New Delhi: MacMillan India limited, 1983.

Tirtha, Ramanand, *Memories of Hyderabad Freedom Struggle,* Bombay: 1967.

Wood, J. R., Rajkot: *Indian Nationalism in the Princely Context; The Rajkot Satyagraha of 1938-39*, in Robin Jeffre, editor, People, Prince and Paramount Power, New Delhi; 1978.

10 and 11

Ahluwalia, S. *Founders of New India*, Manas Publications, New Delhi, 1983.

Brown, J.M. *Modern India: The Origin of an Asian Democracy,* Oxford University Press, Oxford: 1994.

Erdmann, H, *The Swatantra Party and Indian Conservative*, Cambridge, 1967.

Government of India, Report of the States Re-Organisation Commission, New Delhi, 1955.

H. Alexander, *Consider India : An Essay in Values*, Bombay: Asia Publishing House, 1061

Hanson, A.H., *The Processed Planning: A Study of India's Five Years Plans, 1950-1964*, London, 1966.

Indian Journal of Political Science, Vol. 52, No. 2 (April-June 1991), pp. 153-164.

Kashyap, S.C. (edited), *New Delhi*: Lok Sabha Secretariat, 1986.

Keay John, *India: A History*, New Delhi: Harper Collins Publisher, 2004.

Kulke, Hard Rothermund, D., *A History of India* (4th ed), London: Routledge, Taylors and Francis Group, 200.

Lamb, B.P., India: *A World in Transition* (4th Edition), New York: Praeger Publisher, 1975.

Lawrence, J.P, India, New York: Oxford Book Company, Inc. 1971

Nair, T.P.S.(ed.) *Modern India: Society and Politics in Transition*, Inter- India Publication, New Delhi: 1988.

Wolpert, S. *A New History of India* (5th Ed.), Oxford University Press, London:1997.

12

Ahluwalia, S. *Founders of New India,* Manas Publications, New Delhi, 1983.

Kashap, Subharsh C.S.C. (edited), *New Delhi:* Lok Sabha Secretariat, 1986.

Nanda, B.R., *Mahatma Gandhi: A Biography*, New Delhi: Oxford University Press, 1981.s

Royce, T., *The Last Days of the Raj,* New Delhi: John Murray Publishers Ltd., 1997.

Sankar, S., *Modern India 1885-1947*, New Delhi: MacMillan India limited, 1983.

Sarvepally Gropal, *Jawahardal Nehru:* A Biography, New Delhi: Oxford University Press, 1989.

Spear, P., *The Oxford History of Modern India* 1740-1975 (2nd ed). New Delhi, Oxford University Press, 1978.

13

Grover, B.L. and Grover, S. *A New Look at Indian Modern History,* New Delhi: S. Chand & Company Ltd, New Delhi, 2001.

Stein, Burton, *A History of India*, New Delhi: Oxford University Press, 2001.

Kumar, D., Roychandhuri, T., etal (eds), *The Cambridge Economic Hisotry of India*: © 1957, © 1970, Cambridge: Cambridge University Press, 1983.

Appendices

Appendix I

Governor- Generals and Viceroys of British India, 1757-1947

	Name	Year
1.	Robert Clive	1757-67, 1766-67
2.	Warren Hastings	1772-85
3.	Lord Cornwallis	1786-93
4.	Lord Wellesley	1793-98
5.	Lord Minto I	1807-13
6.	Lord Hastings	1813-23
7.	Lord Amherst	1823-28
8.	Lord w. Bentinck	1828-35
9.	Lord Auckland	1836-42
10.	Lord Ellenborough	1842-44
11.	Lord Dalhousie	1849-56
12.	Lord Canning	1856-62
13.	Lord Elgin	1862-63
14.	Lord J. Lawrence	1864-69
15.	Lord Lytton	1876-80
16.	Lord Rippon	1880-84
17.	Lord Dufferin	1884-88
18.	Lord Lansdowne	1888-94
19.	Lord Elgim II	1894-99
20.	Lord Curzon	1899-1905
21.	Lord Minto II	1905-10
22.	Lord Hardinge	1910-16
23.	Lord Chelmsford	1916-21
24.	Lord Reading	1921-26
25.	Lord Irwin	1926-31
26.	Lord Willington	1931-36
27.	Lord Linlithgow	1936-43
28.	Lord Wavell	1943-47
29.	Lord Mountbatten	1947-48

Appendix II

Prime Ministers during the British India 1757-1947

	Name	Party	Year
1.	William Cavendish, Duke of Devonshire	Whig	1756
2.	John Start, Earl of Bute	Tory	1762
3.	George Grenville	Whig	1763
4.	Charles Watson-Wentworth, Marquess of Rockingham	Whig	1765
5.	William Pitt, the Earl of Chatham	Whig	1766
6.	Augustus Fitzrov, Duck of Grafton	Whig	1767
7.	Fredrick North, Lord North	Try	1770
8.	Charles Watson-Wentworth, Marquess of Rockingham	Whig	1782
9.	Thomas Pelham-Holles, Duke of Newcastle	Whig	1775
10.	William FitzMaurice, Earl of Shelburne	Whig	1782
11.	William Bentick, Duke of Portland	Tory	1783
12.	William Pitt, the Younger	Tory	1783
13.	Henry Addington	Tory	1801
14.	William Pitt, the Younger	Tory	1804
15.	Wiliam Grenville, Lord of Grenville	Whig	1806
16.	William Bentinck, Duke if England	Tory	1807
17.	Spencer Percival	Tory	1809
18.	Robert Jenkinson, Earl of Liverpool	Tory	1812
19.	George Canning	Tory	1827
20.	Fredrick Robinson, Viscount of Golderich	Tory	1827
21.	Arthur Wellesley, Duck of Wellington	Tory	1828
22&23.	Charles Gray, Earl Grey	Whig	1830
24.	William Lamb, Viscount Melbourine	Whig	1834
25.	Arthur Wellesley, Duck of Wellington	Tory	1834
26.	Sir Robert Peel	Tory	1834
27.	William Lamb, Viscount of Melbourine	Whig	1835
28.	Lord John Russell	Whig	1846
29.	Edward Stanley, Earl of Derby	Conservative	1852
30.	George Hamilton-Gordon, Earl of Aberdeen	Conservative	1852
31.	Viscount Palmerstone	Liberal	1855

Contd...

	Name	Party	Year
32.	Edward Stanley, Earl of Derby	Conservative	1858
33.	Viscount Palmerstone	Liberal	1858
34.	John Russell, Earl Russell	Liberal	1865
35.	Edward Stanley, Earl of Derby	Conservative	1866
36.	Benjamin Disraeli	Conservative	1868
37.	William E. Gladstone	Liberal	1868
38.	Benjamin Disraeli	Conservative	1874
39.	William E. Gladstone	Liberal	1880
40.	Marquess of Salisbury	Conservative	1885
41.	William E. Gladstone	Liberal	1886
42.	Marquess of Salisbury	Conservative	1886
43.	William E. Gladstone	Liberal	1892
44.	Earl of Rosebery	Liberal	1894
45.	Marquess of Salisbury	Conservative	1895
46.	Arthur Balfour	Conservative	1902
47.	Henry Campbell-Bannerrman	Liberal	1905
48.	Hebrt H. Asqith	Liberal (Collision,1915)	1908
49.	David Llyod George	Liberal (Collision)	1916
50.	Andrew Bonar Law	Conservative	1922
51.	Stanley Baldwin	Conservative	1923
52.	James Ramsay MacDolald	Labour	1924
53.	Stanley Baldwin	Conservative	1924
54.	James Ramsay MacDolald	Labour	1929
55.	James Ramsay MacDolald	National Labour Gov.	1931
56.	Stanley Baldwin	Conservative (National Gov.)	1935
57.	Nevile Chambelian	Conservative (National Gov.)	1937
58.	Winston Churchill	Conservative (Collision Gov.)	1940
59.	Clement Attlee	Labour	1945

Index